LIBRARY OF CONGRESS CATALOGUING-IN-PUBLICATION DATA

Creative technology : essays on the transformation of thought
and society / edited by W. Richard Walker and Douglas J.
Herrmann.
     p.   cm.
    Includes bibliographical references and index.

    ISBN 0-7864-1974-1 (softcover : 50# alkaline paper)

    1. Human-computer interaction.   2. Cognition.   3. Artificial
intelligence.   I. Walker, W. Richard.   II. Herrmann, Douglas J.
QA76.9.H85C645   2005
004'.01'9—dc22   2004019457

British Library cataloguing data are available

Cover photograph ©2005 PhotoSpin

Manufactured in the United States of America

*McFarland & Company, Inc., Publishers
  Box 611, Jefferson, North Carolina 28640
    www.mcfarlandpub.com*

Cognitive Technology

Essays on the Transformation of Thought and Society

Edited by W. Richard Walker
and Douglas J. Herrmann

McFarland & Company, Inc., Publishers
Jefferson, North Carolina, and London

Cognitive Technology

To my dad, Robert Walker, who taught me how to fix things. Believe it or not, Dad, I was listening.

—W. Richard Walker

To my mother, Ruth Ice Herrmann

—Douglas Herrmann

Table of Contents

Preface

Cognitive technologies are technologies that directly or indirectly affect learning, retention, remembering, reasoning, and problem solving. Cognitive technologies include devices such as computers, personal data assistants, cell phones, bank ATMs, and electronic dictionaries. These devices are everywhere. They affect how we manage our personal affairs, conduct business, and socialize. The development of cognitive technologies first became apparent at the 1978 Practical Aspects of Memory Conference. Since then, the creation of new cognitive technologies has been extremely rapid. In recent years, cognitive technologies have invaded many aspects of modern life, and because of their rapid growth, a body of knowledge now exists about applications of cognitive theory to the development of these technologies in a variety of fields. Much more is known now about how cognitive theory may be used to develop cognitive technologies in education, industry, business, the professions, and government. For example, cognitive technologies have been developed to improve such elements as the maintenance of one's daily schedule, with personal data assistants; ease of communication, with portable phones; accuracy of surveys; identification of flaws in commercial software; diagnoses and treatment of cognitive problems due to neuropsychological impairments; analysis and understanding of data; procedures for interviewing witnesses of accidents and crimes; design of understandable statistical maps; training for learning a foreign language; and numerous other products and services that are intended to facilitate performance in a variety of contexts.

Because the growth of cognitive technologies has been so rapid, there has been little chance for psychologists to reflect on the knowledge acquired about their development and use. Many questions that may be asked about cognitive technologies have not been asked or at least not given the attention that they deserve. What cognitive technologies assist cognition the best? What features of a cognitive technology lead to the greatest effectiveness? Do any of the cognitive technologies impair cognition? Are there side effects that disadvantage certain individuals or groups in our society?

As more and more cognitive technologies were being developed so rapidly, it became clear that researchers needed a chance to step back, assess the nature of the developments, and seek to answer the many questions that have arisen about cognitive technologies. Accordingly, we decided in the spring of 2002 to design a conference that would provide leading researchers in cognitive technology with an opportunity to meet, present, and discuss their latest work. It was clear to us and the other participants in this conference that increased communication about cognitive technology was needed in order to attain a better understanding of the science that facilitates the creation and refinements of cognitive technologies.

In June of 2003, the contributors to this volume met at Winston-Salem State University to discuss each other's findings. The research presented at this conference involved new cognitive products, new uses of existing products, and new scientific analyses of products of technology that aid a person's cognitive function. The purpose of this text is to summarize and expand upon the research reported at the 2003 conference and the conclusions drawn there.

Cognitive Technology is the first book that presents the fruits of psychological research on cognitive technology. (Previous books with similar titles present the artificial intelligence—AI—approach to cognitive technology.) This text showcases the paradigms, findings, and theory that have driven the development of new cognitive technologies. In general, this text is organized to address five areas of interest in cognitive technology.

The impact of technology on cognitive psychology. Douglas Herrmann considers the historical roots of cognitive technology and also proposes a framework for categorizing different kinds of cognitive technology.

The impact of technology in the classroom. W. Richard Walker and Reggie Andrews examine how college students are being trained to use personal data assistants. Carol Yoder and Douglas Herrmann examine the impact of new technologies on the prospective memory (remembering "what to do") of college students.

The distracting characteristics of new technologies. The research of David Strayer and Brad Sagarin empirically demonstrates the view that many new technologies have the ability to divert attention in meaningful and potentially dangerous ways. David Strayer and his colleagues have investigated the effects of cell phone use on driving ability while Brad Sagarin and his colleagues have examined the impact of distracting advertisements (e.g., pop-up ads on the Internet) on problem solving.

The impact of technology on social interactions and group problem solving. Katelyn McKenna and Gwendolyn Seidman present an expansive review of the literature in social psychology in order to make the argument that socializing in a virtual environment is fundamentally different from other social interactions. Rod Vogl and his colleagues take an empirical approach to assess the impact of chat-room technologies on group problem solving.

The mass media as cognitive technology. The impact of mass media is usually considered a field of study for sociologists. There are, however, important questions that can be posed about mass media by viewing the media as a cognitive technology. Dick Harris and his colleagues make the argument that the mass media may be studied by assessing people's memory for media experiences. Jeff Gibbons and his colleagues advance the argument that the mass media play an important role in advancing gender and racial prejudices by creating vivid portrayals of heroes and villains.

The research presented in this book attests to the power of cognitive psychology, whose future clearly lies in part in the promise of cognitive technology. Undoubtedly, cognitive technologies elucidate what psychologists can contribute to the public good. It is an unfortunate truth that such applications are not limited to the domains of legitimate business, education, or entertainment, but also include a darker side. Stephen Truhon and W. Richard Walker describe the misuse of cognitive technology in the forms of identity theft and cyberterrorism.

The future. Frank Durso and Catherine Hall consider the future of cognitive psychology as a unique discipline by highlighting a number of key research questions that can be uniquely handled by psychologists.

This text will be of considerable interest to cognitive psychologists, especially those concerned with the formulation of basic theory and the development of cognitive technologies. In addition, the text will also be useful in upper-level undergraduate and graduate courses in cognitive psychology, applied cognitive psychology, human factors, or mass media. Students who study this text will learn a great deal about the fundamentals of cognitive technology and how these cognitive technologies are developed, enhanced, and employed. Additionally, because of the text's focus on applications, students who read *Cognitive Technology* will be better prepared for the workplace. The more that students know about applications of psychology and other sciences, the better prepared they will be for the rapid evolution of technological advances that is occurring in every line of work. By the end of the text, a student will have a much better grasp of how technology affects cognition in daily life.

W. Richard Walker
Douglas J. Herrmann

1

The Potential of Cognitive Technology

Douglas J. Herrmann

Cognitive psychology has grown rapidly since its inception (ca. 1978). Basic research programs in cognitive psychology have been developed at almost all major colleges and universities. In addition, during this period, a sufficient body of basic cognitive research has accumulated such that many applied researchers have begun to apply a basic cognitive approach to everyday problems (Barber, 1988; Berger, Pezdek, and Banks, 1987; Durso, 1999; Gruneberg and Morris, 1992; Gruneberg, Morris, and Sykes, 1978, 1988; Herrmann, McEvoy, Hertzog, Hertel, and Johnson, 1996; Hoffman and Deffenbacher, 1992, 1993; see also Dasgupta, 1996; Schönflug, 1993a, 1993b). The increase in the breadth and depth of cognitive applications and cognitive technologies in just two decades is truly impressive. Contributions have been made for every kind of cognitive process: sensation, perception, attention, comprehension, learning, retention, remembering, reasoning, problem solving, and communication.

The development of applied work involving cognitive psychology has been so fast that we are still formulating the definition, defining characteristics, and assessing the impact of our work on society and science. The present work moves our field forward by giving us the opportunity to articulate our common assumptions, reflect on our history, identify the unique properties of our approach to cognition, conceive a theory of cog-

I thank W. Richard Walker and Carol Yoder for calling my attention to some of the topics discussed here. I apologize to anyone not mentioned here who should have been.

nitive technology, and consider what we want our legacy to be. Therefore, this chapter is devoted to these topics. It will identify some common assumptions; review the history of the cognitive technology field; take note of other groups whose work is related to our own; advance a framework for differentiating different kinds of cognitive technologies; and determine the responsibility of the cognitive technology field to society.

Common Assumptions

Applications versus Technologies

The early efforts to apply cognitive psychology resulted in applications designed to address certain cognitive problems. Subsequent efforts have also resulted in the development of technologies. An application addresses a particular situation. An example of an application would be when a cognitive psychologist has developed a new procedure for conducting lineups by a particular police force. A technology addresses two or more applications at once. An example of a technology would be when a psychologist might develop a new procedure conducting lineups at any police station (Wells, Malpass, et al, 2000).

An application is particular whereas a technology is general. An application is not superior to a technology and a technology is not superior to an application. These two kinds of applied research products differ not in quality but in focus. An application may be altered to become a technology but in order to do so, the application must be stripped of features that pertain to the particular application. Alternatively, a technology may be adapted to a particular situation by adopting features that pertain to the situation.

Devices versus Services

Applications and technologies each can be represented in two ways, either as a device or a service. A cognitive device is a physical object (e.g., a notepad would be one that carries out, or facilitates, the carrying out of a cognitive process such as perception, learning, remembering, or reasoning). For example, certain cognitive devices, such as personal data assistants, remind someone of an intention to be carried out. A cognitive service consists of actions carried out by technicians that facilitate or carry out a cognitive process for a client. For example, there are businesses devoted to reminding people of actions they intend to carry out.

In recent years, numerous cognitive technologies have been developed as devices and services (Yoder and Herrmann, 2003). Consider some further examples. Cognitive devices have been developed to facilitate scheduling of operations in business, to manage individuals' personal data, to enhance medical diagnoses, and provide training to improve cognitive skills. Cognitive services have been devised to improve the accuracy of surveys, resolve legal disputes over trademark infringement, identify flaws in computer screens in commercial software, and develop treatments for cognitive problems due to neuropsychological impairments.

Contexts

Cognitive technologies can be characterized further, beyond that of devices and services. A critical feature of a cognitive technology is the task and domain that the technology addresses. Tasks and domains are critical features of cognitive technologies because cognitive task domains are embedded in specific contexts (Engel, 1999). Indeed, the key to making a cognitive technology truly useful is to make the technology responsive to tasks and the domains of information as found in that context.

Contexts, therefore, provide a heuristic to determining the particular cognitive technology needed. For example, the contexts that may be addressed by cognitive technologies include such areas as personal life, home life, work, recreation, business, industry, government, medicine, the law, media, schools, colleges, or social gatherings. A technology, device, or service is manifested differently when it is transported from one context to another. If a context is understood clearly, then there is a better than average chance that the technology may address the tasks and domains found in that context. If a technology is applied to a task and domain in a context that is different from that intended for the technology, then the technology will not be as effective as it would be in the context appropriate for the technology.

Moreover, if the intended context of a technology is unclear, then it is unlikely that the technology will be that effective. For example, to do lists are most effective when they are context specific. The to do list in a PDA can be used to remember what to buy at a grocery store. However, checklists that show all likely purchases at a grocery store are more likely to remind a person of everything they need. No doubt there are some basic processes that are relevant to products and services such as to do lists. Nevertheless, the appropriate application or technology will be derived faster and more accurately by starting with the process to be aided with the context in mind.

History of Cognitive Technology

The aforementioned assumptions about applications and technologies, devices and services, as well as tasks, domains, and contexts, provide a basis for the development of a theory of cognitive technology. In order to gain more insight into the assumptions underlying cognitive technology, it is useful to examine the history of this field (Herrmann and Yoder, 1998; Hoffman, 1997; Hoffman and Deffenbacher, 1992).

Francis Bacon (1620/1905) advanced the basic applied relationship nearly four centuries ago. In his *Novum Organum*, Bacon distinguished between the "intellectual and practical" understanding of nature while also assuming that these two kinds of understanding are interdependent. Bacon's conception was that basic research has the responsibility for identifying the fundamental principles of our nature (de Wolff, 1993).

The distinction between basic applied research was recognized from the beginning of scientific psychology in the late 1800s. At that time Wundt asserted that the new psychology should not be concerned with applied issues such as the understanding and treatment of the mentally ill (Boring, 1950). A few decades later, Hugo Munsterberg (a Wundt student brought to the United States by William James), dedicated his career to persuading others that applied psychology was possible (Fagan and VandenBos, 1993; Hergenhahn, 1986).

Munsterberg called upon psychologists of his time to apply the knowledge that was emerging from laboratory work (Munsterberg, 1908, 1913, 1914). Munsterberg believed that "Applied psychology would become an independent experimental science which stands related to ordinary experimental psychology as engineering to physics "(1908, p. 9). Munsterberg, often described as the founder of applied psychology, also deserves to be called the founder of applied cognitive psychology and cognitive technology in that his research was largely cognitive and dealt with both applications and technologies. For example, one of his best known works is *On the Witness Stand* (1908), in which he provided an analysis of why children may not make good witnesses in court.

Interest in applied cognitive psychology went underground from about 1910 until the 1940s because behaviorism dominated psychology. Although there was not much overt interest in applied work in this period, there were some exceptions. Notably, Hollingsworth and Poffenberger (1929) wrote an excellent text on applied psychology in 1929. Bartlett published books in the 1930s that further supported what we now call applied cognitive psychology and cognitive technology (Murray and Bandomir, 2002). In the years that followed, dissatisfaction with the stimulus-response approach of behaviorists grew, making psychologists open to other approaches such as the cognitive approach. In World War II there was a need for psychologists to train military personnel in cognitive skills necessary to use various technologies (such as airplanes and radar).

In the 1950s applied cognitive research began addressing practical questions having to do with learning and with language (Baars, 1986). Also, artificial intelligence research began to flourish in the 1950s, programming computers to learn by simulating human processes. The idea that the mind functions something like a computer was compelling to many. This idea has influenced the development of theories of human cognition from the beginning of cognitive psychology into the present (Lachman, Lachman, and Butterfield, 1979; Norman, 1998). Moreover, behaviorism was dealt a crushing blow in 1959 when Chomsky demonstrated that the principles of operant conditioning could not account for the acquisition of language by children (Benjafield, 1997). Soon it was clear that behaviorism was dead.

With the demise of behaviorism, cognitive research became more common and modern cognitive psychology was born in 1967, the date of the publication of Ulric Neisser's textbook *Cognitive Psychology*. Neisser's textbook demonstrated that cognitive psychology was a coherent discipline with a theoretical base and a body of findings that tested that base. Later, Neisser (1976) championed the ecological investigation of cognition; that is, the investigation of how cognition occurs in everyday life. The ecological movement led many psychologists to not only investigate how cognition occurs in everyday life but also to investigate how devices and services may improve how a person adjusts to cognitive challenges in everyday life.

Just as modern cognitive psychology has come to be dated by Neisser's (1967) textbook, applied cognitive psychology and cognitive technology may be dated with the first "Practical Aspects of Memory" conference, which was held in 1978 (Gruneberg, Morris, and Sykes, 1978). One presentation attracted a great deal of attention at the conference, and thereafter was presented by Neisser who argued that basic research had done little or nothing of practical value.

As basic cognitive research grew and matured, applied cognitive research blossomed (Baddeley, 1981; Gillan and Schvaneveldt, 1999; Hoffman, 1997; Hoffman and Deffenbacher, 1992). In 1983, an interdisciplinary group that included applied psychologists, began a program for improving government and private surveys through cognitive investigations of survey methodology (Loftus, Fienberg, and Tanur, 1985; Sirken, et al., 1999). In response to the growing interest in practical applications of cognitive psychological knowledge, the journal *Human Learning* was renamed *Applied Cognitive Psychology* in 1985, with the first issue published in 1986. The first book devoted to applied cognitive research consisted of a collection of research articles that were edited by Berger, Pezdek, and Banks (1987). Psychologists who conducted basic research were interested in determining whether their findings actually did anticipate how people responded in the natural environment (Nickerson, 1999).

Two more conferences on the practical aspects of memory were held, one in 1988 and one in 1994 (Gruneberg, Morris, and Sykes, 1978, 1988; Herrmann, McEvoy, et al., 1995). In 1991, a group of clinicians and cognitive psychologists developed a new cognitive approach to rehabilitating people with cognitive impairments due to head injuries (Gianutsos, 1991; Harrell, Parente, Bellingrath, and Liscia, 1992; Wilson, 1987; see also Parenté, 1998). In 1994 a society was formed (at the 1994 "Practical Aspects of Memory" conference) for investigators interested in cognition in everyday life: the Society for Applied Research in Memory and Cognition (SARMAC). This society has enabled the interests in applied cognition and cognitive technology to continue to grow, with SARMAC holding conferences every couple of years.

A controversy emerged in the 1990s in which basic researchers and applied researchers attacked the validity of each other's work. Banaji and Crowder (1989) criticized Neisser's (1978) conclusion that basic research had not helped the development of practical applications of memory. Banaji and Crowder asserted, instead, that applied research was incapable of discovering the fundamental principles necessary for application, arguing that applications cannot be generalized because they focus on particular topics. Fortunately, the controversy evaporated after the futility of the debate became apparent (Baddeley, 1993; Ceci and Bronfrebrenner, 1991; Gruneberg, Morris, and Sykes, 1991; Loftus, 1991).

In 1995 a Cog Tech Listserve was started at Ege University in Turkey. However, for unknown reasons the Listserve did not last more than a year. In 1995, two web businesses were established that explicitly addressed cognitive technology. One, the Cognitive Technologies Corporation (www.cogtech.com/contacts.html), was established to develop educational applications of cognitive technology. In the same year, the Practical Memory Institute was established to create and market CD-ROM products that provide training to improve memory and cognitive skills (http://www.memoryzine.com). Subsequently, other companies have emerged that also focus on cognitive technologies.

In 1996, the journal *Cognitive Technology* was founded by applied cognitive psychologists to provide a means by which researchers could communicate with each other about the applications that constitute technologies from the perspective of cognitive psychology (e.g., Nickerson, 1997). In 1997, the first conference on cognitive technology (from the psychological perspective) was held at Indiana State University (Herrmann, Yoder, Parente, and Schooler, 1997). During the 1980s and 1990s another controversy emerged among researchers working on cognitive applications and technologies. Many applied cognitive researchers felt it necessary to challenge the traditionally conception of research in which basic researchers have had the responsibility to anticipate the practical situations that basic science might serve. These researchers proposed instead that the traditional formula only works if basic research is conducted on all possible topics that will lead to applications or technologies (Chapanis, 1967; Hoffman and Deffenbacher, 1992; Vincente, 1994). However, these researchers pointed out that society's problems often call for knowledge that has yet to be discovered by basic research (Intons-Peterson, 1997). In such cases, the basic investigation of such problems often falls to applied cognitive psychologists because they need the basic knowledge to develop a sound cognitive application or technology (Herrmann, Raybeck, and Gruneberg, 1999; Intons-Peterson, 1997; Payne, Conrad, and Hager, 1997).

A related issue that was discussed from the 1960s onward, was the relevance of applied research for progress in basic research (Chapanis, 1967). In the grand scheme of science, applications and technologies represent that ultimate test of basic research. If basic science cannot be applied or developed into a technology, this failure suggests at best that basic research has failed to communicate properly with applied researchers. Alternatively, if there are no communication problems, a failure to develop an application or a technology indicates that there is a flaw in the basic science. Thus, the most powerful test of basic findings and theory is provided by applied research.

Allies: Groups Whose Work Is Related to Research on Cognitive Technologies

Applied cognitive psychologists who investigate and develop cognitive technologies are unique. Our approach is similar to and different from the approaches taken by other groups. Nevertheless, it is important to recognize that there are other groups who have similar interests. An appreciation of these other groups is useful to us because it (1) defines our contributions to the world more clearly and (2) it identifies professionals who may provide us with different perspectives on problems that we have difficulty solving (Herrmann and Grant, 1998; Hermann and Raybeck, 1999).

An allied group that deserves special mention is the artificial intelligence (AI) approach to cognitive technology (Russell and Norvig, 2003). In 1994, a group of researchers, primarily concerned with artificial intelligence, formed a Cognitive Technology Society (http:/www.cogtech.org). These researchers seek to understand the effect of understanding the effect of the computer on a person's cognitive functioning (Gorayska, Marsh, and Mey, 1999; Marsh and Gorayska, 1997). However, AI cognitive technology and psychology's cognitive technology differ in method. Psychology develops the field of cognitive technology through experimentation with human participants, whereas the AI cognitive technologies develop their understanding through innovations in AI (Marsh and Gorayska 1997). In the interests of avoiding confusion, I will refer to the research of this group as *AI* cognitive technology and the research reported here as cognitive technology. The AI Cognitive Technology Society held conferences in 1995, 1997, 1999, and 2002. In 2000, the society established a journal to present the AI approach to cognitive technology, *The International Journal of Cognitive Technology*. Nevertheless, both groups clearly value the relationship between technology and cognition, giving researchers such as ourselves another ally.

Finally, because we are working on applied research problems, the cultural differences among professionals are often diverse—more so than in basic research. It is not unusual to encounter people in business and entrepreneurs who know a lot about cognition or at least a lot about how a particular product aids cognition. Regardless of who develops a product, if it aids cognition then it constitutes a cognitive application or technology. Thus, people in business and entrepreneurs are yet another group to whom we must listen in order to achieve our objectives.

A Framework for Understanding Cognitive Technologies

Many devices and services have been created to aid cognitive processing (Harris, 1980; Herrmann and Petro, 1990; Intons-Peterson, 1993; Kapur, 1988; Lynch, 1995; Parente and Anderson-Parenté, 1991; Yoder and Herrmann, chapter 3 this volume). *A psychological principle that has emerged from the cognitive technology field is that products or services almost always are task and domain specific.* No particular aid helps people with any and all cognitive tasks. Different types of cognitive tasks must be approached differently. Consequently, different aids are available for different task. Here are some examples of products or services that represent the different kinds of technological functions.

Cognitive Prostheses

Memos written, checklists, an erasable board, a scheduler on a computer, devices with alarms to remind one to do something, a personal data assistant, phone systems developed to remind people of doctor's appointments and other intended tasks (Walker and Andrews, 2001).

Cognitive Robots

This kind of product does a cognitive job for someone. A thermostat "remembers" to turn a furnace on and off; many modern coffee makers can be programmed to start brewing coffee at a certain time in the morning; many VCRs can be programmed to record a show; auxiliary electrical systems can be set to turn lights on and off in a house.

Cognitive Corrector

This product corrects a cognitive failure before the effect of the failure is final. These products include: key chains that beep when you clap, correcting the cognitive failure of having forgotten where you put the keys; a toilet seat that automatically returns to a horizontal position when the seat has been left in the vertical position (almost always by males).

Social Cognition Facilitation

Important personally and professionally, there are devices and services that facilitate performance of social cognitive tasks. For example, PDAs allow one to retain information about the people one meets. Research has been conducted looking at the impact of these devices in social settings. This research suggests that people use these devices to remember details about social situations (Walker and Andrews, 2001; see also this volume).

Cognitive Self-Care Facilitation

Such facilitation has considerable importance in modern life. Cognitive processes are optimum to the extent that a person's physical and emotional state are optimum. Thus, devices and services exist to facilitate cognitive processes by remedying deficiencies in the physical and emotional states of individuals (Schacter, 2001).

Cognitive Assessors

These devices and services evaluate a person's capability for performing a cognitive task. Examples of such devices are programs that test railroad engineers and airplane pilots for the adequacy of their cognitive functioning. Evaluation of cognitive difficulties due to head injury can be carried out by a psychologist or computerized assessment systems.

Cognitive Trainers

These devices teach people to perform cognitive tasks. Such devices and services instruct a person on how to employ cognitive processes. Trainers are commonly presented in the form of software, CD-ROMS, and how-to videotapes and audiotapes. People can use these products to teach themselves a specific skill (e.g., using a computer) or to learn a more general ability (e.g., language).

Cognitively Friendly Products

Common in many fields of business, these cognitive friendly devices and services are associated with products whose primary purpose has nothing to do with cognition, but which are provided with features that enable people to use the product more effectively. For example, many cars today come with several buzzers that remind the driver to perform chores required by law (such as to buckle up) or to keep the car in running order (such as to turn off the headlights when the car is turned off). Some cars automatically turn off the headlights when the key is removed from the ignition. Thus, the car "remembers" to turn off the lights for the driver. Table 1.1 summarizes the different kinds of cognitive technologies mentioned above.

Societal Impact

Technologies have done wonderful things for the human race, but they have also had damaging consequences as well. For example, nuclear power has had catastrophic effects in the form of bombs and near catastrophic effects in the form of nuclear power used to produce electricity. Pollution, an inevitable side effect of industrialization, has created respiratory illness where illness would not have occurred. Cognitive technologies on the web sometimes facilitate predatory behavior above and beyond what was possible previously (such as identity theft via the Internet or child sexual abuse).

TABLE 1.1 TYPES OF COGNITIVE TECHNOLOGY,
DESCRIPTION OF FUNCTION, AND EXAMPLES

Type of Cognitive Technology	Description of Function	Examples
Cognitive prostheses	Primary function is to externalize the cognitive function; Visual and auditory cues serve as reminders	Alarms, day planners; PDAs, Post-it notes, e-mail reminders
Cognitive robots	Primary function is to carry out a designated task without immediate cognitive participation of the user	Programmable VCRS, programs that back up files
Cognitive corrector	Primary function is to correct the mistakes or oversights of the user	Spell-checks; Finance programs that help to balance accounts
Social cognition facilitator	Primary function is to provide a means to communicate with other users, exchange information, and conversational nuances	Instant messaging, cell phones, pagers, voicemail, chat rooms, e-mail
Cognitive self-care	Primary function is to help user maintain health and lifestyle	Exercise equipment that monitors heart rate and calories burned
Cognitive assessor	Primary function is to assess the capability of a user to carry out a specific task or set of tasks	Devices can assess blood alcohol content for automobile drivers
Cognitive trainers	Primary function is to help people learn a cognitive task	Electronic dictionaries, Instructional videos
Other cognitive friendly products	Functions can include increasing user alertness, Reminding users of needed maintenance, Providing the user with a sense of security	Car and home security systems, check engine lights in automobiles, proximity warnings in aircraft

Cognitive technologies are having an effect on society and that effect is not always a positive one. For example, cognitive technologies are also enhancing differences between the "haves" and the "have nots." Minorities have less access to the web because they do not have funds necessary to purchase computing equipment and time on the Internet (i.e., the "digital divide"). Policies are needed to ensure that certain groups in the future gain access to technology that they do not have now. The explosion of cognitive systems is especially evident in the world today, especially in Iraq. The proliferation of devices (such as laptops and personal data systems) today is overwhelming the world with more information than it can digest. Ultimately, the contribution of cognitive technologies will rest on an adequate theoretical understanding of how the mind may or may not make use of them.

None of us would be so naive as to think that cognitive technologies would only have positive effects (Norman, 1988). Consequently, we need to develop social mechanisms to keep others from using our products for unethical ends. No one who has produced an application or a technology can easily pull it back after it has been distributed. If we hope to influence appropriate use of our products, we will need to organize and collectively address these problems.

References

Baars, B. J. (1986). *The cognitive revolution in psychology*. New York: Guilford.

Bacon, F. (1905). Novum organum. In *The philosophic works of Francis Bacon* (John M. Robertson, Ed.; (R. C. Ellis and J. Spedding, trans.). London: George Routledge. (Original work published 1620).

Baddeley, A. D. (1981). The cognitive psychology of everyday life. *British Journal of Psychology*, 72, 257–269.

_____. (1993). Holy war or wholly unnecessary? Some thoughts on the "conflict" between laboratory studies and everyday memory. In G. M. Davies and R. H. Logie (eds.), *Memory in everyday life*. New York: North Holland.

Banaji, M. R., and Crowder, R. G. (1989). The bankruptcy of everyday memory. *American Psychologist*, 44, 1185–1193.

Barber, D. (1988). *Applied cognitive psychology*. London: Methuen.

Basalla, G. (1988). *The evolution of technology*. Cambridge, U.K.: Cambridge University Press.

Benjafield, J.G. (1997). *Cognitiion*. Englewood Cliffs, NJ: Prentice-Hall.

Berger, D. E., Pezdek, K., and Banks, W. P. (1987). *Applications of cognitive psychology: Problem solving, education, and computing*. Hillsdale, NJ: Erlbaum.

Boring, E. (1950). *A history of experimental psychology*. (2nd ed.) New York: Appleton-Century-Crofts.

Ceci, S.J., and Bronfenbrenner, U. (1991). On the demise of everyday memory: "The rumors of my death are much exaggerated." *American Psychologist*, 46, 27–31.

Chapanis, A. (1967). The relevance of laboratory studies to practical situations. *Ergonomics*, 10, 557–577.

Dasgupta, S. (1996). *Technology and creativity*. New York: Oxford University Press.

deWolff, C. J. (1993). Developments in applied psychology. *Applied Psychology: An International Review*, 42, 46–49.

Durso, F. (ed.). (1999). *Handbook of applied cognition*. Mahwah, NJ: Erlbaum.

Engel, S. (1999). *Context is everything: The nature of memory*. New York: Freeman.

Fagan, T. K., and VandenBos, G. R. (eds.). (1993). *Exploring applied psychology: Origins and critical analyses*. Washington, DC: American Psychological Association.

Gianutsos, R. (1991). Visual field deficits after brain surgery: Computer screening. *Journal of Behaviorial Optometry*. 2, 143–150.

Gillan, D. J., and Schvaneveldt, R. W. (1999). Applying cognitive psychology: Bridging the gulf between basic research and cognitive artifacts. In F. Durso (ed.), *Handbook of applied cognition*. New York: Wiley.

Gorayska, B., Marsh, J. and Mey, J. L. (1999). Methods and practice in cognitive technology: A question of questions. In B. Gorayska (ed.), *Cognitive technology*. Amsterdam: North Holland.

Gruneberg, M. M., and Morris, P. E. (1992). Applying memory research. In M. M. Gruneberg and P. E. Morris (eds.), *Aspects of memory* (Vol. 1, pp. 1–17). London: Routledge.

Gruneberg, M. M., Morris, P. E., and Sykes, R. N. (eds.). (1978). *The practical aspects of memory research*. New York: Academic Press.

_____, _____, and _____ (eds.). (1988). *The practical aspects of memory* (Vols. 1–2). Chichester, U.K.: Wiley.

_____, _____, and _____ (1991). The obituary on everyday memory and its practical applications is premature. *American Psychologist*, 46, 74–76.

Gruneberg, M. M., Morris, P. E., Sykes, R. N., and Herrmann, D. J. (1996). The practical application of memory research: Practical problems in the relationship between theory and practice. In D. J. Herrmann, C. McEvoy, C. Hertzog, P. Hertel, and M. Johnson (eds.), *Basic and_applied memory: Theory and context* (Vol. 1). Hillsdale, NJ: Erlbaum.

Harrell, M., Parente, F.J., Bellingrath, E., and Liscia (1992). *Cognitive rehabilitation of memory: A practical guide*. Aspen, CO: Aspen Pub.

Harris, J.E., (1980). We have ways of helping you to remember. *Journal of the British Association for Service to the Elderly*, 17, 21–27.

Hergenhahn, B. R. (1986). *An introduction to the history of psychology*. Belmont, CA: Wadsworth.

Herrmann, D. J. (1987). The relationship between basic research and applied research in memory and cognition. In C. P. Thompson, D. J. Herrmann, D. G. Payne, J. D. Read, D. Bruce, and M. P. Toglia (eds.), *Autobiographical Memory: Theoretical and applied perspectives*. Mahwah, NJ: Earlbaum.

Herrmann, D., Brubaker, B. Yoder, C., Sheets, V., and Tio, A. (1999). Devices that remind. In F. Durso (ed.), *Handbook of applied cognition*. Mahwah, NJ: Erlbaum.

Herrmann, D. J., McEvoy, Hertzog, C., Hertel, P., and Johnson, M. (eds.). (1996). *Basic and applied memory* (Vols. 1–2). Hillsdale, NJ: Erlbaum.

Herrmann, D. J. and Petro, S., (1990). Commercial memory aids. *Applied Cognitive Psychology*, 4, 439–450.

Herrmann, D. J., and Raybeck, D. (1997a). A clash of cultures: Basic and applied cognitive research. In D. G. Payne and F. G. Conrad (eds.), *Intersections in basic and applied memory research*. Mawah, NJ: Erlbaum.

_____, and _____ (1997). The relationship between basic and applied research cultures. In D. G. Payne and F. G. Conrad (eds.), *Intersections in basic and applied memory research*. Mawah, NJ: Erlbaum.

Herrmann, D., Raybeck, D., and Gruneberg, M. (1999). *A clash between cultures*. Terre Haute, IN: Indiana State University Press.

Herrmann, D., and Yoder, C. (1998). Cognitive technology. In M. Intons-Peterson and D. Best (eds.), *Distortion in memory*. Mahwah, NJ: Erlbaum.

Herrmann, D., Yoder, C., Parente, R., and Schooler, J. (eds.). (1997). The first American Cognitive Technology Conference. Terre Haute: Psychology Department of Indiana State University.

Hoffman, R. R. (1997). How to doom yourself to repeat the past: Some reflections on the history of cognitive technology. *Cognitive Technology*, 2, 4–15.

_____, and Deffenbacher, K. A. (1992). A brief history of applied cognitive psychology. *Applied Cognitive Psychology*, 6, 1–48.

_____, and Deffenbacher, K. A. (1993). An ecological sortie into the relations of basic and applied science: Recent turf wars in human factors and applied cognitive psychology. *Ecological Psychology*, 5, 315–352.

Hollingsworth, H. L., and Poffenberger, A. T. (1929). *Applied psychology*. New York: D. Appleton.

Intons-Peterson, M. J. (1993). External memory aids and their relation to memory. In C. Izawa (ed.), *Cognitive psychology applied*. Hillsdale, NJ: Erlbaum.

_____. (1997). How basic and applied research inform each other. In D. G. Payne, and F. G. Conrad (eds.), *Intersections in basic and applied memory research*. Mahwah, NJ: Erlbaum.

Kapur, N. (1988). *Memory disorders in clinical practice*. London: Butterworth.

Lachman, R., Lachman, J. L., and Butterfield, E. C. (1979). *Cognitive psychology and information processing: An introduction*. Hillsdale, NJ: Erlbaum.

Levi, A. M. and Almog, J. (2000). Cognitive technology and criminal justice: The police composite. *Cognitive Technology*, 5, 26–34.

Loftus, E. F. (1991). The glitter of everyday memory ... and the gold. *American Psychologist*, 46, 16–18.

_____, Fienberg, S. E., and Tanur, J. M. (1985). Cognitive psychology meet the national survey. *American Psychologist*, 40, 175–180.

Lynch, W.J. (1995). You must remember this: Assistive devices for memory impairment. *Journal of Head Trauma Rehabilitation*, 10, 94–97.

Marsh, J. and Gorayska, B. (1997). Cognitive technology: What's in a name? *Cognitive Technology*, 2, 40–43.

Munsterberg, H. (1908). *On the witness stand*. New York: Clark Boardman.

_____ (1913). *Psychology and industrial efficiency*. Boston: Houghton Mifflin.

_____ (1914). *Psychology: General and applied*. New York: Appleton.

Murray, D. J., and Bandomir, C. A. (2002). Bartlett's cognitive technology. *Cognitive Technology*, 7, 13–22.

Neisser, U. (1967). *Cognitive psychology*. New York: Appleton, Century, Crofts.

_____. (1976) *Cognition and reality*. San Francisco: Freeman.

_____. (1978). Memory: What are the important questions? In M.M. Grueneberg, P.E. Morris, and R.N. Sykes (eds.). *Practical aspects of memory*, pp. 3–24. London: Academic Press.

Nickerson, R. S. (1992). *Looking ahead: Human factors challenges in a changing world*. Hillsdale, NJ: Erlbaum.

_____. (1997). Cognitive technology: Reflections on a long history and promising future. *Cognitive Technology*, 2, 6–20.

_____. (1999). The natural environment: Dealing with the threat of detrimental change. In F. Durso (ed.), *Handbook of applied cognition*. New York: Wiley.

Norman, D. (1988). *Psychology of everyday things*. New York: Basic Books.

Norman, D. A. (1998). *The invisible computer*. Cambridge, MA: MIT Press.

Parenté, R. (1998), Cognitive technology and cognitive rehabilitation: A merger of disciplines. *Cognitive Technology*, 3, 53–54.

_____, and Anderson-Parenté, J. (1991). *Retraining memory: Techniques and applications*. Houston, TX: CSY Publishing.

_____, and Herrmann, D. (2003). *Retraining cognition* (2nd ed.). Austin, TX: Pro Ed.

Payne, D. G., Conrad, F. G., and Hager, D. (1997). Basic and applied memory research: Empirical, theoretical, and metatheoretical issues. In D. G. Payne and F. G. Conrad (eds.), *Intersections in basic and applied memory research*. Mawah, NJ: Erlbaum.

Russell, S. J. and Norvig, P. (2003). *Artificial intelligence: A modern approach*. Upper Saddle River, NJ: Pearson Education.

Schacter, D.L. (2001). *The seven sins of memory: How the mind forgets and remembers*. Boston: Houghton-Mifflin.

Schönflug, W. (1993a). Applied psychology: Newcomer with a long tradition. *Applied Psychology: An International Review*, 42, 5–30.

_____ (1993b). Practical and theoretical psychology: Singles with wedding rings? *Applied Psychology: An International Review*, 42, 58–60.

Sirken, M., Herrmann, D., Schecter, S., Schwarz, N., Tanur, J., and Tourangeau, R.(1999). *Cognition and survey research*. Boston: Wiley.

Vincente, K. J. (1994). A pragmatic conception of basic and applied research: Commentary on Hoffman and Deffenbacher (1993). *Ecological Psychology*, 6, 65–81.

Walker, W. R., and Andrews, R. Y. (2001). External memory aids and the use of personal data assistants in improving everyday memory. *Cognitive Technology*, 6, 15–25.

Wells, G. L., Malpass, R. S., Lindsay, R. C. L., Fisher, R. P., Turtle, J. W., and Fulero, S. M. (2000). Mistakes in eyewitness identification that are caused by known factors. Collaboration between criminal justice experts and research psychologists may lower the number of errors. *American Psychologist*, 55, 581–598.

Wilson, B. A. (1987). *Rehabilitation of Memory*. New York: Guilford.

Yoder, C. and Hermann, D. (in press). The utility of commercial memory aids as a function of the kind of aid and individual differences. *Psychologia*.

2

Training College Students to Use Personal Data Assistants

W. RICHARD WALKER *and*
REGGIE Y. ANDREWS

The relationship between pedagogy and technology is a tenuous one. On the one hand, technology has much to offer in raising the profile of educational pursuits. Technology enables students to gather large quantities of material quickly, contact their instructors and fellow students through e-mail and on-line instant messaging systems, and organize their materials using electronic scheduling programs or spreadsheet files. On the other hand, technology may overwhelm students with waves of irrelevant material, create anxiety in students who are not technologically savvy, or serve as an inadvertent barrier to education by forcing students to spend time learning about technology rather than focusing on course content. Further, some technologies may force people into rigid patterns of thought that are difficult to overcome (Barshi and Healy, 1993).

Of course, the debate of whether or not technology should be used in higher education is a false one. There is ample evidence to suggest that students are using technology. Even before the advent of modern technologies such as the Internet, research showed that many students relied upon external aids over traditional learning techniques to enhance their performance on everyday memory tasks. Harris (1980) interviewed 30 students and asked them to rate how frequently they used various memory aids on a 7-point scale ranging from 0 (never used) to 6 (used more than 10 times in the last 2 weeks). Some of these memory aids were external memory aids, such as diaries and shopping lists; others were internal memory aids, such as the method of loci and the peg-word method. The results clearly showed that most people rely upon external memory aids more often than mnemonics or retrieval strategies (see also, Harris and Morris, 1984). Given recent advances in technology and the willingness of students to use this technology in everyday situations, these external reminders are likely to include an array of electronic devices (e.g., cell phones, pagers, software). Cognitive psychologists have considered the general implications of these devices on mental functions such as memory improvement (Herrmann and Petro, 1990; Herrmann, Sheets, Wells, and Yoder, 1997; Herrmann, Yoder, Wells, and Raybeck, 1996; see also Yoder and Herrmann, chapter 3 this volume). There has also been some investigation into how these devices can be used in special populations (e.g., Jackson, Bogers, and Kerstholt, 1988; Wilson, Emslie, Quirk, and Evans, 2001), although there is some debate about the effectiveness of such interventions (Cooley and Singer, 1991; Herrmann, chapter 1 this volume). However, there has been little research into how these devices affect performance of typical college students.

In a recent replication of Harris's (1980) study, we supported the finding that students show an overwhelming tendency to rely upon external aids to boost their memory rather than use traditional learning styles (Walker and Andrews, 2001). Fifty students were given a list of external memory aids (e.g., notes to self, calendars, cell phones/pagers) and internal memory aids (e.g., mnemonics, study strategies) and asked to rate each item in terms of how each aid was used for helping them remember things. Not only did students show a preference for external aids, they rated cell phones and pagers as the most frequently used memory aid. In follow-up interviews, these students clearly expressed interest in using new technologies to help them in their daily academic tasks.

Our previous research has also shown that personal data assistants (PDAs) can be useful devices in the hands of students. We have examined the impact of PDAs on everyday memory and aspects of classroom participants (Walker and Andrews, 2001). This research tracked two groups of students for six weeks. The first group was given PDAs to use during the six-week period. The second group served as controls. Several tests of everyday memory were administered at the beginning and end of the experimental period. These tests included memory for names, telephone numbers, and events in student's schedule (e.g., exam dates, term paper due dates). The attendance records of the students were also recorded for two freshman level courses. Finally, the use of the PDAs was tracked by accessing the memory functions of the devices and by having students keep a written record of the troubles they experienced using the devices. In contrast to the control group, the PDA group showed increased memory for telephone numbers and events in their weekly schedules, but no change in other memory tests. Course attendance records indicated that the PDA group missed fewer days than the control group. Finally, students in the PDA group reported the greatest amount of difficulty entering data into the PDA, particularly during the initial phase of the experiment.

The overarching goal of the current research is to better understand the circumstances that lead to the successful use of technology by college students. This research will consist of two parts. First, a brief survey to understand what technologies students are using as part of their studies and what technologies they use for other purposes. The results of this survey should offer insights into the technological preferences of students. The second part is a quasi-experiment that studies how students learn to use new technologies as part of their curriculum. Specifically, freshmen students were given the opportunity to use a personal data assistant (PDA) for six weeks while their use of the device was monitored. The results of this experiment should help identify methods that instructors could use to more successfully integrate technology into their coursework.

Experiment 1

We asked participants to report the frequency with which they used various types of technology for purposes related to coursework and for other purposes. In all, we assessed the use of 12 different technologies. While this list is by no means exhaustive, we feel that it adequately captures the variety of technologies used by most college students.

We made two predictions. First, we predicted that students would report using e-mail, instant messaging, VCRs, and cell phones more often for personal reasons than for reasons related to coursework. Second, we hypothesized that the personal use of the aforementioned devices would dwarf other technologies such that students would report using technology more often for personal reasons than for reasons related to coursework.

Method

Participants. Fifty-two undergraduates from a historically African-American university participated in this experiment in exchange for extra credit in an introductory psychology class. All participants were first or second semester freshmen who were enrolled full time at the university.

Procedure. Participants were surveyed in three mass testing sessions (15 in session 1; 26 in session 2; 11 in session 3). Prior to being given the survey materials, participants were given five minutes to write down a brief description of some of the different kinds of technology they used in their coursework and in everyday life. The purpose of this task was simply to get the students focused on the topic of technology.

Materials. Participants were given a 12-item questionnaire that asked about their use of various technologies. Participants were provided with a two- to three-sentence description of each technology. Participants were asked to work on the survey for 10 minutes.

Frequency of Use. Participants were asked to make two ratings as to how frequently they used these technologies. The first rating was how frequently they used each technology for purposes related to coursework and the second rating was a frequency of use rating for purposes other than coursework (personal reasons). Participants made this judgment on a scale ranging from 0 (never used) to 6 (used more than 10 times in last 2 weeks).

Posttest Interviews. After completing the survey, students were asked to write down their telephone number or e-mail address for a brief open-ended question-and-answer period. Students were primarily asked about their experiences with technology in the college setting, which courses employed what kinds of technologies, and where they saw weaknesses. Thirty-three of the participants were able to be contacted within one week of completing the survey.

Results

Data Analysis. We performed two sets of analyses on the rating scale data. The first set of analyses was designed to compare the use of each technology for coursework and for personal reasons. We entered the rating data into a series of repeated measures t-tests. The second analysis examined if there was an overall difference in the use of technology for coursework or personal reasons. In this case, we calculated mean rating for each reason (Coursework vs. Personal Reasons) for each participant and entered these data into a repeated measures t-test. Table 2.1 presents the mean rating for each technology type for coursework and personal reasons as well as the t-values for each comparison.

Technologies used more often for personal reasons. As expected, technologies designed for communication (e-mail, cell phone, instant messaging) or entertainment (VCR or DVD) were more likely used for personal reasons than for coursework. An interesting point, however, is that with the exception of cell phones, these technologies were used for coursework. Post-test interviews suggest that the majority of university instructors employed video presentations in class and often correspond with students via e-mail.

Technologies Used More Often for Coursework. Students reported using scientific calculators, data analysis programs (e.g., SPSS), spreadsheet programs (e.g., EXCEL), and audiovisual programs (e.g., Powerpoint) significantly more for coursework than for personal reasons. Posttest interviews suggest that the students gained experience with the calculators, spreadsheet programs, and data analysis programs in math and science courses while they gained experience with audiovisual programs in English and social science courses.

TABLE 2.1 AVERAGE FREQUENCY OF USE RATING
FOR TECHNOLOGY USED FOR CLASS PURPOSES
AND PERSONAL REASONS IN EXPERIMENT 1 (N = 62)

Frequency of Use (0–6 scale)

Technology Type	Coursework	Personal	T-Value
Word processing programs	5.8	5.5	1.37, n.s.
Spreadsheet programs	4.2	2.3	2.20, p < .05
Data analysis programs	4.1	1.9	3.05, p < .01
Audio/visual display programs	4.0	1.7	3.30, p < .01
E-mail	3.5	5.5	2.51, p < .01
Instant messaging systems	1.5	4.9	2.96, p < .01
Scientific/graphing calculators	3.3	1.5	2.04, p < .05
Cell phones	0	5.6	9.89, p < .001
VCR/DVD player	3.4	6.0	3.38, p < .01
Personal data assistants	2.3	2.0	1.45, n.s.
Internet search engines	6.0	6.0	0.00, n.s.
Electronic dictionaries	1.7	1.2	1.55, n.s.
Overall	3.31	3.68	1.42, n.s.

Rating Scale. 0 = never used; 6 = used more than 10 times in the last 2 weeks.

Technologies Used Equally Often for Coursework and Personal Reasons. Students reported using word processing programs (e.g., Word), PDAs, and the Internet at approximately equal rates for purposes related to coursework or for personal reasons. Posttest interviews suggest that students use the Internet and word processors for entertainment and in job related tasks. In fact, some students seemed to have difficulty distinguishing these technologies from each other. The interviews also suggested that most of the students had little or no experience using a PDA (only four of the participants reported owning a PDA).

Discussion

We would like to focus on three findings from this experiment. First, technologies designed for communication and entertainment were used significantly more for personal reasons than for reasons related to coursework. Cell phones and instant messaging systems are two good examples of such technologies (see Strayer et al., chapter 4, and Vogl et al., chapter 7, this volume). Second, technologies related to data analysis and audiovisual presentations were more likely to be used for coursework than for personal reasons. Third, there was no overall difference in the use of technology for coursework or personal reasons. While there was a trend for technology to be used more for personal reasons, this trend was not significant. Taken together, these data suggest that academia has done a reasonably good job integrating a variety of technologies into the college classroom. This conclusion should be taken with a cautionary note. Most of the students in the postinterview sessions advocated even greater integration of technology into the learning environment.

The view adopted by many of our participants is consistent with Baddeley's (1990) claim that external memory aids have a legitimate role in improving memory. For instance, Gibbons and Thompson (2001) found that using a calendar during event recall dramatically increased the ability of a person to place events in time. This view, in conjunction with the results of experiment 1, led us to consider how beginning university students might be trained to use new technologies in the classroom. We decided to focus on the use of PDAs in the classroom for two reasons. First, the vast majority of our sample had little experience using these devices. This naiveté would allow us to better observe the factors that affected their learning, with less fear that their learning would be biased by prior experience with similar devices. Second, our prior research suggests that the use of PDAs can be linked to gains in everyday memory and moderate decreases in absenteeism (Walker and Andrews, 2001).

Experiment 2

The primary goal of experiment 2 was to identify the factors that helped students learn to use the basic functions of a PDA. We collected data over a six-week period in order to evaluate how often students used their PDAs and what kinds of problems they experienced with the devices. The experiment employed several methods to minimize the effects of confounding variables and to keep participants on task during the lengthy data collection period. This experiment consisted of three separate stages: Initial training, weekly interviews, and final evaluation of PDA use. Each stage was designed to keep participants in continuous contact with the laboratory and on task.

Method

Participants. Twenty-three undergraduates from an historically African-American university participated in this experiment in exchange for a cash payment of $20. All participants were freshmen who were enrolled full time at the university.

Procedure. The present experiment had three stages: initial training, weekly interviews, and final assessment. Participants were tested individually during each stage of the experiment. The initial training consisted of a one-hour session in which participants were trained to use their new PDAs and given tips on time management and mnemonics. The weekly interviews consisted of a brief interview by the researcher during which participants reported any problems they had experienced during the week.

At this time, participants were randomly assigned to two conditions. The PDA control condition (11 participants) and the PDA training condition (12 participants). The PDA training condition differed from the control condition because participants in this group received additional training throughout the course of the project.

Training. Participants received a Sharp EL-6790. While this device came with multiple functions, participants were explicitly trained in how to use four features. (1) The weekly planner can be used for scheduling weekly events by date, day of week, and time. (2) The personal memo can be used for making quick notes consisting of one to three sentences. (3) The telephone number bank can be used to store telephone numbers. (4) The e-mail address bank can be used to store e-mail addresses. Participants were shown how to enter information into the PDA, how to modify the information already in the PDA, and how to retrieve information from the PDA. Participants were given an example for each function and tested for proficiency by the researcher. Specifically, the researcher recorded the number of trials that participants required to successfully use the PDA function. Prior to leaving this session, participants were encouraged to use the PDA as much as possible over the next six weeks for whatever reason they felt necessary. Participants were cautioned that the memory of the devices would be checked at the end of the experiment to evaluate the overall use of the device.

Weekly Interviews. Participants in both conditions met with researchers during the six weeks following the training period. In the PDA control condition, participants were asked to keep a record of any problems they experienced during the previous week with the PDA, specifically focusing on problems they had inputting data and recalling data from the PDA. In the PDA training condition, participants were probed about any input or recall problems they experienced. Participants in this condition also received additional instruction. They were instructed how to use supplementary functions of the PDA, including the alarm function, The URL/website function, and the computer link (which allows the PDA to be linked to a personal computer).

Final Evaluation. At the end of the six-week period, participants were scheduled for a 30-minute evaluation. During this stage of the experiment, the memory of each PDA was checked so that the number of entries for each function could be recorded. Participants were again asked to report any problems they had experienced with the PDA. Participants were debriefed and then paid for their participation.

Results

Data Analysis. We performed two sets of analyses on these data. The first set of analyses were aimed at determining whether the additional training had any impact on the use of any of the PDA functions. The dependent variable in these analyses was either the number of entries for each function in the PDA memory at the end of the six-week period or the number of problems participants experienced during the six-week period. These data were entered into a series of independent-samples t-tests. If the training had an impact on PDA use, then participants in the training condition should have significantly more PDA entries and significantly fewer problems.

The second set of analyses were aimed at determining whether the use of the PDA functions during the six-week period was associated with the participants' initial experience with the PDA. That is, we wanted to determine if a person's initial ease or difficulty using the PDA predicted later use. To determine this, we performed a series of Pearson-product moment correlations between the number of trials that a participant needed to gain proficiency for each PDA function during the initial training period and the number of entries for each PDA function during the six-week period. If initial experience had an impact on later use, then one should expect a series of negative correlations between trials to proficiency and PDA entries (people who learned quickly should use the PDA more often) and a series of positive correlations between trials to proficiency and problems using the PDA (people who learned slowly should experience more problems during the six-week experiment).

PDA Training Had No Impact on Subsequent PDA Use or PDA Problems. Participants in the PDA control condition and PDA training condition did not differ in the use of any of the PDA functions ("strongest" effect was for the telephone function, $t(11) = 1.29$, *n.s.*). Likewise, PDA training did not have any effect on the number of problems that participants experienced inputting data, $t(11) = .85$, *n.s.*, or recalling data, $t(11) = .63$, *n.s.*, from their PDAs.

Initial PDA Experience Does Predict Subsequent PDA Use and PDA Problems. The initial experience participants had with the PDAs was a significant predictor of subsequent use. Participants who initially learned to use their PDA functions in fewer trials were significantly more likely to use their PDA during the six-week experiment. Table 2.2 presents a partial correlation matrix highlighting the relations between the number of trials to learn each PDA function, the use of each PDA function, and the number of problems experienced by participants. In general, fewer trials to proficiency were associated with greater use and fewer problems inputting data.

To further illustrate this finding, we combined the total number of trials to proficiency across the four functions and correlated this measure with the total number of entries across the four functions. There was a significant negative correlation between trials and usage, $r(22) = -.737$, $p < .001$. We then correlated the total number of trials to proficiency with the number of input and recall problems experienced during the 6-week experiment. There was a significant positive correlation between trials to proficiency and the number of input problems, $r(22) = .844$, $p < .001$, but a nonsignificant relation between trials to proficiency and recall problems, $r(22) = .213$, n.s.

TABLE 2.2. PARTIAL CORRELATION MATRIX HIGHLIGHTING THE RELA-
TIONS BETWEEN THE NUMBER OF TRIALS TO LEARN EACH PDA FUNC-
TION, THE USE OF EACH PDA FUNCTION, AND THE NUMBER OF
PROBLEMS EXPERIENCED BY PARTICIPANTS IN EXPERIMENT 2 (N = 23).

Number of Trials to Proficiency

ActualUse of PDA Function	*Schedule Trials*	*Telephone Trials*	*E-Mail Trials*	*Memo Trials*
Schedule use	-.702 $p<.001$	-.496 $p<.05$	-.654 $p<.001$	-.653 $p<.001$
Telephone use	-.16 *n.s.*	-.425 $p<.05$	-.458 $p<.05$	-.464 $p<.05$
E-mail use	-.341 *n.s.*	.336 *n.s.*	-.647 $p<.01$	-.520 $p<.05$
Memo use	-.392 *n.s.*	-.315 *n.s.*	-.301 *n.s.*	-.49 $p<.05$
Input problems	.713 $p<.001$	.868 $p<.001$	.832 $p<.001$	.749 $p<.001$
Retrieval problems	.059 *n.s.*	.147 *n.s.*	.321 *n.s.*	.184 *n.s.*

Note: All Function Trials to Proficiency were positively correlated with each other (lowest r^2=.496, $p < .02$). The Function Uses were also positively correlated with each other,
although not as strongly (lowest r^2=.22, *n.s.*). This is due to the fact that the Schedule
and Telephone Functions were used significantly more than the other functions.

Discussion

We would like to focus on two results from this experiment. First, the
additional PDA training failed to have any impact on PDA use or problems associated with the device. The goal of these training sessions was to
teach students more about their PDA so that they could make better use
of it. These sessions included several question-and-answer discussions
and examples of how the PDA functions could be used for coursework.
Based upon the participant-experimenter interactions during these sessions, the participants were actively engaged in the training tasks. If training would have produced more PDA use, one might attribute the increase
to a simple placebo effect. However, the fact that the training produced
no reliable increase in PDA use underscores the second result of this experiment; namely, that participants' initial experience with the PDA was
significantly correlated with later use of the device. This means that when
participants experienced initial problems learning to use the device, this

was associated with reduced use during the subsequent six-week period. Conversely, initial success with the device was associated with increased use of the device.

Implications for Technology in Higher Education

One question that can be readily posed is, "How well is academia keeping pace with technology use?" Academia is doing fairly well keeping pace with technology use in the classroom relative to the use of technology outside of the classroom. Although some technologies are used significantly more outside the classroom, a number of technologies are used more frequently for coursework than for other purposes. This makes sense, technologies such as cell phones and instant messaging systems will likely have limited use in a traditional classroom environment, which is more conducive to technologies that facilitate problem solving (e.g., data analysis) and the presentation of course material (e.g., VCRs, audiovisual displays). It is also interesting to note that some technologies are used equally often both in and outside of the classroom. The use of word processing programs and Internet search engines have become so commonplace in our society that students use these technologies for many courses as well as for entertainment purposes. However, it should be noted that, like all survey data, these results are tentative and may change depending upon the availability of new technologies. For now, the use of technology in higher education seems to be on a par with technology use outside the ivory tower.

A second question that can be posed is, "What advice can be given to instructors wanting to use technology in the classroom?" Instructors who are interested in incorporating new technologies into their coursework should heed the key finding of experiment 2. The first contact that a student has with a new technology is likely to determine his or her successful use of that technology during the course of an academic semester. Although our research did not find an effect of PDA training, it seems likely that subsequent instruction may help students grasp the new technology, especially when device proficiency is linked to course grades, the importance of first contact should not be overlooked. This means that an instructor must take the greatest care when preparing the initial lesson plans that employ new devices, programs, or technological protocol. Examples should be specific and executed by the instructor with as much proficiency as possible. Brief written instructions should be prepared to accompany verbal instructions. Finally, a prepared instructor should expect the unavoidable truth: All technologies will inevitably fail from time to time.

Implications for Technology Interfaces

Another question that can be posed is, "What can technology providers do to enhance technology use among college students?" While this research does not speak to this directly, consider some of the insights offered by Marvin Cetron and Owen Davies (1997). These authors examined both the technical and socioeconomic trends in technology. They observed that engineers continue to make stunning technological advances, many of which will never see the marketplace because of mundane constraints of human capacity and taste. For instance, they speculate that technology will soon exist to create personal computers that will fit neatly into a shirt pocket. The difficulty facing technology providers is not in the development of this technology (which they view as "simple"), but instead will be adapting these technologies to fit the needs and sensibilities of the users. In critiquing the future of science and technology, they offered many suggestions for technology interfaces. We would like to emphasize two of these suggestions.

First, the interface system should be constructed with the abilities of the user in mind. This means keeping in mind that if a person has to tax his or her memory to use a device, the individual will probably not use the device. Our data suggest that students experienced difficulty inputting data into their PDAs. We suggest that PDA interfaces should be constructed to allow easier data entry. Specifically, the data entry processes should be limited to four steps (there were as many as six steps for some functions).

Second, the interface system should be constructed with the goals of the user in mind. Too many functions may hurt the overall utility of the product. In the case of students, technology providers should keep in mind that the needs of a student center around *basic* time management and information organization. Almost all of the students in our study reported that their PDAs had too many functions that seemed redundant with other technologies. For instance, the URL function of the PDA, which stores web page addresses was thought to be useless by most of students. Students were quick to point out that web browsers typically save the addresses in memory which allows for immediate website access. Because the PDA essentially did the same (without granting immediate website access), this function was deemed unnecessary.

Future Research

The next step in this research is to establish a causal linkage between the first contact with a new technology and subsequent device use. We predict that students who are confronted with initial difficulties with a technology (e.g., a dysfunctional keypad or a blinking screen) will use the device less often over an observation period than students who are not confronted with such difficulties. Conversely, students who experience early success (e.g., successfully finding and opening a prewritten memo from the experimenter) should use the device more often than students who do not experience such success. Of course, because of its applied nature, this research paradigm will never reach the complete control of laboratory experiment. Even now, the SHARP-EL 6790 is obsolete and has been replaced with a new generation of handheld devices.

References

Baddeley, A. (1990). *Human memory: Theory and practice.* Needham Heights, MA: Allyn and Bacon.

Barshi, I., and Healy, A. F. (1993). Checklist procedures and the cost of automaticity. *Memory and Cognition*, 21, 496–505.

Cetron, M., and Davies, O. (1997). *Probable tomorrows: How technology will transform our lives in the next 20 years.* New York: St. Martin's Press.

Cooley, E., and Singer, G. (1991). On serving students with head injuries: Are we reinventing the wheel that doesn't roll? *Journal of Head Trauma Rehabilitation*, 6, 47–55.

Gibbons, J. A., and Thompson, C. P. (2001). Using a calendar in event dating. *Applied Cognitive Psychology*, 15, 33–44.

Harris, J. E. (1980). Memory aids people use: Two interview studies. *Memory and Cognition*, 8, 31–38.

_____, and Morris, P. E. (eds.). (1984). *Everyday memory, actions, and absent-mindedness.* London: Academic Press.

Herrmann, D. J., and Petro, S. (1990). Commercial memory aids. *Applied Cognitive Psychology*, 4, 439–450.

Herrmann, D. J., Sheets, V., Wells, J., and Yoder, C. Y. (1997). Palmtop computerized reminding devices: The effectiveness of the temporal properties of warning signals. *AI and Society*, 11, 71–84.

Herrmann, D. J., Yoder, C. Y., Wells, J., and Raybeck, D. (1996). Portable electronic scheduling/reminding devices. *Cognitive Technology*, 1, 36–44.

Jackson, J.L., Bogers, H., and Kersholt, J. (1988). Do memory aids aid the elderly in their day to day remembering? In M.M. Gruneberg, P.E. Morris, and R.N. Sykes (eds.), *Practical aspects of memory: Current research and issues, Vol. 2: Clinical and education implications*, pp. 137–142. Chichester: John Wiley and Sons.

Walker, W. R., and Andrews, R. Y. (2001). External memory aids and the use of personal data assistants in improving everyday memory. *Cognitive Technology*, 6 (2), 15–25.

Wilson, B. A., Emslie, H. C., Quirk, K., and Evans, J. J. (2001). Reducing everyday memory and planning problems by means of a paging system: A randomised control crossover study. *Journal of Neurology, Neurosurgery, and Psychiatry*, 70, 477–482.

3

Remembering What to Do: Using Conventional and Technology-Based Aids to Facilitate Self-Reported and Actual Prospective Memory

Carol Y. Yoder *and*
Douglas J. Herrmann

Cognitive demands today differ from what was expected just a decade or two ago. With increasing technological advances, information is available to anyone who knows how to find it quickly and effectively. In former times, having a vast store of personal knowledge about one's environment was essential for successful living. Today, knowing how to access information efficiently is increasingly important for managing the environment. Throughout much of the world, human-machine interactions have become a routine and expected component in how people live (Weil and Rosen, 1995). As people become increasingly reliant on technology-based products in their work and personal lives, it is important to develop a better understanding of how technologies and strategies impact how we approach and execute tasks. Computer-mediated memory aids are increasingly used by people who do not want to expend processing resources on trivial, but resource-demanding memory tasks.

Memory for upcoming events and actions, termed *prospective mem-*

ory, is a concern for many busy people today. Although there has been debate as to whether prospective memory is distinct from retrospective memory (Roediger, 1996), there is no question that prospective memory is important to everyday professional and personal lives. Failing to remember intentions contributes to on-the-job errors as well as many interpersonal problems. Remembering prospective events can require considerable effort. One reason is that prospective memory has at least two components: The actual intention of remembering and the content of what is to be remembered (Kvavilashvili, 1987; Meacham and Leiman, 1982); under some circumstances these components are independent (Kvavilashvili, 1987). That is, remembering to stop at the store also needs to be accompanied by the retrospective memory of what needs to be delivered or retrieved. A variety of strategies and a wide range of external reminding devices have been developed to manage prospective memory demands (as well as retrospective memory). Although external aids are often used to help people who experience brain injury, surveys indicate that most adults report using some kinds of memory aids (Intons-Peterson and Fournier, 1986; Yoder and Herrmann, 2003). In general, memory aids provide context cues, often associated with the targeted memory at the time of initial encoding or near the time of retrieval (Einstein, McDaniel, Manzi, Cochran, and Baker, 2000; Ellis, Kvavilashvili, and Milne, 1999). In order to remember prospective events and activities, people use internal aids such as imagery and mental strategies and external aids, such as reminding devices or environmental manipulations, to facilitate memory. External aids are considered more reliable for helping avoid memory failures, especially in situations where there is too much information to accurately remember with internal strategies (Herrmann and Petro, 1990; Intons-Peterson and Fournier, 1986; Yoder and Herrmann, 2003). Some external aids are specific to a particular situation (e.g., medication reminder alarm), while others have broader utility (e.g., PDA, lists).

External aids can be used to improve performance when remembering to do certain activities (event-based) or when remembering certain times with specific commitments (time-based) (Einstein and McDaniel, 1990; Rendell and Thomson, 1999). Although most external aids can be used for either time- or event-based tasks, event-based tasks are often prompted by lists and Post-it notes, while time-based tasks are often cued by timers or electronic devices. The latter devices, in particular, can be classified as commercial memory aids, devices created for the purpose of reminding. Analyses of the amount of commercial memory aids over the past couple of decades indicate that the variety and numbers of commercial memory aids are increasing (Herrmann and Petro, 1990; Yoder and Herrmann, 2003). While many of these devices provide a variety of ways to cue the individual about particular events, research indicates that there are an optimal number of external cues to improve memory, and use of too many external aids or too much signaling actually impedes memory performance (Herrmann, Sheets, Wells, and Yoder, 1997; Herrmann, Yoder, Sheets, Wells, and Brubaker,1999).

College students today represent a generation that has grown up with ever-developing computer technologies that have supported and enhanced their learning opportunities throughout their lives. In the studies we report on in this chapter, we were interested in looking at the strategies and devices students used to organize their intentions. We were interested in strategies students used to remember scheduled appointments, academic and personal responsibilities/chores, as well as how individual differences might impact planning and scheduling activities.

Although not extensively researched, differences in the attributes and attitudes of people can impact memory performance. Individual differences are rarely a focus of research in cognitive psychology, because most efforts are made to minimize or randomize this type of variation; however, these differences have been linked to prospective memory and aid use. Heffernan and Ling (2001) found that extraverts remember more short-term and long-term prospective memories than introverts. They suggested that extraverts are more motivated to engage in planning for events than introverts. Searleman and Gaydusek (1989) found people with type A personality type tend to use more external aids relative to type B individuals. There is little doubt that external aid use can enhance prospective memory performance, in that cues can remind us of obligations. Other research has begun to explore who is most likely to benefit from external aids in what type of circumstances (e.g., Park and Kidder, 1996).

As previously noted, many of today's external aids have a technological component. In order to use these aids, a person must be interested in taking the time to learn how to use them effectively, and to figure out their various features. People who are less comfortable with technology probably use fewer technology-based external aids (Herrmann and Petro, 1990). Little research has directly explored the relationship between external aid use, especially technology-based devices, and comfort with technology. However, some research has looked at computer anxiety, and because many memory devices contain computers, this research provides some related information. Chua, Chen, and Wong (1999) conducted a meta-analysis looking at computer anxiety, gender, and age. Computer anxiety is a complex type of state anxiety involving fear of computers, which can be assessed with a variety of observations, learning, or performance measures (Chua et al., 1999; Weil and Rosen, 1995). Chua et al. reported that computer anxiety was inversely related to computer experience, but was dependent on the type of experiences people had. Females were less comfortable than males, but individual experience with computers was the more reliable predictor of anxiety (Chua et al., 1999). Even more recently, DeYoung and Spence (in press) created a technology profile inventory to predict how individuals respond to different types of technology. Their analyses yielded seven factors (e.g., interest, approval, confidence, anxiety, internet transitions, entertainment, complex design preference) and also found user experience was related to overall score. Of note, these authors separated the interest and liking function and found that women were more anxious than men about technology although they were equally approving of technology. DeYoung and Spence (in press) suggested that this distinction may be due to differential gender support for using technology.

External aids encompass a broad range of devices and strategies ranging from written planners to palmtops. Contrary to much of the information on computing technologies, research suggests that women report using more external memory aids than men (Herrmann, Crawford, and Holdsworth, 1992; Long, Cameron, Harju, Lutz and Means, 1999). Herrmann et al. have suggested that this may reflect different societal roles and expectations in that women are more likely to take responsibility for remembering social events and many time-based prospective intentions. Analogous to research reported by Chua et al. and DeYoung and Spence, we might expect that technology-based external aid use in particular would be dependent largely on computer experience and comfort and that gender may play a role in availability or motivation to seek out that experience.

Apart from anxiety about technology and gender, other individual differences are likely to impact use as well. There are various personality-related variables that could influence memory performance and external aid use, such as extraversion (Yoder and Herrmann, 2003). As previously noted, extraverts have been found to remember more short-term and long-term prospective memories than introverts (Heffernan and Ling, 2001). One proposed explanation is that extraverts are motivated to engage in more planning and thinking about events than introverts. If extraverts do plan more, they may also be more inclined to use memory aids. People also differ in their interest in detail. Need for cognition is defined as the need to understand and make reasonable the experiential world. Those with a high need for cognition like to think, solve problems, and understand issues in their lives (Caccioppo and Petty, 1982), and they might think more about tasks that should be done, and therefore might use external aids more frequently to remember prospective tasks.

The level of commitment to activities, the regularity of an individual's schedule, and the importance of remembering events, impact memory load and may in turn influence memory performance. Research suggests that salient prospective memory tasks are more likely to be remembered than less significant tasks, and that a greater prospective memory load increases memory failure (Kvavilashvili, 1987). Expectations about reminders may also be salient as Schaefer and Laing (2000) reported that people who expected to be cued were more likely to fail to remember prospective memory tasks relative to people who were asked to cue others or people who served as controls.

In this study we explored perceptions of external aid use, prospective memory, and individual differences. Based on limited research and our observations, we hypothesized that people with more memory demands will be more likely to report using external aids and that participants who report more memory failures will be more likely to report using external aids (Long et al., 1999). We also hypothesized that women and more extraverted individuals will be more likely to use aids, because of differential investment in the importance of remembering prospective commitments, particularly those involving people. However, if we consider only technology-based aids such as PDAs, software reminder systems, and reminder beeper systems, that relationship may change. We also proposed that people with a higher need for cognition are likely to report using more external memory aids because they will think more about the task at hand, and invest more mental effort to ensure that tasks are executed effectively. Other central personality characteristics may also affect prospective task execution such as consciousness and neuroticism.

Because concerns about technology may be related to less frequent use of technology-based external aids, comfort with technology and individual preferences about planning were also measured. Since the complexity of a person's schedule, the regularity of the obligation, and the relative importance of the prospective memory task may influence external aid use and prospective memory performance, these characteristics were also assessed.

Method

Participants

Eighty-nine undergraduates (61 women and 28 men, mean age = 18.57 years (SD=.93), enrolled in an average of 15.38 (SD = 1.35) credit hours at a selective liberal arts college, participated in this study. Seventy-four percent were first year and 22 percent were sophomore students with an average of 9.8 (SD = 8.22) estimated number of hours in organized activities per week outside of classes. Students earned extra credit for their hour-long testing session, as well as the opportunity to win a $25 gift certificate if they completed the prospective memory task, assigned several hours after the experiment.

Materials

SIME. To assess past experiences and future expectations about memory, participants completed Herrmann and Neisser's revised Inventory of Memory Experiences called the Short Inventory of Memory Experiences (SIME; Herrmann and Neisser, 1979).

NEO-FFI. Participants were also asked to complete the five-choice 60-item NEO-FFI (Costa and McCrae, 1990), which assesses individual differences in personality. Factors measured in this well-researched scale include: (1) extraversion; (2) agreeableness; (3) conscientiousness; (4) neuroticism; and (5) openness to experience. Higher scores indicated more of the targeted trait.

CAS. The Computer Attitude Scale (Bandalos and Benson, 1990) assesses computer anxiety, confidence with computers, and liking of computers. Higher scores indicate less comfort with computer technology.

Need for Cognition. The Need for Cognition scale (Cacioppo and Petty, 1984) was devised to assess individual need for information and understanding when performing difficult or challenging tasks. Questions focused on enjoyment of situations requiring complex and abstract thinking or puzzle solving. Higher scores indicated greater interest in thinking and understanding.

External Memory Aid Questionnaire. Participants also responded to the modified External Memory Aid questionnaire (Harris, 1980; Walker and Andrews, 2001), which assessed how the participants use external aids in order to remember future events, as well as the specific aids that were used in completing everyday tasks. Questions were also included that evaluated the types of events most likely to trigger the use of external aids. Participants were asked to indicate, relative to others, how much responsibility or how many chores they had to remember, as well as the regularity of their schedule and perceived importance of their appointments and meetings compared to others.

Procedure

Data for this study was assessed through self-reports and through two prospective memory tasks. Upon arrival, all participants were told about the purpose of the study. Participants then received two consent forms along with a test protocol containing assessment instruments that dealt with many different aspects of participants' daily lives concerning memory performances, as well as other individual and personal characteristics. Participants were instructed to sign one of the consent forms and return it to the experimenter (the second consent form was theirs to keep for record of participation in the study). Standardized instructions were read aloud to the participants, who were then informed they should feel free to ask about any problems with the format or specific questions on the testing protocol at any point during the testing period. The experimenter explained the purpose of the study, indicated the kinds of questions involved, and described two prospective memory tasks. These prospective memory tasks involved writing one's mother's maiden name in a rectangular box when seen in the test protocol packet and sending an e-mail that same evening to one of the experimenters between 8:30 and 11:30 p.m. Participants were judged to have failed the first prospective memory task if they did not write the name at all, if the name is written somewhere other than the box, or if they asked questions about the task. The second task required an e-mail response during the designated hours. Objective and straightforward assistance was given to participants with any questions during the experimental session. However, after the initial instructions were explained, any follow-up questions about the two prospective memory tasks were duly noted, and these participant prospective memory responses were not counted as correct prospective completions (n =2).

After providing informed consent, participants were handed a packet of questionnaires arranged in the same order for all participants. Participants responded to the SIME (Herrmann and Neisser, 1979), the NEO-FFI (Costa and McCrae, 1990), the Computer Attitude Scale (Bandalos and Benson, 1990), the Need for Cognition scale (Caccioppo, Petty and Kao, 1984), and the modified External Memory Aid questionnaire (Harris,1980; Walker and Andrews, 2001).

Participants were thanked for their participation, given extra credit, but with the still outstanding final prospective memory task to complete, to be entered in the $25 gift certificate raffle.

Results

Frequencies were calculated on all dichotomous and continuous questions related to participants' demographics. Means and standard deviations were calculated on total scores for each assessment instrument and for some continuous measures. An alpha level of .05 was used as the significance level for all statistical tests and primary assessment instruments maintained between a .8 and .83 power level, indicating sufficient power to detect significant relationships between variables.

Causes of Memory Failure and External Aid Use

Using self-report data, the most prevalent causes for prospective memory failure were that participants had other things on their mind (n = 45, 51 percent) or they were doing something else (n = 19, 21 percent). Somewhat less frequently used explanations provided by the respondents attributed their memory failure to the event being less important or their own laziness. The most commonly used external aids were writing down a reminder in a planner or on Post-it notes (n = 74, 83 percent), making changes to personal body space (n = 13, 15 percent), and engaging in verbal repetition with others (n = 11, 12 percent). Only 51 percent of the sample had *any* experience with more technologically sophisticated aids such as palmtops, software reminding systems, and beepers from cells used as reminding signals, and fewer than 20 percent had regular use of one or more of these devices for reminders. Only two individuals consistently used these systems.

Strategies for remembering academic responsibilities primarily involved using a planner or calendar, with over two-thirds (*n* = 65, 73 percent) of the sample preferring this method to writing intentions in their notebooks (*n* = 22, 25 percent), or using mental notes (*n* = 6, 7 percent). When responsibilities focused around more recreational activities such as renting a movie, making mental notes were more prevalent (*n* = 17, 19 percent), but were not used as heavily as visible placement (*n* = 29, 33 percent) or writing a reminder (*n* = 26, 29 percent). Individual characteristics of the objects or events themselves may have influenced heavily people's choice of strategy.

Reported External Aid Use

To explore individual characteristics of people who chose to use external aids, we categorized participants into high and low extracurricular commitments, using a median split. Because of several outlier commitment scores, external aid use data was analyzed with a 2 (Gender) X 2 (Commitment) ANCOVA, with importance level of organized activities serving as the covariate. Participants with more memory demands reported higher levels of external aid use than those categorized as having low commitments to organized activities, $F(1,85) = 8.59$, $p = .004$. Level of importance, however, did not affect this relationship. As seen in Figure 3.1, women also reported higher external aid use than men, $F(1,85) = 12.634$, $p = .001$. Although these variables were significantly related to the levels of reported external aid use, they did not show a statistically significant interaction with each other in predicting external aids use. Essentially what we found was that female participants reported using more external aids than did male participants regardless of commitment. We also found that individuals with more time commitments to organized activities reported using more external aids as well. Total external aid use was predicted by the NEO-FFI, $F(5, 83) = 3.28$, $p = .009$, with extraversion ($\beta = .28$), neuroticism ($\beta = .22$), and openness ($\beta = -.20$) all contributing unique variance to the relationship. Need for cognition was not related to overall aid use.

Comfort with Technology and Reported External Aid Use

A separate standardized regression analysis was performed for the participants' comfort level with computer technology and use of external

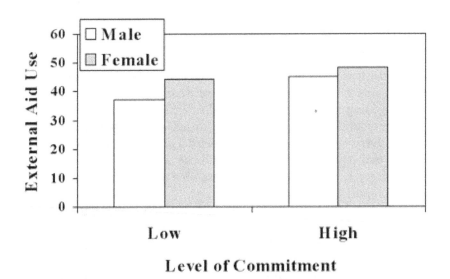

Figure 3.1. External aid use by gender and level of activity commitment.

aids. Although overall external aid use was not related to comfort level with computer technology, a statistically significant relationship between comfort level with computer technology and reported technology based external aid use was supported, $F(1,85) = 9.75$, $p = .002$.

Gender did discriminate technology use. Relative to females ($M = 4.4$), males ($M = 6.1$) were more likely to use technology-based aids, $t(87) = 2.6$, $p = .01$ although overall use was low. When overall commitment level, comfort with technology, and gender were used to predict overall use, all three factors independently contributed to this relationship, $F(3,82)$, 7.97, $p = .001$, with commitment yielding a $\beta = .31$, comfort with technology yielding a $\beta = -.24$, and gender yielding a $\beta = .20$. Personality factors did not predict use of technology aids, but this may partially reflect the low level of use overall in this sample.

Prospective Memory Failures

As noted, need for cognition did not significantly predict reported overall external aid use but was significantly related to self-reported prospective memory failures, $F(4,82) = 2.76$, $p = .007$. Participants with a higher need for cognition reported more prospective memory failures than participants with lower levels of need for cognition. However, reports about prospective memory performance were not related to actual prospective memory performance.

Discussion

Consistent with our predictions, women tended to report using more external aids than men, students who were comfortable with technology reported using more technology-based external aids, and busy students with higher levels of commitment to organized activities reported a greater use of external aids. Students who reported a greater number of memory failures also reported more external aid use, and individuals who were more extraverted, more neurotic, and less open to experience were all most likely to report greater use of external aids.

It is not surprising that people with more commitments use more external aids, because busy people are sufficiently concerned about failing to keep commitments that they do not exclusively rely on memory. People with more to remember may look for ways to counteract forgetting, and find the use of external aids is a helpful solution. Alternatively, busy people may report using more memory aids than they realistically use.

Consistent with existing published literature, women reported using significantly more external aids than men (Crawford, Herrmann, Holdsworth, Randall, and Robbins, 1989; Herrmann, Crawford, and Holdsworth, 1992; Long et al., 1999). In this society, women often expect to be social planners and organizers, and this outcome may reflect society-induced self-report biases that are often found in questionnaire studies (Crawford et al., 1989; Herrmann et al., 1992).

One of the interesting relationships we found in this study is between comfort with computer technology and the use of technology-based external aids. As expected, people who are more comfortable with technology report using more technology-based aids, such as palmtops and software, which remind people about prospective tasks. Men were more likely to use technology-based aids compared to women. It is possible that we did not find a relationship between self-reported memory performance and the use of technology-based aids because perceptions and performance are not related. Alternatively perhaps, first-year students are just entering into the academic and social scene and have not yet incorporated these technologies into their scheduling and planning.

We also hypothesized that need for cognition would influence prospective memory and external aid use. We predicted, based on Cacioppo and Petty's research (1982), that people with a higher need for cognition would have fewer memory failures due to an increased amount of mental capacity given to remembering. We found the opposite result. Our data showed that people who report a higher need for cognition reported more memory failures; however, higher need for cognition was not related to actual prospective memory performance as operationalized in this study. Do people with a higher need for cognition truly have more memory failures, or do they notice failures more than people with a lower need for cognition? Perhaps people with a low cognitive need have fewer memory failures, remain unaware of memory failures, or dismiss forgetting as unimportant.

People in this sample tended to use very few technology-based aids. While computer anxiety was related to technology use, personality factors were not. Anxiety is a highly salient factor in aid use although other individual differences were not sufficient to discriminate technology use. Self-reported prospective memory was not related to actual prospective memory performance.

Contrary to expectations, the prospective memory tasks that we chose to include in our study were not related to self-reported memory performance or other individual differences. This could be due to confounds commonly found in prospective memory tasks, where other study participants provided cues or reminders to complete the prospective memory tasks (e.g., classmates reported sending the requested e-mail). Alternatively, what people report about memory may bear little resemblance to actual behavior.

Study 2 investigated a second sample of students to compare external aid use and prospective memory. Here we wanted to look at the relationship between actual prospective memory performance and prospective memory reporting, with attention to need for cognition. In addition, we wanted to continue to explore the relationship between individual differences and external aid use, hypothesizing that external aid users would perform prospective memory tasks better, and that commitments, gender and personality would also affect reported aid use.

Method

Participants

Twenty-one undergraduates (11 women and 10 men, mean age = 19.24 years (SD = .93), enrolled in an average of 16.3 (SD = 1.23) credit hours, participated in this study. Fifty-six percent were first year and 44 percent were sophomore students with an average of 9.8 (SD = 8.22) estimated number of hours in organized activities per week outside of classes. Students were recruited from an introductory cognition class at a selective liberal arts college; for many of the participants, this was their second class in psychology.

Measures

Academic Motivation Scale. In addition to the measures previously described, an Academic Motivation scale, initially developed by Scott (1965), was revised to a Likert-format. This measure contains face valid questions regarding one's interest in academic endeavor.

Prospective Memory Performance. Eleven tasks embedded in class activities were used as measures of actual memory performance. Tasks included bringing books, articles, or other items to class, as well as a room change, and out-of-class meetings. Activities were chosen which fit into the context of the class but would not seem overly intrusive or demanding. Data were collected on each participant's success at prospective memory completion, adjusted for absences on day of assigned task and due date, and summarized into a percent correct prospective performance.

Final Interview—Debriefing. Questions were developed to assess participants' awareness of the relevance of prospective memory, their specific aid use, and reasoning regarding prospective recall. Besides explaining the complete rationale for the study, participants were also asked for their permission to use their in-class prospective memory data.

Procedure

After providing informed consent, participants responded to the SIME, the NEO-FFI, the Need for Cognition scale, and the Academic Achievement measure, which were administered in a small group format. Time 2 involved a 20-minute interview, scheduled individually, to assess task demands and external aid use in the context of this study. Participants were also debriefed about the study and were asked for permission to use prospective memory data collected in their cognitive class.

All participants were enrolled in a cognitive class and they received extra credit for their participation in this study. Twenty-one of the 32 students enrolled in the class opted to participate in the two-session study. Across the entire semester, 11 different activities or events were scheduled that required prospective memory. These prospective memory events were distributed throughout the semester and were expected of everyone who was enrolled in the class. In the final interview, students were asked about class activities. None of the students was aware that these activities were related to the study nor were they aware that the instructor monitored their success or failure in each in-class task. All students who volunteered for the external aid study gave permission to use their in-class prospective memory data.

Results

External Aids and Individual Differences

Overall use of external aids varied based on several participant characteristics. Because of the popularity of the planner and the small sample size, planner was used as a general proxy for external aid use. Females were more likely to use planners, as were individuals who scored high on conscientiousness, and high on academic achievement. External aid use was positively related to higher levels of conscientiousness, $r(19) = .48, p < .03$, and negatively related to openness, $r(19) = -.56, p < .01$. Similar to study 1, need for cognition was not related to overall external aid use. Contrary to expectations, no relationship was found between overall external aid use and actual prospective memory performance.

Technology-Based Aids

Standard regression was used to predict characteristics of those who used technology-based aids. These aids were used by those who were more extraverted ($\beta = .43, p < .05$) and those with greater need for cognition ($\beta = .49, p < .03$). In study 1, a similar relationship was found between extraversion and technology use, but not between technology use and need for cognition. Although technology-based aids were used more in this sample than in study 1, usage was low. Males ($M = 9.2$) and females ($M=8.2$) did not significantly differ in use of technology based aids, $t(19) = -.512, p > .05$ n.s., but sample size was small and relationships were in the expected direction.

Prospective Remembering

Prospective memory success, defined as percentage of completed tasks based on individual student performance, was not predicted by academic achievement although there was a trend for conscientiousness to be predictive. Contrary to the hypothesis suggested by Study 1, need for cognition did not predict prospective task success, although postmeasure interviewing indicated that participants did not feel that it mattered whether or not they remembered or executed the assigned tasks. Obviously, this perspective, which was articulated by several participants in the debriefing interview, provides a possible explanation for why prospective memory performances were not generally predictive of self-assessment or individual characteristics.

Discussion

Study 2 once again indicated that women use more external aids overall, although men appeared to be more likely to use technology based aids. External aid use was related to some individual difference characteristics, even with the small number of participants. Similar to study 1, aid use was negatively related to openness; additionally, aid use was related to greater consciousness. Individuals who were more inclined to use technology-based aids, liked having more information about the world and scored higher on extraversion. Self-reported perceptions of memory were not related to actual prospective memory performance. While this has been reported before, it reiterates again the need to individually assess both perception and behavior as many people fail to be aware of or correctly describe memory failures and successes. Conscientiousness may be a factor in actual performance, perhaps because the differential motivation to follow-through with responsibilities in service of maintaining one's self-concept. However, some participants perceived that they did not really need to execute the prospective tasks, reporting they remembered but did not follow through with the assigned task. This information, verified during debriefing, underscores the importance of motivation in executing prospective memories that were recalled but not completed due to perceived unimportance of the task; however, self-reported academic motivation did not capture this important value.

General Discussion

Because there is so little published literature regarding various aspects of prospective memory and external aid use, the implications for future research are numerous. While several studies have documented brain-injured individuals' use of external aids and benefits to prospective memory, most studies of individual differences have focused on gender and age differences. Research on age differences has been inconsistent, in that it appears to depend on the resource demands of the tasks, especially for older adults (Kidder, Park, Hertzog, and Morrell, 1997; Park, Hertzog, Morrell, and Mayhorn, 1997). Older adults are often more motivated and more interested in remembering than younger adults. While we did not explore age differences, our results on gender were consistent with previous work on external aid use and technology use (DeYoung and Spence, in press). Longitudinal tracking of changes in types of memory failures and external aid use and how this central executive process develops over the college years as business and social scheduling skills evolve, might be quite informative. DeYoung and Spence's work, previously described as females reporting similar interests in technology, but lessened motivation to actually use technological devices, suggests that targeting females for training and advertising may increase overall technology use. External memory aids may be an excellent way to involve females in more technology-enhanced use.

Traditional-aged college students provide an interesting sample to monitor cognitive aid use, especially technology-oriented ones, because these individuals have grown up with ever-changing computer-enhanced environments. While these people generally exhibit cognitive functioning at its best, how college students choose to navigate and manage prospective memories will impact how cognitive technologies evolve. Although our sample did not rely heavily on technology aids, that is likely to change with increased responsibilities and more demanding memory loads. Because samples such as these are not as affected by technology exposure and familiarity, relative to older groups, considering how individual difference variables impact aid use, perceived memory effectiveness, and performance-based memory may provide useful information about real-world aspects of memory.

Using aids to enhance and support our memory activities is rapidly becoming a primary way of getting work done, so investigating how aids improve memory is increasingly important if we want to comprehend how memory really works. Ultimately, if we want to develop a realistic assessment of practical memory we need to look at individual differences and how the environment supports memory and other cognitive activity. Until we consider cognition from a multimodal point of view, where individual characteristics of the rememberer are considered when analyzing memory processes (Herrmann, Plude, Yoder, and Mullin, 1999), our understanding of how cognition works in everyday settings will necessarily be limited. While minimizing individual differences through randomization and through focus on basic processes has been a productive approach within cognitive psychology, looking at user characteristics is increasingly important to understand naturally occurring differences in how people approach everyday prospective functioning. Even though our efforts to understand cognition in a more holistic way did not account for a great deal of variance, they are a small step toward understanding some of the more subtle influences that impact memory.

References

Bandalos, D. L., and Benson, J. (1990). A test of the factor structure invariance of the Computer Attitude scale over grouping conditions. *Educational and Psychological Measurement*, 51, 49–60.

Cacioppo, J. T., and Petty, R. E. (1982). The need for cognition. *Journal of Personality and Social Psychology*, 42, 116–131.

Cacioppo, J. T., Petty, R. E., and Kao, C. F. (1984). The efficient assessment of need for cognition. *Journal of Personality Assessment*, 48, 306–307.

Chua, S. L., Chen, D., and Wong, A. F. (1999). Computer anxiety and its correlates: A meta-analysis. *Computers in Human Behavior*, 15 (5), 609–623.

Costa, P. T., and McCrae, R. R. (1990). The five-factor model of personality. *Journal of Personality Disorders*, 4, 362–371.

Crawford, M., Herrmann, D. J., Holdsworth, M., Randall, E., and Robbins, D. (1989). Gender and beliefs about memory. *British Journal of Psychology*, 80, 391–401.

DeYoung, C. F., and Spence, I. (2004). Profiling information technology users: En route to dynamic personalization. *Computers in Human Behavior*, 20, 55–65.

Einstein, G. O., and McDaniel, M. A. (1990). Normal aging and prospective memory. *Journal of Experimental Psychology: Learning, Memory and Cognition*, 16, 717–726.

Einstein, G. O., McDaniel, M. A., Manzi, M., Cochran, B., and Baker, M. (2000). Prospective memory and aging: Forgetting over short delays. *Psychology and Aging*, 15, 671–683.

Ellis, J., Kvavilashvili, L., and Milne, A. (1999) Experimental tests of prospective remembering : The influence of cue-event frequency on performance. *British Journal of Psychology*, 90, 9–23.

Harris, J. E. (1980). Memory aids people use: Two interview studies. *Memory and Cognition*, 8, 31–38.

Heffernan, T., and Ling, J. (2001). The impact of Eysenck's extraversion-introversion personality dimension on prospective memory. *Scandinavian Journal of Psychology*, 42, 321–325.

Herrmann, D. J., Crawford, M., and Holdsworth, M. (1992). Gender-linked differences in everyday memory performance. *British Journal of Psychology*, 83, 221–231.

Herrmann. D. J., and Neisser, U. (1979). An inventory of everyday memory experiences. In *Proceedings of the Practical Aspects of Memory*, Cardiff. New York: Academic Press.

Herrmann, D., and Petro, S. (1990). Commercial memory aids. *Applied Cognitive Psychology*, 4, 439–450.

Herrmann, D., Plude, D., Yoder, C., and Mullin, P. (1999). Cognitive processing and psychological systems: A holistic model of cognition. *Zeitscrift für Psychologie*, 207, 123–147.

Herrmann, D., Sheets, V., Wells, J. and Yoder, C. (1997). Palmtop computerized reminding devices: The effectiveness of the temporal properties of warning signals. *Artificial Intelligence and Society*, 11, 71–84.

Herrmann, D, Yoder, C., Sheets, V., Wells, J., and Brubaker, B. (1999). Palmtop reminding devices—Capabilities and limitations. In J. P. Marsh, B. Gorayska, and J.L. Mey (eds.), *Humane interfaces: Questions of method and practice in cognitive technology*. New York: Elsevier.

Intons-Peterson, M., and Fournier, J. (1986). External and internal memory aids: When and how often do we use them? *Journal of Experimental Psychology: General*, 115, 267–280.

Kidder, D. P., Park, D. C., Hertzog, C., and Murrell, R. (1997). Prospective memory and aging: The effects of working memory and prospective task load. *Aging, Neuropsychology, and Cognition*, 4, 93–112.

Kvavilashvili, L. (1987). Remembering intentions as a distinct form of memory. *British Journal of Psychology*, 78, 507–518.

Long, T., Cameron, K., Harju, B., Lutz, J., and Means, L. (1999). Women and middle-aged individuals report using more prospective memory aids. *Psychological Reports*, 85, 1139–1153.

Meacham, J. A., and Leiman, B. (1982). Remembering to perform future actions. In U. Neisser (ed.), *Memory observed: Remembering in natural contexts*. San Francisco: Freeman.

Park, D., and Kidder, D. (1996). Prospective memory and medication adherence. In M. Brandimonte, G. O. Einstein, and M. A. McDaniel (eds.), *Prospective memory: Theory and application* (pp. 369–390). Mahwah, NJ: Erlbaum.

Park, D. C., Hertzog, C., Kidder, D. P., Murrell, R., and Mayhorn (1997). Effect of age on event-based and time-based prospective memory. *Psychology and Aging*, 12, 314–327.

Rendell, P. G., and Thomson, D. M. (1999). Aging and prospective memory: Differences between naturalistic and laboratory tasks. *Journal of Gerontology: Psychological Sciences*, 43B, 256–269.

Roediger, H. L. (1996). Prospective memory and episodic memory. In M. Brandimonte,

G. O. Einstein and M. A. McDaniel (eds.), *Prospective memory: Theory and application* (pp. 149–155). Mahwah, NJ: Erlbaum.

Schaefer, E. G., and Laing, M. L. (2000). "Please, remind me...": The role of others in prospective remembering. *Applied Cognitive Psychology*, 14, S99–S114.

Scott, J. (1965). The academic motivation scale. *Journal of General Psychology*, 72, 221–229.

Searleman and Gaydusek, K. A. (1989). Relationship between prospective memory ability and selective personality variables. Paper presented at the annual meeting of the Psychonomics Society, Atlanta.

Walker, W. R., and Andrews, R. Y. (2001). External memory aids and the use of personal data assistants in improving everyday memory. *International Journal of Cognitive Technology*, 6, 15–25.

Weil, M. M., and Rosen, L. D., (1995). The psychological impact of technology from a global perspective: A study of technological sophistication and technophobia in university students from twenty-three countries. *Computers in Human Behavior*, 11, 95–133.

Yoder, C. Y., and Herrmann, D. J. (2003). The utility of commercial memory aids as a function of the kind of aid and individual differences. *Psychologia*, 46, 83–103.

4

Why Do Cell Phone Conversations Interfere with Driving?

DAVID L. STRAYER, FRANK A. DREWS,
DENNIS J. CROUCH, *and* WILLIAM A. JOHNSTON

While often being reminded to pay full attention to driving, people regularly engage in a wide variety of multitasking activities when they are behind the wheel. Indeed, as the average time spent commuting increases, there is a growing interest in trying to make the time spent on the roadway more productive. Unfortunately, due to the inherently limited capacity of human attention, engaging in these multitasking activities often comes at a cost of diverting attention away from the primary task of driving. There are a number of more traditional sources of driver distraction. These "old standards" include talking to passengers, eating, drinking, lighting a cigarette, applying makeup, or listening to the radio (Stutts et al., 2003). However, since the mid–1990s, many new electronic devices have been developed and are making their way into the vehicle. In most cases, these new technologies are engaging, interactive information delivery systems. For example, drivers can now surf the Internet, send and receive e-mail or fax, communicate via cellular device, and even watch television. There is good reason to believe that some of these new multitasking activities may be substantially more distracting than the old standards because they are more cognitively engaging and because they are performed over longer periods of time.

This chapter focuses on how driving is impacted by cellular communication because this is one of the most prevalent exemplars of this new class of multitasking activity. Here we summarize research from our lab (e.g., Strayer, Drews, and Johnston, 2003; Strayer, Drews, and Crouch, in press; Strayer and Johnston, 2001), that addressed four interrelated questions related to cell phone use while driving. First, does cell phone use interfere with driving? There is ample anecdotal evidence suggesting that it does. However, multiple resource models of dual-task performance (e.g., Wickens, 1984; but see Wickens, 1999) can be interpreted as suggesting that an auditory/verbal/vocal cell phone conversation may be performed concurrently with little or no cost with a visual/spatial/manual driving task. Unfortunately, there is a paucity of empirical evidence to definitively answer the question. Second, if using a cell phone does interfere with driving, what are the bases of this interference? For example, how much of this interference can be attributed to manual manipulation of the phone (e.g., dialing, holding the phone) and how much can be attributed to the demands placed on attention by the cell phone conversation itself? This question is of practical importance: If the interference is primarily due to manual manipulation of the phone, then policies such as those enacted by New York State (chapter 69 of the Laws of 2001, section 1225c State of New York) discouraging drivers from using hand-held devices while permitting the use of hands-free units, would be well grounded in science. On the other hand, if significant interference is observed, even when all the interference from manual manipulation of the cell phone has been eliminated, then these regulatory policies would not be supported by the scientific data. Third, to the extent that the cell phone conversation itself interferes with driving, what are the mechanisms underlying this interference? One possibility that we explored is that the cell phone conversation causes a withdrawal of attention from the visual scene, yielding a form of inattention blindness (Rensink, Oregan, and Clark, 1997; Simons and Chabris, 1999). Finally, what is the real-world significance of the interference produced by cell phone use? That is, when controlling for frequency and duration of use, how do the risks compare with other activities commonly engaged in while driving? The benchmark that we employed is that of the driver who is intoxicated at the legal limit (.08 wt/vol). Do the impairments caused by cell phone conversations rise above this benchmark?

Background

In their seminal article, Redelmeier and Tibshirani (1997) evaluated the cellular records of 699 individuals involved in motor vehicle accidents. It was found that 24 percent of these individuals were using their cell phone within the 10-minute period preceding the accident, and this was associated with a fourfold increase in the likelihood of getting into an accident. Moreover, these authors suggested that the interference associated with cell phone use was due to attentional factors rather than to peripheral factors such as holding the phone. However, there are several limitations to this study. First, while the study established a strong association between cell phone use and motor vehicle accidents, it did not demonstrate a *causal link* between cell phone use and increased accident rates. For example, there may be self-selection factors underlying the association: People who use their cell phone may be more likely to engage in risky behavior. It may also be the case that a person's emotional state may simultaneously increase the likelihood of using a cell phone and driving erratically. Finally, limitations on establishing the exact time of the accident lead to uncertainty regarding the precise relationship between talking on a cell phone while driving and increased traffic accidents.

Other researchers have established that the manual manipulation of equipment (e.g., dialing or answering the phone) has a negative impact on driving (e.g., Briem and Hedman, 1995; Brookhuis, De Vries, and De Waard, 1991). However, the effects of the phone *conversation* on driving are not as well understood, despite the fact that the duration of a typical phone conversation is often significantly greater than the time required to dial or answer the phone. Briem and Hedman (1995) reported that simple conversations did not adversely affect the ability to maintain road position. On the other hand, several studies have found that working memory tasks (Alm and Nilsson, 1995; Briem and Hedman, 1995), mental arithmetic tasks (McKnight and McKnight, 1993), and reasoning tasks (Brown, Tickner, and Simmonds, 1969) disrupt simulated driving performance.

Experiment 1

Our first study was designed to contrast the effects of hand-held and hands-free cell phone conversations on responses to traffic signals in a simulated driving situation. We also included control groups who either listened to the radio or listened to a book on tape while performing the driving task. As participants performed the driving task, occasional red and green lights were flashed on the computer display. If participants saw a green light, they were instructed to continue as normal. However, if a red light was presented they were to make a braking response as quickly as possible. This manipulation was included to determine how quickly participants could react to the red light as well as to determine the likelihood of detecting simulated traffic signals under the assumption that these measures would contribute significantly to any increase in the risks associated with driving and using a cell phone.

Method

Participants. Sixty-four undergraduates (32 male, 32 female) from the University of Utah participated in the experiment. Participants ranged in age from 18 to 30. All had normal or corrected-to-normal vision and a valid driver's license. Participants were randomly assigned to one of the radio control, book-on-tape control, hand-held cell phone, or hands-free cell phone groups.

Stimuli and Apparatus. Participants performed a pursuit tracking task in which they used a joystick to maneuver the cursor on a computer display to keep it aligned as closely as possible to a moving target. The target position was updated every 33 msec and was determined by the sum of three sine waves (0.07 hz, 0.15 hz, and 0.23 hz). The target movement was smooth and continuous, yet essentially unpredictable. At intervals ranging from 10 to 20 sec (mean = 15 sec), the target flashed red or green and participants were instructed to press a "brake button," located in the thumb position on top of the joystick, as rapidly as possible when they detected the red light. Red and green lights were equiprobable and were presented in an unpredictable order.

Procedure. An experimental session consisted of three phases. The first phase was a warm-up interval that lasted 7 minutes and was used to acquaint participants with the tracking task. The second phase was the single-task portion of the study and was comprised of the 7.5-minute segment immediately preceding and the 7.5-minute segment immediately following the dual-task portion of the study. During the single-task phase, participants performed the tracking task by itself. The third phase was the dual-task portion of the study, lasting 15 minutes. Dual-task conditions required the participant to engage in a conversation with a confederate (or listen to a radio broadcast of their choosing or a book on tape) while concurrently performing the tracking task. The confederate's task was to facilitate the conversation and also to ensure that the participant listened and spoke in approximately equal proportions during the dual-task portions of the experiment. Participants in the radio control group listened to a radio broadcast of their choice during the dual-task portions of the experiment. Participants in the book-on-tape control group listened to selected portions from a book on tape during the dual-task portions of the experiment.

Results and Discussion

A preliminary analysis of detection rates and reaction times to traffic signals indicated that there were no reliable differences between hands-free and hand-held cell phone groups (all p's > .8). Neither were there reliable differences between radio control and book-on-tape control groups (all p's > .3). Therefore, the data were aggregated to form a 2 (Group: Cell Phone vs. Control) X 2 (Task: Single vs. Dual) factorial design. Table 4.1 presents both the probability of missing simulated traffic signals and the reaction time to the simulated traffic signals that were detected. Overall, miss rates were low; however, the probability of a miss significantly increased when participants were engaged in conversations on the cell phone, $F(1,31)=8.8, p < .01$. By contrast, the difference between single and dual-task conditions was not reliable for the control group, $F(1,31)=0.9, p > .3$. Analysis of the RT data revealed that participants in the cell phone group responded slower to simulated traffic signals while engaged in conversation on the cell phone, $F(1,31)=29.8, p < .01$. There again was no indication of a dual-task decrement for the control group, $F(1,31)=2.7, p > .1$.

These data demonstrate that the phone conversation itself resulted in significant slowing in the response to simulated traffic signals, as well as an increase in the likelihood of missing these signals. Moreover, the fact that hand-held and hands-free cell phones resulted in equivalent dual-task deficits indicates that the interference was not due to peripheral factors such as holding the phone while conversing. These findings also rule out interpretations that attribute the deficits associated with a cell phone conversation to simply attending to verbal material, because dual-task deficits were not observed in the book-on-tape and radio controls. Active engagement in the cell phone conversation appears to be necessary to produce the observed dual-task interference.

Experiment 2

Experiment 1 found that participants driving and conversing on a cell phone missed more traffic signals than when they were driving with-

TABLE 4.1. THE PROBABILITY OF MISSING THE SIMULATED TRAFFIC SIGNALS AND
THE MEAN REACTION TIME TO THE SIGNALS THAT WERE DETECTED IN
SINGLE AND DUAL-TASK CONDITIONS FOR THE CELL PHONE AND CONTROL
GROUPS IN EXPERIMENT 1. STANDARD ERRORS ARE PRESENTED IN PARENTHESES.

Probability of Missing Signal	Single-Task	Dual-Task
Cell Phone	0.028 (.009)	0.070 (.015)
Control	0.027 (.007)	0.034 (.007)
Reaction Time (msec)		
Cell Phone	534 (12)	585 (16)
Control	543 (12)	533 (12)

out the distraction caused by cell phone use. One possible interpretation
of these findings is that participants using a cell phone detected the imperative signals, but that their responses to them were suppressed. However,
a potentially more dangerous possibility is that the cell phone conversation actually inhibited attention to the external environment. Our second
study was designed to examine how cell phone conversations affect the driver's attention to objects that are encountered while driving. We contrasted
performance when participants were driving but not conversing (single-
task conditions) with that when participants were driving and conversing
on a hands-free cell phone (dual-task conditions).

Experiment 2 used an incidental recognition memory paradigm to
determine what information in the driving scene participants attended to
while driving. The procedure required participants to perform a simulated
driving task without the foreknowledge that their memory for objects in
the driving scene would be subsequently tested. Later, the participants
were given a surprise recognition memory task in which they were shown
objects that were presented while they were driving and were asked to discriminate these objects from foils that were not in the driving scene. The
difference in incidental recognition memory between single- and dual-task
conditions provides an estimate of the degree to which attention to visual
information in the driving environment is distracted by cell phone conversations.

Method

Participants. Twenty undergraduates (15 male, 5 female) from the
University of Utah participated in the experiment. Participants ranged in
age from 18 to 23. All had normal or corrected-to-normal vision and a
valid driver's license.

Figure 1. The PatrolSim Driving Simulator Used in Experiments 2 and 4.

Stimuli and Apparatus. A PatrolSim high-fidelity driving simulator, illustrated in Figure 4.1, was used in the study. The simulator incorporates proprietary vehicle dynamics, traffic scenario, and road surface software to provide realistic scenes and traffic conditions. The dashboard instrumentation, steering wheel, gas, and brake pedal were taken from a Ford Crown Victoria® sedan with an automatic transmission.

A key manipulation in the study was the placement of five billboards in each of the scenarios. The billboards were positioned so that they were clearly in view as participants drove past them. A total of 45 digital images of real-world billboards were created using a digital camera. A random assignment of billboards to conditions and locations within the scenarios was created for each participant.

Eye movement data were recorded using an Applied Science Laboratories eye and head tracker (ASL Model 501). The ASL Model 501 eye tracker is a video-based unit that allows free range of head and eye movements, thereby affording naturalistic viewing conditions for the participants as they negotiated the driving environment.

Procedure. When participants arrived for the experiment, they were familiarized with the driving simulator using a standardized 20-minute adaptation sequence. The experiment involved driving six 1.2-mile sections of a suburban section of a city. Half of the scenarios were used in the single-task condition and half were used in the dual-task condition. Single- and dual-task conditions were blocked and both task order (single- vs. dual-task) and driving scenario were counterbalanced across participants. For data analysis purposes, the data were aggregated across scenario in both the single- and dual-task conditions.

The participant's task was to drive through each scenario, following all the rules of the road. Participants were given directions to turn left or right at intersections by using left or right arrow signs that were placed in clear view of the roadway. Within each scenario, participants made an average of two left-hand and two right-hand turns.

The dual-task condition involved conversing on a cell phone with a confederate. To avoid any possible interference from manual components of cell phone use, participants used a hands-free cell phone that was positioned and adjusted before driving began. Additionally, the call was initiated before participants began the dual-task scenarios. Thus, any dual-task interference that we observed must be due to the cell phone conversation itself, because there was no manual manipulation of the cell phone during the dual-task portions of the study.

Immediately following the driving portion of the study, participants performed an incidental recognition memory task in which they judged whether each of the 45 billboards had been presented in the driving scenario (15 of the billboards had been presented in the single-task condition, 15 in the dual-task condition, and 15 were control billboards that had not been presented in the driving portion of the study). Each billboard was presented separately on a computer display and remained in view until the participants made their old/new judgment. There was no relationship between the order of presentation of the billboards in the driving task and the order of presentation in the recognition memory task. Participants were not informed about the recognition memory test until after they had completed the driving portions of the experiment.

Analysis. Eye-tracking data were analyzed to determine whether or not the participant fixated on each billboard. We required the participant's eyes to be directed at the center of the billboard for at least 100 msec for the billboard to be classified as having been fixated.

Results and Discussion

Table 4.2 presents the recognition memory data. The classification of control billboards as "old" was infrequent, indicating a low base rate of guessing. Billboards presented in single-task conditions were correctly recognized more often than billboards from dual-task conditions, $t(19)=4.53$, $p < .01$. These data are consistent with the hypothesis that the cell phone conversation disrupts performance by diverting attention from the external environment associated with the driving task to an engaging internal context associated with the cell phone conversation. However, it is possible that the impaired recognition memory performance may be due, at least in part, to a disruption of the visual scanning of the driving environment while conversing on the cell phone. This possibility is addressed in the following analyses.

We next assessed whether the differences in recognition memory may be due to differences in eye fixations on billboards. The eye-tracking data indicated that participants fixated on approximately two-thirds of the billboards and that the difference in the probability of fixating on billboards from single- to dual-task conditions was not significant, $t(19) = 0.76, p >$ .4. Thus, the contribution of fixation probability on recognition memory performance would appear to be negligible. We also measured total fixation duration in single- and dual-task conditions to ensure that the observed differences in recognition memory were not due to longer fixation times in single-task conditions. The difference in fixation duration between single- and dual-task conditions was also not significant, $t(19) = 0.75, p > .4$. Thus, the differences in recognition memory performance that we observed in single- and dual-task conditions cannot be attributed to alterations in visual scanning of the driving environment.

Finally, we computed the conditional probability of recognizing a billboard given that participants fixated on it while driving. This analysis is important because it specifically tests for memory of objects that were presented where the driver's eyes were directed. The conditional probability analysis revealed that participants were more than twice as likely to recognize billboards presented in the single-task condition than in the

TABLE 4.2. RECOGNITION MEMORY PERFORMANCE FOR EXPERIMENT 2. STANDARD ERRORS ARE PRESENTED IN PARENTHESES.

	Single-Task	Dual-Task	Control
Number of billboards classified as old	6.9 (0.5)	3.9 (0.6)	1.2 (0.5)
Fixation probability	0.66 (0.06)	0.62 (0.06)	
Fixation duration (msec)	1122 (99)	1009 (115)	
Conditional probability of recognition billboard fixation	0.50 (0.05)	0.24 (0.04)	

dual-task condition, $t(19) = 4.53$, $p < .01$. That is, when we ensured that participants fixated on a billboard, we found significant differences in recognition memory between single- and dual-task conditions.

The results indicate that conversing on a cellular phone disrupts the driver's attention to the visual environment. Even when participants looked directly at objects in the driving environment, they were less likely to have explicit memory of those objects if they were conversing on a cell phone. The data are consistent with an inattention-blindness hypothesis whereby the cell phone conversation disrupts performance by diverting attention from the external environment associated with the driving task to an engaging internal context associated with the cell phone conversation.

Experiment 3

To more thoroughly evaluate the inattention-blindness hypothesis, our third study measured the implicit perceptual memory for words that were presented at fixation during the pursuit-tracking task originally used in experiment 1. Perceptual memory was measured immediately after the tracking task using a dot-clearing procedure. In the dot-clearing procedure, words were initially masked by an array of dots and then slowly faded into view as the dots were gradually removed. We estimated the perceptual memory for an item by the time taken by participants to correctly report the identity of that item. One advantage of the dot-clearing task is that it does not rely on the participant's explicit memory of objects in the driving scene. Indeed, evidence for implicit perceptual memory has been obtained even when observers have no explicit memory for old items (Johnston, Dark, and Jacoby, 1985). However, This form of memory is obtained only if attention is directed to fixated words (Hawley and Johnston, 1991). Thus, the dot-clearing task provides an index of the initial data-driven processing of the visual scene.

Method

Participants. Thirty undergraduates (17 male and 13 female) from the University of Utah participated in the experiment. Participants ranged in age from 18 to 25. All had normal or corrected-to-normal vision and a valid driver's license.

Stimuli and Apparatus. The task was adapted from that used in Experiment 1 as follows. At intervals ranging from 10 to 20 sec (mean = 15 sec), a four- to five-letter word, selected without replacement from the Kucera and Francis (1967) word norms, was presented at the location of the target. Each word subtended an approximate visual angle of 0.5 degrees vertically and 2.0 degrees horizontally. Altogether, 200 words were presented during the driving task and an additional 100 words were presented as new words in the subsequent dot-clearing phase. A random assignment of words to conditions was generated for each participant. The latencies of responses in the dot-clearing phase were measured with msec precision using a voice-activated response device and response accuracy was manually recorded.

Procedure. The tracking portion of the study was identical to experiment 1, with the exception that during the tracking task words were presented for 500 msec at the center of fixation. Participants were asked to press a button on the joystick if the word was an animal name. Only 3 percent of the words were animal names and these items were excluded from the dot-clearing phase of the experiment.

Immediately following the tracking task, participants performed the dot-clearing task. The dot-clearing procedure was used to measure the perceptual memory for old words, that is, those previously presented in the single- and dual-task conditions. New words that had not been previously presented were included to provide a baseline against which to assess perceptual memory for the old words. In the dot-clearing task, words were initially masked with random pixels and the mask was gradually removed pixel by pixel until participants could report the identity of the word. A pixel from the mask was removed every 33 msec, rendering the word completely in view after 5 sec. The words from the three categories (i.e., single-task, dual-task, and control) were presented in a randomized order in the dot-clearing phase of the study.

Results and Discussion

Participants named old words from the single-task condition faster than control words, $t(29) = 4.97$, $p < .01$ ($M_{Control} = 3252$ msec, $M_{Single} = 3114$ msec), replicating prior demonstrations of implicit perceptual memory. Old words from the dual-task condition were also identified faster than control words, $t(29) = 2.31, p < .05, M_{Control} = 3252$ msec, $M_{Dual} = 3175$ msec). However, most importantly, identification was slower for old words from the dual-task condition than those from the single-task condition, $t(29) = 2.39, p < .05$ ($M_{Single} = 3114$ msec, $M_{Dual} = 3175$ msec). These data indicate that cell phone conversations reduce attention to external inputs, even of those presented at fixation.

Experiment 4

Our fourth study was designed to evaluate the real-world risks associated with conversing on a cell phone while driving. One way to evaluate these risks is by comparison with other activities commonly engaged in while driving (e.g., listening to the radio, talking to a passenger in the car). The benchmark that we used in the current study was driving while intoxicated from ethanol at the legal limit (.08 wt/vol). We selected this benchmark because there are well-established societal norms and laws regarding drinking and driving. How does conversing on a cell phone compare with the drunk driving benchmark?

Redelmeier and Tibshirani (1997) concluded that "the relative risk [of being in a traffic accident while using a cell phone] is similar to the hazard associated with driving with a blood alcohol level at the legal limit" (p. 465). If this finding can be substantiated in a controlled laboratory experiment, then these data would be of immense importance for public safety. Here we report the result of a controlled study that directly compared the performance of drivers who were conversing on a cell phone with the performance of drivers who were legally intoxicated with ethanol. We used a car-following paradigm in which participants followed an intermittently braking pace car while they were driving on a multilane freeway. Three conditions were studied: single-task driving (baseline condition), driving while conversing on a cell phone (cell phone condition), and driving with a blood alcohol concentration of 0.08 wt/vol (alcohol condition).

Method

Participants. Forty-one adults (26 male and 15 female) participated in the study. Participants ranged in age from 22 to 45. All had normal or corrected-to-normal vision and a valid driver's license.

Stimuli and Apparatus. The PatrolSim high-fidelity driving simulator used in experiment 2 was used in the study. A freeway road database simulated a 24-mile multilane beltway with on and off-ramps, overpasses, and two- and three-lane traffic in each direction. A pace car, programmed to travel in the right-hand lane, braked intermittently throughout the scenario. Distractor vehicles were programmed to drive between 5 and 10 percent faster than the pace car in the left lane, providing the impression of a steady flow of traffic. Unique driving scenarios, counterbalanced across participants, were used for each condition in the study. Measures of real-time driving performance, including driving speed, distance from other vehicles, and brake inputs, were sampled at 30 Hz and stored for later analysis. Blood alcohol concentration levels were measured using an Intox-ilyzer 5000, manufactured by CMI Inc.

Procedure. The experiment was conducted in three sessions on differ-ent days. The first session familiarized participants with the driving sim-ulator using a standardized adaptation sequence. The order of subsequent alcohol and cell phone sessions was counterbalanced across participants. In these latter sessions, the participant's task was to follow the intermit-tently braking pace car driving in the right-hand lane of the highway. When the participant stepped on the brake pedal in response to the brak-ing pace car, the pace car released its brake and accelerated to normal highway speed. If the participant failed to depress the brake, they would eventually collide with the pace car. That is, like real highway stop and go traffic, the participant was required to react in a timely and appropriate manner to a vehicle slowing in front of them.

In the alcohol session, participants drank a mixture of orange juice and vodka (40 percent alcohol by volume) calculated to achieve a blood alcohol concentration of 0.08 wt/vol. Participants then drove in the car-following scenario while legally intoxicated. Blood alcohol concentrations were verified using infrared spectrometry breath analysis both before and after driving in the simulator.

In the cell-phone session, three counterbalanced conditions were included: single-task baseline driving, driving while conversing on a hand-held cell phone, and driving while conversing on a hands-free cell phone. The call was initiated before participants began driving to minimize inter-ference from manual components of cell phone use.

Performance Variables. Six performance variables, presented in Table 4.3, were measured to determine how participants reacted to the vehicle braking in front of them. *Brake-onset time* is the time interval between the onset of the pace car's brake lights and the onset of the participant's brak-ing response (expressed in milliseconds). *Braking force* is the maximum force that the participant applied to the brake pedal in response to the braking pace car (expressed as a percentage of maximum). *Speed* is the average driving speed of the participant's vehicle (expressed in miles per hour). *Following distance* is the distance between the pace car and the par-ticipant's car (expressed in meters). *Half-recovery time* is the time for par-ticipants to recover 50 percent of the speed that was lost during braking (expressed in seconds). Also shown in Table 4.3 is the total number of col-lisions in each phase of the study. We used a Multivariate Analysis of Vari-ance (MANOVA) followed by planned contrasts to provide an overall assessment of driver performance in each of the experimental conditions.

TABLE 4.3. MEANS FOR THE ALCOHOL, BASELINE, AND CELL PHONE
CONDITIONS OF EXPERIMENT 4. STANDARD ERRORS ARE IN PARENTHESES.

	Alcohol	Baseline	Cell Phone
Total accidents	0	0	3
Brake onset time (msec)	888 (51)	943 (58)	1022 (61)
Braking force (% of maximum)	69.6 (3.6)	56.4 (2.5)	55.2 (2.9)
Speed (MPH)	52.8 (.08)	54.9 (.08)	53.2 (.07)
Following distance (m)	26.5 (1.7)	27.3 (1.3)	28.5 (1.6)
½ Recovery time (sec)	5.4 (0.3)	5.4 (0.3)	6.2 (0.4)

Results and Discussion

We performed an initial comparison of driving while using a hand-held versus hands-free cell phone. Both hand-held and hands-free cell phone conversations impaired driving. However, there were no significant differences in the impairments caused by these two modes of cellular communication, $F(5,36)=1.33, p > .3$. Therefore, we collapsed across the hand-held and hands-free conditions for all subsequent analyses reported in this chapter. The observed similarity between hand-held and hands-free cell phone conversations is consistent with the preceding experiments and suggests that the impairments to driving are mediated by a withdrawal of attention from the processing of information in the driving environment necessary for safe operation of a motor vehicle

MANOVAs indicated that both cell phone and alcohol conditions differed significantly from the single-task baseline, $F(5,36) = 3.44, p < .01$ and $F(5,36) = 3.90, p < .01$, respectively. When drivers were conversing on a cell phone, they were involved in more rear-end collisions and their initial reaction to vehicles braking in front of them was slowed by 8.4 percent, relative to baseline. In addition, compared to baseline it took participants who were talking on the cell phone 14.8 percent longer to recover the speed that was lost during braking. Drivers using a cell phone attempted to compensate for their increased reaction time by driving 3.1 percent slower than baseline and increasing their following distance by 4.4 percent.

By contrast, when participants were legally intoxicated, neither accident rates, reaction time to vehicles braking in front of the participant, nor recovery of lost speed following braking differed significantly from baseline. Overall, drivers in the alcohol condition exhibited a more aggressive driving style. They followed 3.0 percent closer to the pace vehicle and braked with 23.4 percent more force than in baseline conditions. Most importantly, our study found that accident rates in the alcohol condition did not differ from baseline; however, the increase in hard braking that we observed is likely to be predictive of increased accident rates in the long run (e.g., Lee, Vaven, Haake, and Brown, 2001).

The MANOVA also indicated that the cell-phone and alcohol conditions differed significantly from each other, $F(5,36)=4.66$, $p < .01$. When drivers were conversing on a cell phone, they were involved in more rear-end collisions, had a 7.5 percent greater following distance, and took 14.8 percent longer to recover the speed that they had lost during braking than when they were legally intoxicated. Drivers in the alcohol condition also applied 26.1 percent greater braking pressure than drivers in the cell phone condition.

Taken together, we found that both intoxicated drivers and cell phone drivers performed differently from baseline, and that the driving profiles of these two conditions differed. Drivers in the cell phone condition exhibited a sluggish behavior (i.e., slower reactions) which they attempted to compensate for by increasing their following distance. Drivers in the alcohol condition exhibited a more aggressive driving style, in which they followed closer, necessitating braking with greater force. With respect to traffic safety, our data are consistent with Redelmeier and Tibshirani's (1997) earlier estimates. In fact, when controlling for driving difficulty and time on task, cell phone drivers may actually exhibit greater impairments (i.e., more accidents and less responsive driving behavior) than legally intoxicated drivers.

General Discussion

Our research provided a controlled laboratory environment for assessing the impact of cell phone conversations on driving. We found that when drivers talk on a cell phone, their reactions to imperative events (e.g., braking in response to traffic lights or a decelerating vehicle) were significantly slower than when they were not talking on the cell phone. In several cases, the driver's reactions were impaired to such an extent that they were involved in a traffic accident. By contrast, listening to radio broadcasts or books on tape did not impair driving performance. Together, these findings are important because they demonstrate that listening to auditory or verbal material, by itself, is not sufficient to produce the interference associated with using a cell phone while driving. The data indicate that when drivers become involved in a cell phone conversation, attention is withdrawn from the processing of the information in the driving environment necessary for safe operation of a motor vehicle.

We found that cell phone conversations alter how well drivers perceive the driving environment. For example, cell phone drivers were more likely to miss traffic signals and often failed to see billboards and other signs in the driving environment. In our studies, we used an eye-tracking device to measure exactly where drivers were looking while driving. We found that even when drivers were directing their gaze at objects in the driving environment that they often failed to see them because attention was directed elsewhere. Thus, talking on a cell phone creates a form of inattention blindness, making drivers less aware of important information in the driving scene.

We also compared hand-held and hands-free cell phones and found that the impairments to driving are identical for these two modes of communication. There was no evidence that hands-free cell phones were any safer to use while driving than hand-held devices. In fact, we have consistently found significant interference even when we removed any possible interference from manual components of cell phone use (e.g., by having drivers place a call on a hands-free cell phone that was positioned and adjusted before driving began). Although there is good evidence that manual manipulation of equipment (e.g., dialing the phone, answering the phone, etc.) has a negative impact on driving, the distracting effects of cell phone conversation persist even when these manual sources are removed. Moreover, the duration of a typical phone conversation is often significantly greater than the time required to dial or answer the phone. Thus, these data call into question driving regulations that prohibit hand-held cell-phones and permit hands-free devices, because no significant differences were found in the impairments caused by these two modes of cellular communication.

What is the real-world risk associated with using on a cell phone while driving? An important epidemiological study by Redelmeier and Tibshirani (1997) found that cell phone use was associated with a fourfold increase in the likelihood of getting into an accident and that this increased risk was comparable to that observed when driving with a blood alcohol level at the legal limit. In a similar vein, our simulator-based research controlling for time on task and driving conditions found that driving performance was more impaired when drivers were conversing on a cell phone than when these same drivers were legally intoxicated. Taken together, these observations provide converging evidence indicating that driving while conversing on a either a hand-held or hands-free cell phone poses significant risks both to the driver and to the general public.

We have found it useful to conceptualize the problem of driver distraction along several dimensions, because not all multitasking activities are equal in distraction. First, is the source of interference from sources outside the vehicle "stealing" attention from the driver (e.g., Sagarin, Britt, Heider, Wood, and Lynch, chapter 5 this volume; Stutts et al., 2003), from manual manipulation of equipment inside the vehicle, or from cognitive distraction? While few activities are exclusively manual or cognitive, the primary source of interference often stems from one source or the other and methods to combat such distraction are likely to differ. Second, is the multitasking activity relevant to the primary goal of driving or is the secondary task less relevant to driving? Some activities may be higher in task-relevance (e.g., using an electronic navigation system) whereas others may be quite low in relevance to driving (e.g., surfing the Internet). Third, what are the time constraints imposed by these multitasking activities? Some tasks can be accomplished quickly, such as changing radio stations, whereas others may take place over extended periods of time, like cell phone conversations. The difference in timing can significantly compromise the ability of the driver to schedule these secondary activities during lulls in traffic. Fourth, what is the frequency of use in real life? Some activities may be quite risky, but low in frequency, such as changing clothes while driving. By contrast, other activities may be lower in risk, but engaged in by a large segment of the public (e.g., NHTSA estimates that at any point in time that 3 percent of drivers are using their cell phone while driving). Together, the frequency, duration, task relevance, and basis of interference combine to determine the impact of a particular source of distraction on traffic safety.

In sum, our research indicates that the use of cell phones disrupts driving performance by diverting attention from the information processing immediately associated with the safe operation of a motor vehicle. Similar patterns of interference were observed for hand-held and hands-free cell phones. These findings suggest that policies that restrict hand-held devices but permit hands-free devices are not well grounded in science. We are often asked what our position is on regulatory issues concerning cell-phone induced driver distraction. Clearly, the safest course of action is to pull over and park in a safe location before one makes or takes a call. However, regulatory issues are best left to legislators who are provided with the latest scientific evidence (for more on the interplay between cognitive technology and the legal system, see Truhon and Walker, chapter 10 this volume). We caution, however, that as more cognitively engaging technology makes its way into the vehicle, the potential for even more severe driver distraction will increase. In the long run, skillfully crafted regulation and better driver education addressing driver distraction will be essential to keep our roadways safe.

References

Alm, H., and Nilsson, L. (1995). The effects of a mobile telephone task on driver behaviour in a car following situation. *Accident Analysis and Prevention*, 27(5), 707–715.

Briem, V., and Hedman, L. R. (1995). Behavioural effects of mobile telephone use during simulated driving. *Ergonomics*, 38(12), 2536–2562.

Brookhuis, K. A., De Vries, G., and De Waard, D. (1991). The effects of mobile telephoning on driving performance. *Accident Analysis and Prevention*, 23, 309–316.

Brown, I. D., Tickner, A. H., and Simmonds, D. C. V. (1969). Interference between concurrent tasks of driving and telephoning. *Journal of Applied Psychology*, 53(5), 419–424.

Hawley, K. J., and Johnston, W. A. (1991). Long-term perceptual memory for briefly exposed words as a function of awareness and attention. *Journal of Experimental Psychology: Human Perception and Performance*, 17, 807–815.

Johnston, W. A., Dark, V. J., and Jacoby, L. L. (1985). Perceptual fluency and recognition judgments. *Journal of Experimental Psychology: Learning, Memory, and Cognition*, 11, 3–11.

Kucera, H., and Francis, W. N. (1967). *Computational analysis of present-day American English*. Providence, RI: Brown University Press.

Lee, J. D., Vaven, B., Haake, S., Brown, T. L. (2001). Speech-based interaction with in-vehicle computers: The effects of speech-based e-mail on drivers' attention to the roadway. *Human Factors*, 43, 631–640.

McKnight, A. J., and McKnight, A. S. (1993). The effect of cellular phone use upon driver attention. *Accident Analysis and Prevention*, 25(3), 259–265.

Redelmeier, D. A., and Tibshirani, R. J. (1997) Association between cellular-telephone calls and motor vehicle collisions. *The New England Journal of Medicine*, 336, 453–458.

Rensink, R. A., Oregan, J. K., and Clark, J. J. (1997). To see or not see: The need for attention to perceive changes in scenes. *Psychological Sciences*, 8, 368–373.

Simons, D. J., and Chabris, C. F. (1999). Gorillas in our midst: Sustained inattentional blindness for dynamic events. *Perception*, 28, 1059–1074.

Strayer, D. L., Drews, F. A., and Crouch, D. J. (in press). Fatal distraction? A comparison of the cell-phone driver and the drunk driver. In D. V. McGehee, J. D. Lee, and M. Rizzo (eds.) *Driving assessment 2003: International symposium on human factors in driver assessment, training, and vehicle design*. Iowa City: Public Policy Center, University of Iowa.

Strayer, D. L., Drews, F. A., and Johnston, W. A. (2003). Cell phone induced failures of visual attention during simulated driving. *Journal of Experimental Psychology: Applied*, 9, 23–52.

Strayer, D. L., and Johnston, W. A. (2001). Driven to distraction: Dual-task studies of simulated driving and conversing on a cellular phone. *Psychological Science*, 12, 462–466.

Stutts, J., Feaganes, J., Rodman, E., Hamlet, C., Meadows, T., Rinfurt, D., Gish, K., Mercadante, M., and Staplin, L. (2003). Distractions in everyday driving. AAA Foundation for Traffic Safety. http://www.aaafoundation.org

Wickens, C. D. (1984). Processing resources in attention. In R. Parasuraman and R. Davies (eds.), *Varieties of attention*. (pp. 63–101). New York: Academic Press.

_____ (1999). Letter to the Editor. *Transportation Human Factors*, 1, 205–206.

5

Intrusive Technology: Bartering and Stealing Consumer Attention

BRAD J. SAGARIN, M. ANNE BRITT,
JEREMY D. HEIDER, SARAH E. WOOD,
and JOEL E. LYNCH

When you eat, just eat. When you read the newspaper, just read the newspaper. Don't do anything other than what you are doing. — Zen teacher Seung Sahn

We live in an age full of distractions with an ever-increasing number of stimuli competing for our attention. Our cell phones ring, our pagers beep, our computers herald the arrival of instant messages and e-mail. When we watch television, the bottom third of the screen is often devoted to advertisements for upcoming shows. On the typical TV news program, we must simultaneously parse the main story, the news ticker running underneath, the stock market indexes in the corner, as well as the ubiquitous network logo or "bug."

Marketers, well aware of the myriad of competing stimuli, have

Some of the findings reported here were initially presented at the February 2002 meeting of the Society for Personality and Social Psychology in Savannah, GA, and at the May 2002 meeting of the Midwestern Psychological Association in Chicago. We thank Kimberly Arthur, Julie Bonini, Joanne Comiskey, Anndrea Dixon, Reyna Gilbert, Thomas Millar, and Jennifer Shewalter for their help in running the experiments and Rosanna Guadagno, John Skowronski, and Kimberly Lawler-Sagarin for their helpful comments on an earlier draft of this paper.

become quite adept at placing ads anywhere our eyes may stray. Advertisements now adorn supermarket floors, the screens of exercise bikes, airport baggage carousels, the stickers on bananas, even the bottoms of urinals (although one might wonder what symbolic associations that type of ad elicits). Unfortunately, as Seung Sahn's words highlight, there are costs associated with distraction and divided attention—costs vividly demonstrated in Strayer, Drews, Crouch and Johnston's (chapter 4 this volume) work on cell phone use while driving. However, despite their differences, there is one point on which marketers, Zen masters, and psychological researchers are in full agreement: Attention is a limited and valuable resource.

The recognition that attention is a limited and valuable resource has a number of ethical implications for marketing. First, because attention to advertisements represents an allocation of limited resources, consumers should receive something of worth in exchange for their attention. Thus, an ethical distinction may be drawn between situations in which consumers barter their attention (e.g., commercial television, ad-sponsored web sites) and situations in which marketers steal consumer attention (e.g., unsolicited telemarketing, billboards). Second, for bartering-related arrangements to be truly ethical, both consumers and marketers must have an accurate sense of the worth of the resources being exchanged. This chapter begins by considering the distinction between bartering and stealing attention and the ways in which consumers perceive their own attentional resources. These points are then examined empirically in a series of studies that explore the distraction and persuasion effects of online advertisements.

Bartering and Stealing Consumer Attention

Bartering attention refers to situations in which consumers opt to attend to advertisements in exchange for products or services they receive at reduced or no monetary cost. Bartered attention can be seen most prominently in the mass media. Television programs are broadcast along with the sponsoring commercials. Newspapers and magazines are subsidized in part by the ads interspersed with the articles. Internet web sites are paid for by the banner ads that border each page. In these cases, consumers receive desired content in exchange for their attention.

Over time, however, marketers have steadily eroded the exchange rate by demanding more attention for less content. The half-hour television program today is substantially shorter than it was 30 years ago. Technologies such as CASH (Kuczynski, 2000) are used to harvest up to four minutes of extra advertising time out of an hour of talk radio by cutting superfluous pauses between words and shortening extended phonemes within words. On the Internet, yesterday's rectangular banner ads have evolved into today's pop-ups, "skyscraper" ads, and sponsored links atop a page of search engine results.

By providing the same (or, in some cases, reduced) content in exchange for greater quantities of attention, these developments could be seen as questionably ethical alterations to the consumer-marketer relationship. Of course, consumers retain the option to reject the content if the attentional cost grows too high. But marketers often attempt to phase in additional advertisements gradually, so the change will not be noticed by consumers. Even more clearly unethical are situations in which marketers obtain consumer attention but consumers receive nothing in return—in other words, situations in which marketers steal consumer attention. Telemarketing and unsolicited commercial e-mail ("spam") are probably the most salient and reviled examples of this type of advertising, but they are far from the only ones. Ads steal consumers' attention while consumers ride the bus, drive down the highway, wait on hold, and stand in line at the supermarket.

It has been argued that consumers receive valuable information in exchange for their attention to these types of ads. However, this exchange differs in an important respect from the bartering transactions described earlier. Consumers bartering their attention retain the option to say no— to turn off the TV, to close their web browser. Consumers whose attention is stolen cannot opt out. Their resources are allocated and expended without their consent. It is notable, in this regard, that junk faxes were outlawed because the lost resources (e.g., paper, telephone lines) were tangible. Cognitive resources, in contrast, enjoy far less protection. How do consumers perceive the distinction between bartering and stealing attention? It seems to depend on whether the advertisement is focal (i.e., in the center of attention) or peripheral (i.e., in the visual or sensory periphery).

Focal versus Peripheral Advertisements

Consumers seem to have little patience for focal media that steal their attention. Consumer sentiment against telemarketing and spam—two highly focal media—is sufficiently negative that both media have been targeted by legislation. Consumers also seem to resent attempts to add an attentional cost to a product that already has a monetary cost. For example, New York City recently ended a pilot program that placed television sets with custom programming and advertisements in taxis, in part because of negative reactions to the ads (Feuer, 2003). There has also been a backlash, publicized by organizations such as Commercial Alert and the aptly named didntialreadypayforthismovie.com, against movie theaters that show commercials before the previews. However, both of these examples consisted of focal advertisements targeted at a captive audience, and as such, they are precisely the type of ad likely to incur consumer ire.

Consumers appear to have substantially greater tolerance for peripheral ads, even those for which they get nothing in return. Billboards, for example, are considered quite innocuous (Wood et al., 2002). Why do consumers care so much less about peripheral advertising? Perhaps because they perceive that the presence of peripheral ads costs them nothing. This stands in contrast to the visceral experience of expending resources attending to unwanted focal advertisements (e.g., a telephone solicitation during dinner). Such perceptions would have both practical and ethical implications for consumers' decisions to barter their attention. First, if consumers perceive that peripheral ads consume no attentional resources, they may require little in return for their attention to such ads. Second, if consumers are incorrect in their perceptions, then they cannot barter their attention knowledgeably and ethically.

These considerations are particularly relevant in the context of a new marketing model that enables individual consumers to choose whether to pay money for a product or to barter their attention for an ad-sponsored version (e.g., Eudora in "Paid mode" versus "Sponsored mode," Qualcomm, 2000; NetZero's "Platinum Service" versus "free service," NetZero, n.d.). Eudora's "Sponsored mode," for example, provides the same functionality as the "Paid mode," but instead of paying $49.95, customers accept the presence of visually peripheral ads that appear whenever the product is used.

To examine consumers' perceptions of ads similar to those found in these ad-sponsored products, we asked 90 undergraduate Internet users how much they believe they are affected by Internet banner ads. On a 7-point scale, with 1 indicating that "Banner ads don't affect me at all" and 7 indicating "Banner ads have a very strong effect on me," respondents reported that Internet banner ads were almost completely ineffective, with fully 49 percent reporting that banner ads had no effect whatsoever. Interestingly, this invulnerability to advertising appears to apply only to the respondents themselves and not to their peers. Participants indicated that a comparable peer-group member ("the typical NIU student") is significantly more affected by Internet banner ads than they are themselves.

Clearly, marketers and consumers have very different perspectives regarding consumers' attentional resources. By forgoing monetary payment, marketers demonstrate that they believe they are getting something of value (consumer attention) in exchange for the products they are providing. The results of our survey suggest that consumers, in contrast, perceive that they are getting something of value (desired products) at no cost whatsoever—a perspective that marketers may encourage by describing the products as "free" (e.g., "The Eudora 4.3 release offers three user-selectable modes, including a new sponsor-supported mode that provides the full-featured program to consumers for free"; Qualcomm, 2000, ¶1).

The Present Experiments

To test whether marketers or consumers are correct in their beliefs regarding consumers' attentional resources, we conducted a series of studies that examined the distraction and persuasion effects of online advertising. In order to provide the most stringent test of the effects of online advertising, we modeled our ads after the least intrusive type of online advertising we could find: the nonanimated, static, visually peripheral ads that appear in Eudora's "Sponsored Mode" (about which one reviewer explained, "Personally, I find the little ads so inoffensive that I can't imagine why anyone would choose the partly disabled Light mode over the ad-sponsored one"; Moore, 2000, ¶36).

We focused on three possible effects of online ads: distraction, recognition, and persuasion. Significant distraction and persuasion effects would suggest that consumers are affected by visually peripheral ads in ways they currently deny, whereas significant recognition and persuasion effects would suggest that marketers are correct in their assumptions regarding the efficacy of visually peripheral ads.

In the present experiments, participants performed a focal task (solving anagrams) in the center of a computer screen while, depending upon condition, zero, one, or more than one advertisement appeared in the periphery. In order to examine the effects of ad competition and ad clutter (a problem of increasing concern for Internet advertisers), three ad-present conditions were included. The first ad-present condition (one ad) had one static ad on the screen. The second ad-present condition (two ads) introduced ad competition by simultaneously placing a second static ad on the screen. In the third ad-present condition (dynamic ads), the ads moved across the screen and became animated when the participant moved the mouse over either ad.

The focal task consisted of solving a series of anagrams. An anagram is a word puzzle that consists of a series of scrambled letters that can be reordered to form one or more words. For example, "rissneoapu" can be rearranged to form the word *persuasion*. Anagrams were selected because (1) they are cognitively demanding; (2) they require complex input from the participant to solve; (3) they require visual attention to the center of the screen, but only for a limited portion of the solving time; and (4) they are engaging and enjoyable, as suggested by the variety of anagram-related web sites on Google's (n.d.) Recreation > Humor > Wordplay > Anagrams directory and as rated by participants in our studies.

We manipulated the difficulty of the focal task by increasing the number of letters in the anagram. Participants in the difficult anagram condition solved five-letter anagrams (which are frequently used in other studies—see Mayzner and Tresselt, 1958), while those in the easy anagram condition solved four-letter anagrams. Several factors are known to influence anagram solution speed, the most important of which are, word frequency (Mayzner and Tresselt, 1958; Tresselt and Mayzner, 1968), word imagery (Dewing and Hetherington, 1974), and letter repetition (Mayzner and Tresselt, 1966). Therefore, word frequency and word imagery were equated across difficulty conditions. Words with repeated letters were not used.

Participants were instructed to solve as many anagrams as possible in 10 minutes. After one minute, participants were given the option to skip to the next anagram. This provided two measures of distraction: the number of anagrams solved and the number of anagrams skipped.

After the anagram task, recognition and persuasion were assessed. It was predicted that the presence of ads would distract participants from the focal task. It was further predicted that participants would show significant recognition of the ads displayed during the anagram task compared to a set of distractors, and that the displayed ads would be rated as significantly more persuasive than the distractors. Finally, it was predicted that competition would reduce an ad's effectiveness (as measured by recognition and persuasion), but that this reduced effectiveness would be mitigated, at least in part, by increased ad salience. Specifically, it was predicted that making the competing ads dynamic and interactive would increase recognition and persuasion, possibly to the level of a single static ad presented without competition. This latter prediction is consistent with Li and Bukovac (1999), who found that animation increased recall for banner ads.

Distraction-related predictions were tested using between-subjects ANOVAs that examined the number of anagrams solved (and, separately, the number of anagrams skipped) across the anagram difficulty and ad type conditions. Recognition-related predictions were tested using mixed-model ANOVAs that examined recognition accuracy for viewed versus unviewed ads across the anagram difficulty and ad type conditions. Persuasion-related predictions were tested with analogous mixed-model ANOVAs.

Experiment 1

Three hundred forty-three Northern Illinois University undergraduates were randomly assigned to solve either easy (4-letter) or difficult (5-letter) anagrams in the presence of no ads, one static ad, two static ads, or two dynamic ads. The ads varied in size from 143 × 144 pixels to 153 × 150 pixels. Each ad consisted of the name of a fictitious web site printed next to a picture (e.g., professor.com with a drawing of professor lecturing to students; see Sagarin, Britt, Heider, Wood, and Lynch, in press, for an extended discussion of the materials and results of these studies). Eight stimulus ads were created for the experiment, and four additional distractor ads were created for the two static ads and two dynamic ads conditions.

Upon entering the laboratory, participants were seated in front of a computer running a custom computer program written in Microsoft Visual Basic. The experimenter typed in the participant's randomly assigned participant number, which indicated the difficulty of the anagrams the participant would solve and whether there would be advertisements on the screen while the participant solved the anagrams. The experimenter then left the room, and the participant completed the experiment at his or her own pace. The initial screen contained the following instructions:

> Hi. Welcome to the Software Study. In this study, you will be using a custom software program written to simulate the types of software that people typically use on personal computers (such as the Eudora e-mail program or software to connect to the Internet and surf the Web). As with some of these other programs, this program was available for free because it contains advertisements.

For participants in the no ads condition, the instructions then said, "After finishing the task (described below) you will be asked to rate a short series of ads." The rest of the instructions were the same for all participants:

The experiment should take approximately 30 minutes to complete. During the experiment, you'll be solving a series of anagrams. Each anagram consists of a word with the letters rearranged. Your task is to figure out what the word is. Anagrams will appear one at a time on the screen. When you've figured out the word, type it in and press the button. If you're correct, the next anagram will appear. Each anagram will remain on the screen for a maximum of 3 minutes, but if you get stuck, you can skip to the next anagram after 1 minute. If you take longer than 3 minutes on an anagram, the next one will appear automatically. You'll have a total of 10 minutes to finish as many anagrams as possible.

When the participant finished reading the instructions, a practice screen appeared. The practice screen was included to ensure that participants knew what anagrams were and how to solve them before beginning the anagram task. In a Preliminary Experiment that did not have a practice screen, a substantially higher proportion of participants skipped the first anagram than any subsequent anagrams, suggesting that participants may not have fully understood the anagram task until the answer to the first anagram was revealed. The number of letters in the practice anagrams corresponded to the participant's Anagram Difficulty condition. For example, a participant in the easy anagram condition saw the following instructions, "Here are some practice anagrams. For example, if the anagram is 'adso,' you can rearrange the letters to make the word 'soda.'" Below these instructions were two anagrams for the participant to solve. When he or she had solved both anagrams (or pressed the corresponding "Show the solution to this anagram" button), the anagram task began.

The anagram task consisted of a series of anagrams presented in the same order for all participants. As described in the instructions, participants had 10 minutes to solve as many anagrams as possible. If the participant took longer than one minute to solve an anagram, the "Skip to next anagram" button became active. If participants solved the anagram correctly, the next anagram appeared. If participants entered an incorrect answer, the program indicated that the answer was incorrect and highlighted the incorrect answer so participants could type in a new answer without having to erase the old one. If participants pressed the "Skip to next anagram" button after it was activated, the answer to the current anagram was revealed and the next anagram appeared. The program was designed so that an anagram was skipped automatically after three minutes. Messages to the participant were displayed on the screen above the "Anagram" field, and these messages disappeared automatically after 10 seconds. Within each anagram difficulty condition, all participants solved the same anagrams in the same order.

For participants in the one ad condition, an ad appeared in the upper left corner of the screen throughout the anagram task. The program randomly selected four of the eight stimulus ads to display and randomly selected an order in which to display the four ads. The ads appeared one at a time, with the next ad replacing the current one every 45 seconds (a replacement rate corresponding to the approximate rate of ad replacement in Eudora's "Sponsored Mode").

In the two ads condition, a second ad appeared in the upper right-hand corner of the screen. Like the ad in the upper left-hand corner, this ad changed to a new ad every 45 seconds. These ads appeared in a random order, and they only appeared during the anagram task. These distractor ads were not rated for recognition or persuasion.

In the dynamic ads condition, the first ad was placed at the top of the screen to the left. Throughout the anagram task, the ad moved slowly right and left from one side to the other. Similarly, the second ad was placed at the bottom of the screen to the right. This ad moved slowly left and right, always in the opposite direction of the ad at the top of the screen. When the participant moved the mouse over either ad, the ad would change to one of seven randomly selected transformations (90, 180, and 270 degree rotations, vertical and horizontal reflections, color inversion, and embossing), and if the participant clicked on either ad, a message would appear (either "Visit us on the web!" or "Hey, shouldn't you be solving anagrams!" with this latter message included to simulate the type of humor often found in online advertising). Results indicated that 86.5 percent of participants in the dynamic ads condition moused over one of the ads and 10.1 percent of participants clicked on one of the ads.

Participants in the no ad condition completed the task without ads appearing on the screen.

After 10 minutes, the program displayed a dialog box that indicated that time was up and gave the answer to the final anagram. Once the participant acknowledged the dialog box by pressing a button, the participant was prompted to begin the ad-rating task.

In this task, eight ads were presented to participants in a random order. Participants in the ad condition were asked, "Did you see this ad while doing the anagrams?" (answered yes or no) and "How confident are you about whether or not you saw this ad?" (answered on a 7-point scale from "I definitely saw this ad" to "I definitely did not see this ad"). All participants were asked "What do you think would be the quality of the web site advertised above?" (answered on a 7-point scale from "Low quality" to "High quality"), "How interested are you in visiting this web site?" (answered on a 7-point scale from "Uninterested" to "Interested"), and

"Please indicate how you feel about this ad" (answered on a 7-point scale from "Bad" to "Good"). The final page consisted of a debriefing letter that thanked the participant, provided some background on the study, and instructed the participant to get a credit slip from the experimenter.

Results

Experiment 1 consisted of a 2 (Anagram Difficulty: easy vs. difficult) × 4 (Ad Type: no ads, one ad, two ads, vs. dynamic ads) × 2 (Ad Experience: previously viewed vs. unviewed) factorial design. Anagram Difficulty and Ad Type were between-subjects; Ad Experience was within-subject. Ad Experience was manipulated only for participants in the one ad, two ads, and dynamic ads conditions.

Distraction. Distraction was assessed using two dependent variables: the number of anagrams solved and the number of anagrams skipped. Participants solved significantly more four-letter anagrams ($M = 51.54$, $SD = 23.78$) than five-letter anagrams ($M = 14.34$, $SD = 7.00$), and skipped significantly fewer four-letter anagrams ($M = 1.47$, $SD = 1.25$) than five-letter anagrams ($M = 3.81$, $SD = 1.83$), $F(1, 335) = 372.58$, $p < .001$, $F(1, 335) = 201.53$, $p < .001$, respectively (see Table 5.1). Ad Type (i.e., no ads, one ad, two ads, vs. dynamic ads) did not impact the number of anagrams solved, but Ad Type significantly affected the number of anagrams skipped, $F(3, 335) = 4.15$, $p = .007$. An examination of the means reveals that the results were opposite to those predicted: Participants who completed anagrams while one static ad was on the screen skipped significantly fewer anagrams compared to participants in the control condition, $F(1, 335) = 6.48$, $p = .011$. Two static ads showed a similar, non-significant effect, $F(1, 335) = 2.31$, $p = .13$.

These results suggest that minor distractions have the potential to facilitate task performance. While solving anagrams, solvers may get into a "mental set" resulting in a lack of flexibility necessary to make transformations to produce hypothesized solution word sets. Like other problems of functional fixedness, this may require a fresh perspective to help break out of the set (Duncker, 1945), and a minor distraction such as an advertisement may facilitate this fresh perspective. Indeed, people have more difficulty solving anagrams that require them to break up highly frequent letter pairs (e.g., "gatuch" to form "caught") (Mayzner and Tresselt, 1959, 1966), and distractions may break the mental sets induced by those frequent letter pairs.

Recognition. Recognition was assessed by examining participants' responses to the question asking whether they had seen the ad while doing

TABLE 5.1. NUMBER OF ANAGRAMS SOLVED AND SKIPPED, AND
NUMBER OF HINTS REQUESTED IN EXPERIMENTS 1 AND 2

Anagrams	Ads	Solved	Skipped	Hints
Experiment 1				
Easy	No ads ($n = 42$)	48.07 (23.08)	1.55 (1.47)	
	One ad ($n = 44$)	53.07 (22.34)	1.18 (1.08)	
	Two ads ($n = 42$)	53.40 (21.41)	1.50 (1.25)	
	Dynamic ads ($n = 48$)	51.54 (27.73)	1.62 (1.16)	
Difficult	No ads ($n = 40$)	14.58 (6.66)	4.15 (1.61)	
	One ad ($n = 42$)	14.60 (5.46)	3.31 (1.69)	
	Two ads ($n = 44$)	14.70 (8.54)	3.48 (2.04)	
	Dynamic ads ($n = 41$)	13.46 (7.08)	4.34 (1.77)	
Experiment 2				
Difficult	No ads ($n = 48$)	18.00 (7.48)	2.06 (1.38)	6.27 (2.08)
	One ad ($n = 47$)	18.26 (9.40)	2.36 (1.61)	7.13 (1.78)
	Two ads ($n = 48$)	18.56 (9.85)	2.25 (1.64)	6.83 (1.68)
	Dynamic ads ($n = 48$)	18.00 (7.01)	1.71 (1.29)	6.31 (1.84)

Note. After 1 minute, participants were given the option to skip to the next anagram. In experiment 2, after 30 seconds, participants were given the option to request a hint.

the anagrams. Responses were coded as 0 if the participant indicated that he or she had not seen the ad while doing the anagrams and 1 if the participant reported having seen the ad. Composite scores for recognition of viewed and unviewed ads were created by averaging the responses for the four viewed ads and the four unviewed ads. Perfect recognition would be indicated by a composite score of 1 for viewed ads and 0 for unviewed ads. Because recognition was not assessed in the no ads condition, recognition analyses include only participants in the 1 ad, 2 ads, and dynamic ads conditions.

Participants displayed highly accurate recognition of previously viewed ($M = .54$, $SD = .32$) versus unviewed ($M = .09$, $SD = .17$) ads, $F(1, 248) = 439.54$, $p < .001$ (see Table 5.2 and Figure 5.2). However, recognition was moderated by anagram difficulty, $F(1, 248) = 24.83$, $p < .001$. Participants solving difficult anagrams displayed significantly more accurate recognition compared to participants solving easy anagrams. This result offers additional evidence that participants may have glanced at the advertisements when they became stuck on a difficult anagram, leading to increased recognition of the ad. Consistent with this explanation, recognition accuracy was positively correlated with the number of anagrams skipped, $r(252) = .26$, $p < .001$. In other words, participants who were more distracted (i.e., participants who skipped more anagrams) displayed more accurate ad recognition.

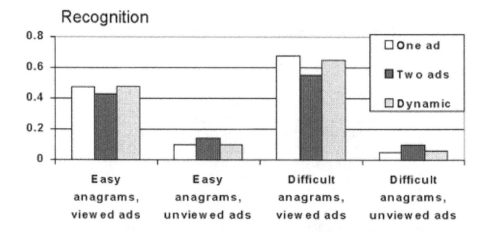

Figure 5.2. Recognition of viewed and unviewed ads in Experiment 1.

TABLE 5.2. RECOGNITION OF VIEWED AND
UNVIEWED ADS IN EXPERIMENTS 1 AND 2

Anagrams	Ads	Recognition of Viewed Ads	Recognition of Unviewed Ads
Experiment 1			
Easy	One ad ($n = 44$)	.47 (.35)	.10 (.20)***
	Two ads ($n = 42$)	.43 (.32)	.14 (.19)***
	Dynamic ads ($n = 48$)	.48 (.33)	.10 (.15)***
Difficult	One ad ($n = 42$)	.68 (.31)	.05 (.10)***
	Two ads ($n = 44$)	.55 (.29)	.10 (.21)***
	Dynamic ads ($n = 41$)	.65 (.27)	.06 (.12)***
Experiment 2			
Difficult	One ad ($n = 47$)	.58 (.30)	.04 (.10)***
	Two ads ($n = 48$)	.42 (.25)	.12(.20)***
	Dynamic ads ($n = 48$)	.56 (.33)	.13 (.21)***

Note. Recognition measures for each participant represent the mean of the four viewed ads and the four unviewed ads. Recognition scores ranged from 0 to 1, with 0 indicating that the participant reported not having seen the ad, and 1 indicating that the participant reported having seen the ad. Perfect recognition was represented by a 1 for viewed ads and a 0 for unviewed ads. Significant simple effects of Ad Exposure (i.e., viewed vs. unviewed ads) within each condition are indicated by ***$p < .001$.

Recognition was also moderated by the number and type of ads present, as reflected in a significant interaction between Ad Type and Ad Experience, $F(2, 248) = 3.80, p = .024$. Comparisons between conditions within this significant omnibus interaction were tested with a series of interactions between Ad Experience and contrasts that compare two Ad Type conditions against each other (e.g., the one ad vs. two ads contrast was represented by a vector with 1 for participants in the one ad condition, -1 for participants in the two ads condition, and 0 for participants in the dynamic ads condition).

An examination of the means reveals that, as predicted, recognition accuracy was highest in the one ad condition. Recognition accuracy suffered when a second ad was displayed, as reflected in a significant interaction between a one ad vs. two ads contrast and Ad Experience, $F(1, 248) = 6.02, p = .015$. This decrease was mitigated by making the ads dynamic and interactive; the interaction between a one ad vs. dynamic ads contrast and Ad Experience was nonsignificant.

Persuasion. Persuasion was assessed using the three questions regarding perceived quality of the web site, interest in visiting the web site, and feelings about the ad (Cronbach's alphas ranged from .86 to .88). Because exploratory factor analyses suggested that the three questions formed one factor, the questions were averaged to form a persuasion score. Then, as with recognition, composite persuasion scores were created that averaged across the four previously viewed ads and the four unviewed ads (see Table 5.3). As with the recognition variables, the analyses of the persuasion variables include only participants in the one ad, two ads, and dynamic ads conditions.

Overall, viewed ads were rated as significantly more persuasive ($M = 2.66, SD = 1.14$) than unviewed ads ($M = 2.35, SD = 1.10$), $F(1, 254) = 26.68, p < .001$, but this relationship was moderated by a significant 3-way Anagram Difficulty by Ad Type by Ad Experience interaction, $F(2, 254) = 4.23, p = .016$ (see Table 5.3 and Figure 5.3). An examination of the means reveals that, as predicted, a second ad reduces the persuasiveness of the first ad, as reflected in an interaction between a one ad versus two ads contrast and Ad Experience, $F(1, 254) = 2.70, p = .102$. The effects of two dynamic ads were moderated by anagram difficulty. For participants solving easy anagrams, two dynamic ads were no less persuasive than one static ad. For participants solving difficult anagrams, however, dynamic ads were significantly less persuasive than one ad, $F(1, 254) = 5.63, p = .018$.

In sum, Experiment 1 demonstrated that even relatively unobtrusive advertisements in the visual periphery are memorable and persuasive, but that ad competition reduces both recognition and persuasion. Increasing the salience of the ads by making them dynamic and interactive partially mitigated the effects of ad competition, but persuasion still suffered among participants solving difficult anagrams. Finally, experiment 1 demonstrated that static ads can facilitate performance on the focal task, possibly by helping participants break out of a mental set.

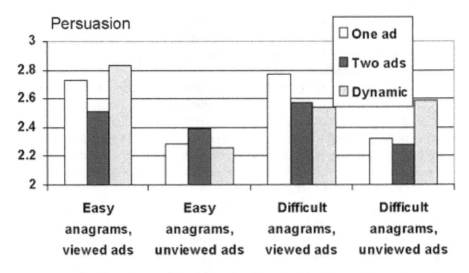

Figure 5.3. Persuasion of viewed and unviewed ads in experiment 1.

Experiment 2

The facilitation effect found in experiment 1 was particularly surprising in the context of a significant distraction effect found in the Preliminary Experiment mentioned earlier. The Preliminary Experiment was
similar to experiment 1 with one notable exception: Participants did not
complete any practice anagrams before beginning the anagram task. As a
result, a substantial portion of participants skipped the first difficult anagram. Interestingly, while only 14.3 percent (2/14) of participants skipped
the first anagram when there were no ads on the screen, 56.2 percent (9/16)
of participants skipped the first anagram in the presence of an ad, $\chi^2(1, N
= 30) = 5.66, p = .017$. For participants facing the difficult, ambiguous task
of solving their first five-letter anagram, the ad apparently provided a welcome distraction, with over half the participants waiting 60 seconds until
they were able to skip the anagram. However, the 85.7 percent success rate
in the no ads condition suggests that most participants could have solved
the problem had the presence of an advertisement not sapped their motivation to persevere.

The results of experiment 1 demonstrate that advertisements can
facilitate task performance. The results of the Preliminary Experiment
suggest that advertisements may also impact performance negatively by
facilitating procrastination. Thus, by facilitating procrastination, the presence of an ad may cause individuals to fail to complete a task that they
would have been able to accomplish had the ad not been present. This

hypothesized procrastination effect is reminiscent of the concern among employers that high-speed Internet connections distract employees from work. Support for the procrastination explanation would suggest that employers should be concerned not only with the availability of work-irrelevant web sites, but also with distracting ads in work-related software and on work-relevant web pages.

Experiment 2 was designed to replicate and extend the findings of experiment 1—most notably by providing a rigorous test of the procrastination explanation for the negative impact of peripheral ads on the focal task. To test this explanation, we modified the task to include a "procrastination option" that would help participants solve the current anagram if they were willing to procrastinate for a short time. This was operationalized as a hint button that became active after 30 seconds. When the hint button was pressed, the program revealed the first letter of the solution. Consistent with the procrastination explanation, it was predicted that participants solving difficult anagrams would request more hints in the presence of ads than in the absence of ads. Because the distraction effect in the Preliminary Study appeared only for participants solving difficult anagrams, all participants in experiment 2 solved difficult anagrams.

One hundred ninety-one Northern Illinois University undergraduates were randomly assigned to solve difficult (5-letter) anagrams in the presence of no ads, one static ad, two static ads, or two dynamic ads. After completing the anagram task, participants were asked to indicate how distracting the ads were on a 7-point scale from 0 ("not at all distracting") to 6 ("very distracting").

Results

Distraction. As in experiment 1, presence of an ad had no effect on the number of anagrams solved (see Table 5.1). In contrast to the results of experiment 1, presence of an ad also had no effect on the number of anagrams skipped, $F(3, 187) = 1.77, p = .154$. An examination of the means reveals that, if anything, participants skipped somewhat more anagrams with one or two ads on the screen than when there were no ads on the screen. The presence of an ad had a marginal effect on the number of hints requested, $F(3, 187) = 2.40, p = .069$. As predicted, participants in the one ad condition requested significantly more hints than participants in the no ads condition, $F(1, 187) = 5.10, p = .025$. Participants in the two ads condition also requested more hints than participants in the no ads condition, but this difference did not achieve statistical significance, $F(1, 187) = 2.22, p = .138$. Participants in the dynamic ads condition did not differ from participants in the no ads condition with respect to hint request frequency.

Apparently, when participants encountered an anagram that they had trouble solving, the presence of an ad provided a ready distraction until they could request a hint. This result supports the procrastination explanation of the distracting effect of peripheral ads. Such ads facilitate procrastination by providing an available stimulus toward which individuals gravitate when the focal task becomes challenging.

Interestingly, although the static ads elicited greater distraction than the dynamic ads, participants rated the static ads as substantially less distracting (one ad: $M = .85$, $SD = 1.23$; two ads: $M = .77$, $SD = 1.15$) than the dynamic ads ($M = 1.96$, $SD = 1.99$), $F(1, 140) = 18.46$, $p < .001$. This suggests that participants were unaware that the static ads were facilitating procrastination. Instead, participants' experience of distraction seemed to be based on the challenge of maintaining focus on the anagram task in the presence of the ads (a challenge made substantially more difficult when the ads were animated).

Recognition. Overall, participants showed highly accurate recognition of previously viewed ($M = .52$, $SD = .30$) versus unviewed ($M = .10$, $SD = .18$) ads, $F(1, 133) = 247.73$, $p < .001$ (see Table 5.2). This effect was qualified by a significant interaction between Ad Type and Ad Experience, $F(2, 133) = 6.87$, $p = .001$. An examination of the means reveals that, compared to the one ad condition, recognition suffered significantly in the two ads condition, $F(1, 133) = 13.48$, $p < .001$, and non-significantly in the dynamic ads condition, $F(1, 133) = 1.98$, $p = .162$.

Persuasion. As in Experiment 1, previously viewed ads were significantly more persuasive ($M = 2.53$, $SD = 1.08$) than unviewed ads ($M = 2.31$, $SD = 1.10$), $F(1, 137) = 10.06$, $p = .002$ (see Table 5.3). This effect was not moderated by Ad Type, $F(1, 137) < 1$.

Overall, experiment 2 demonstrated that visually peripheral ads can facilitate procrastination by distracting people from a challenging focal task. Experiment 2 also replicated the findings from experiment 1 that visually peripheral ads are memorable and persuasive.

The Ethics of Attention

This chapter began by distinguishing marketing contexts in which consumers barter their attention for desired products from other contexts in which marketers steal consumers' attention without providing anything in return. We argued that, because attention is a limited and valuable

TABLE 3. PERSUASION OF VIEWED AND
UNVIEWED ADS IN EXPERIMENTS 1 AND 2.

Anagrams	Ads	Persuasion of Viewed Ads	Persuasion of Unviewed Ads
Experiment 1			
Easy	One ad ($n = 44$)	2.73 (1.26)	2.29 (1.19)**
	Two ads ($n = 42$)	2.51 (1.12)	2.39 (1.18)
	Dynamic ads ($n = 48$)	2.83 (1.15)	2.26 (1.00)***
Difficult	One ad ($n = 42$)	2.77 (1.21)	2.32 (1.12)**
	Two ads ($n = 44$)	2.57 (.99)	2.28 (.81)*
	Dynamic ads ($n = 41$)	2.54 (1.12)	2.59 (1.29)
Experiment 2			
Difficult	One ad ($n = 47$)	2.57 (1.08)	2.29 (1.04)*
	Two ads ($n = 48$)	2.52 (1.11)	2.33 (1.16)
	Dynamic ads ($n = 48$)	2.52 (1.07)	2.31 (1.11)+

Note. Persuasion measures for each participant represent the mean of the four viewed ads and the four unviewed ads. Persuasion scores ranged from 0 to 6 with a higher number indicating greater persuasion. Significant simple effects of Ad Exposure (i.e., viewed vs. unviewed ads) within each condition are indicated by *: * indicating p ⅝ .05; ** indicating $p < .01$; *** indicating $p < .001$; + indicating a marginal effect at $p < .10$.

resource, stealing attention is unethical. This distinction clearly differentiates marketing media such as TV and radio commercials (both of which sponsor content that consumers may desire, and both of which can be avoided by consumers who also reject the associated content) from marketing media such as telemarketing and billboards (which are neither sponsors of desired content nor avoidable by consumers).

Recent technological innovations have created a new marketing model that appears, at first glance, to provide a remarkably ethical opportunity for consumers to barter their attention. Companies such as Qualcomm, NetZero, and Salon.com, have begun offering their products and services for free in exchange for consumers' willingness to view and, in some cases, interact with advertisements (Qualcomm, 2000; Ives, 2003).

It appears, however, that marketers and consumers have very different perceptions of this relationship. Marketers clearly perceive it as a profitable reciprocal relationship in which consumers receive a desired product or service, and in exchange, marketers receive a highly prized and increasingly scarce commodity: consumer attention. Consumers may believe, in contrast, that they are receiving a desired product or service at no cost whatsoever—a belief exacerbated by their illusions of personal invulnerability to advertising (Perloff, 1987; Sagarin, Cialdini, Rice, and Serna, 2002).

If consumers underestimate the effects that the sponsoring advertisements have on them, then the ethics of the situation become somewhat murky—consumers may have an accurate idea of the value of the product offered to them, but they are misinformed of its cost. Unfortunately, the results of the present experiments suggest that this is the case. Despite the claim by participants that online ads have little effect on them (including 49 percent who claimed that such ads have no effect whatsoever), across both experiments, peripheral ads had substantial persuasive and subtle distracting effects.

Distraction. The results of experiment 2 and our Preliminary Experiment suggest that advertisements may distract individuals from a difficult focal task by encouraging procrastination. In the Preliminary Experiment, 56.2 percent of participants solving difficult anagrams skipped the first anagram when there was an ad on the screen. This relatively high proportion may seem unsurprising at first, given that participants may not have fully understood the task they were asked to perform. However, it is notable that only 14.3 percent of participants skipped the identical first anagram when there were no ads on the screen. Apparently, the first anagram was solvable by the vast majority of participants, but the presence of an ad led over half of participants to fail on a task that most could have performed in the absence of the ad.

Experiment 2 confirmed this procrastination explanation. In experiment 2, participants were given the option of receiving a hint 30 seconds after an anagram first appeared. Consistent with the prediction that advertisements facilitate procrastination, participants requested significantly more hints in the presence of an advertisement compared to the absence of an advertisement. Participants solving anagrams in the presence of two ads showed a similar, but nonsignificant trend toward requesting more hints.

Ironically, the presence of an advertisement may also sometimes facilitate task performance. In experiment 1, participants skipped significantly fewer anagrams in the presence of one static ad than in the absence of ads. This facilitation effect may be specific to tasks such as anagrams during which participants may get stuck in a mental set. Glancing briefly at an advertisement may help participants break out of this mental set and achieve fresh insight into the anagram. Although facilitation may have been present in experiment 2, it seems likely that the addition of the hint option caused the procrastination effect to overwhelm any facilitative effects of advertisements.

Persuasion. A clear finding across both experiments is that visually peripheral ads are highly memorable and persuasive. Participants in all nine conditions showed significant recognition effects, and participants in five out of nine conditions showed significant persuasion effects, with three of the remaining four conditions showing nonsignificant effects in the direction of increased persuasiveness (see Tables 5.2 and 5.3). Although the effects occurred most strongly when participants were exposed to a single, static ad, increases in ad persuasiveness also tended to occur when two static ads were presented or when the ads were dynamic. In sum, visually peripheral advertisements can have substantial persuasive impact, particularly if they are presented without simultaneous competition from other ads.

Epilogue

> One day a student saw [Seung Sahn] reading the newspaper while he was eating. The student asked if this did not contradict his teaching. Seung Sahn said, "When you eat and read the newspaper, just eat and read the newspaper" [Tanahashi and Schneider, 1996, p. 15].

There is nothing inherently wrong with divided attention. Indeed, such a state may be impossible to avoid. But as Seung Sahn's response to the student suggests, when we choose to divide our attention, we should make an informed choice. Unfortunately, the results of the present experiments, as well as the results of Strayer et al. (chapter 4 this volume), demonstrate that we may chronically underestimate the costs of divided attention. This is not to say that we should never barter our attention. But unless we are aware of the value and scarcity of the commodity we bring to the table, we are likely to demand far too low a price.

References

Dewing, K., and Hetherington, P. (1974). Anagram solving as a function of word imagery. *Journal of Experimental Psychology*, 102, 764–767.

Duncker, K. (1945). On problem solving. *Psychological Monographs*, 58, 113.

Feuer, A. (2003, August 28). City pulls TV sets from cabs [Electronic version]. *The New York Times*.

Google (n.d.). *Google directory—Recreation > Humor > Wordplay > Anagrams.* Retrieved June 18, 2003, from http://directory.google.com/Top/Recreation/Humor/Wordplay/Anagrams

Ives, N. (2003, February 11). Marketers shift tactics on web ads [Electronic version]. *The New York Times*.

Kuczynski, A. (2000, January 6). Radio squeezes empty air space for profit. *The New York Times*, A1, C8.

Li, H. R., and Bukovac, J. L. (1999). Cognitive impact of banner ad characteristics: An experimental study. *Journalism and Mass Communication Quarterly*, 76, 341–353.

Mayzner, M. S., and Tresselt, M. E. (1958). Anagram solution times: A function of letter order and word frequency. *Journal of Experimental Psychology*. 56, 376–379.

_____, and _____ (1959). Anagram solution times: A function of transition probabilities. *Journal of Psychology*, 47, 117–125.

_____, and _____ (1966). Anagram solution times: A function of multiple-solution anagrams. *Journal of Experimental Psychology*, 71, 66–73.

Moore, C. W. (2000, February 24). [Moore's views and reviews] Checking out Eudora 4.3, plus an interview with Eudora products' David Ross. *Applelinks.com*. Retrieved January 23, 2001, from http://www.applelinks.com/articles/2000/02/2000022423926.shtml

NetZero (n.d.). *Welcome to NetZero*. Retrieved April 1, 2003, from http://www.netzero.net

Perloff, L. S. (1987). Social comparison and illusions of invulnerability to negative life events. In C. R. Snyder and C. E. Ford (eds.), *Coping with negative life events: Clinical and social psychological perspectives* (pp. 217-242). New York: Plenum.

Qualcomm (2000, February 15). *Qualcomm's new Eudora 4.3 provides industrial-strength e-mail for free*. Retrieved January 24, 2001, from http://www.eudora.com/press/2000/2_15_00.htm

Sagarin, B. J., Britt, M. A., Heider, J. D., Wood, S. E., and Lynch, J. E. (2003). Bartering our attention: The distraction and persuasion effects of on-line advertisements. *Cognitive Technology*, 8, 4–17.

Sagarin, B. J., Cialdini, R. B., Rice, W. E., and Serna, S. B. (2002). Dispelling the illusion of invulnerability: The motivations and mechanisms of resistance to persuasion. *Journal of Personality and Social Psychology*, 83, 526–541.

Tanahashi, K., and Schneider, T. D. (1996). *Essential zen*. Edison, NJ: Castle Books.

Tresselt, M. E., and Mayzner, M. S. (1968). Anagram solution times: A function of single- and double-letter solution words. *Journal of Verbal Learning and Verbal Behavior*, 7, 128–132.

Wood, S. E., Panchal, A. J., Houle, B. J., Scherer, C. R., Heider, J. D., Lynch, J. E., Dixon, A., and Sagarin, B. J. (2002, May). *"If that phone rings one more time..."*: *Consumer perceptions of intrusive marketing*. Paper presented at the Midwestern Psychological Association's annual meeting, Chicago, Illinois.

6

Social Identity and the Self: Getting Connected Online

KATELYN Y. A. MCKENNA *and*
GWENDOLYN SEIDMAN

Belonging

After basic needs of survival such as food, water, and shelter have been met, the need to connect with others becomes of primary concern (Baumeister and Leary, 1994). Yet it is not enough for individuals to achieve a sense of belonging based only on tenuous connections, nor to only feel identification with broad social groups. Rather, one needs to feel an integral member of a group who share similar interests and goals (Baumeister and Leary, 1994). People are motivated to forge connections with others who see them as they see themselves (Swann, 1990). Moreover, one needs to feel unique and valued among those members (Brewer, 1991).

We will argue that the Internet is a prime venue for the expression and exploration of important aspects of identity that one may be barred from sharing in everyday life. That is, one may be able to meet important needs for belonging and acceptance over the Internet that one is lacking in one's daily life. We begin with a discussion of some of the reasons why one's need to belong may be being inadequately met in daily life. Next, we discuss the qualities of electronic media that facilitate social identification and belonging. We then discuss some of the social identification processes that appear to be particularly important for the attainment of effective and self-transformative group membership online. Finally, we discuss the social

and psychological consequences that may result when one finds a sense
of belonging and acceptance in cyberspace.

Issues of Identity: Why Belonging
Needs May be Inadequately Met

Social Anxiety and Loneliness

Forging relationships with others that would allow one to express
important self-qualities is often quite difficult for those who experience
high levels of social anxiety when meeting new people, taking part in social
group activities, or talking with someone whom they find attractive (e.g.,
Leary and Atherton, 1986). As Leary (1988) and others have shown,
the socially anxious are often less socially skilled and more reticent with
self-disclosure. As a result, they tend to be less liked and accepted by
others. Ironically, the self-inhibition brought about by the very fear of
saying or doing something that might create a negative impression often
results in others forming a negative impression of the socially anxious
individual. Chronically experiencing high levels of social anxiety in interpersonal situations can significantly interfere with an individual's pursuit and achievement of his or her interpersonal goals (e.g., Henderson and Zimbardo, 1999). Thus the socially anxious may find themselves
barred from the benefits (e.g., feelings of belonging, acceptance; increases
in self-esteem) that close relationships and group memberships often
bring, including the opportunity to reveal and have validated identity-
important aspects of the self (e.g., Deaux, 1996; McKenna and Bargh,
1998).

Similarly, those who are lonely and without a satisfactory social circle may also lack the chance to express important aspects of self and identity with others. Those who experience high levels of social anxiety often
are among the "lonely crowd." However, there are many other reasons why
an individual may find him or herself in a lonely and isolated situation.
Loneliness can be chronic or brought about by situational circumstances.
For instance, those who are homebound because of physical disabilities
or illness, those who have just moved to a new city and have yet to forge
new social connections there, and those whose social circles are rapidly
shrinking due to death and illness can often feel quite lonely indeed. These
individuals are likely to be highly motivated to establish meaningful relationships with others, if they only could.

Socially Stigmatized Identities

Brewer (1991) argued that people have the need to feel connected to others, to have a sense of group belonging, and to feel like a valued member of a group. Opportunities for such group identification are readily available for those with mainstream identities. Such is not the case for those who possess stigmatized identities, particularly those that are concealable from others (Frable, 1993; E. E. Jones et al., 1984).

Because of the potentially embarrassing nature of concealable culturally stigmatized identities (e.g., former prison inmates, those with non-mainstream views), it is often difficult for an individual to disclose this identity-aspect, even should he or she suspect that another may share it. There can be very real risks of such self-disclosure to one's important relationships, both at home and at work (Derlega, Metts, Petronio, and Margulis, 1993). For the reason that people do tend to conceal socially stigmatized identities when possible, one is generally not able to identify others who are similar to oneself in this important way without being the one to make the first move in self-disclosure. Thus, those with such stigmatized aspects of self often feel isolated and different from those around them. Such conflicts between the public persona and the private self are the major cause of unhappiness and neuroses (Homey, 1946).

While those with conspicuous culturally stigmatized identities (e.g., obesity) are often made abundantly aware of the fact that they differ from mainstream society, they do have the benefit of being able to readily identify similar others. Because they are able to see that there are others who share this marginalized aspect of self, they do not feel so unique or alone. Frable (1993) found that, compared to those with conspicuous marginalized qualities and those with wholly mainstream qualities, people with stigmatized but concealable self-aspects demonstrated a considerably reduced tendency toward false consensus. They were the least likely to feel that others shared their preferences for such mundane items as tuna salad. They were also more likely to describe themselves in terms of items related to uniqueness and alienation (e.g., rare, outsider).

Further, the important relationships that an individual with a conspicuous stigmatized identity forges are often premised on the knowledge that the other is aware of this marginalized identity aspect and nonetheless accepts him or her. In other words, there is often a sense that these important others "like me for who I am." In contrast, when relationships are forged with a marginalized aspect of identity well-concealed, the concealer may well feel that these relationships are not authentic. In other words, the individual may feel that "I'm liked and accepted only because they don't know what I'm really like." Thus, when relationships are formed based on mutual mainstream aspects of self, the individual with a concealed stigmatized identity may not gain the same benefits of belonging as do members who are not concealing stigmatized self-qualities.

Thus the motivations for group identification and authentic relationships are likely to be strongly operative for the individual with a marginalized and concealable identity. The fundamental need to belong to the society at large is frustrated because the individual feels different from others. Lacking a comparison group of similar others, the individual is likely to be uncertain about this important aspect of identity and will be motivated to reduce this uncertainty (Archer, 1987; Hogg and Abrams, 1993). Because this negative aspect of identity is included in the individual's sense of self, one's motive to hold a positive self-image (e.g., Sedikides, 1993) is likely to be thwarted. The individual is thus likely to be highly motivated to try to connect with others who share that identity and who do not view it negatively, in order to reduce the stigma and thereby increase self-esteem (Jones et al., 1984, p. 133).

Health Problems and Grief

While serious illness and bereavement will touch most of us at some point in our lives, these are issues that people are loath to dwell on. Following such an unfortunate event, friends and family members (and even strangers when something like the terrorist attacks of September 11, 2001 occur) generally rally around—for a time. However, as Pennebaker and others (e.g., Rimé, Mesquita, Philippot, and Boca, 1991; Pennebaker and Harber, 1993) have shown, the pattern of social sharing tends to be far more short-lived than those affected need and desire.

Being able to openly discuss one's feelings and fears about traumatic life events has been shown to result in improved physical and mental health (Pennebaker, 1997; Smyth, 1998). Yet, those around the individual in need of support quickly become weighed down with their own emotional responses and so wish to avoid reminders of the subject. In other words, the conflicting needs to talk about and to avoid talking about the issue result in social constraints to inhibit personal disclosure (e.g., Pennebaker, 1989).

The message that this is now a taboo topic can come across in a variety of ways. People in one's supportive social network may put a stop to discussions about the issue by literally asking (demanding) that one stops talking about the painful subject or by changing the subject whenever it arises (e.g., Dakof and Taylor, 1990; Lehman and Hemphill, 1990; Helmrath and Steinitz, 1978). Friends and family members may begin to ignore or avoid the sufferer in an effort to avoid dealing with the issue (Lepore, 1997) or they may minimize the problems or offer inept support attempts (e.g., Lepore and Hegelson, 1998; Lepore, Silver, Wortman, and Wayment, 1996). Even when the members of an individual's social network are willing to discuss the issue as much as the sufferer desires, he or she may not perceive that such is the case. The individual may feel that it is wrong to burden others with one's own problems, that talking about it would only add to the distress that others are already experiencing, or he or she may have difficulty expressing emotions. No matter how one gets the "don't go there" message, the person in need of social support is left feeling isolated and alienated from their social network.

Role Expectancies and Constraints

People define themselves and are defined by others to a great extent by their social roles and obligations. An individual may consider many roles to be identity-important—for instance, those of husband, father, businessman, Harvard graduate, golfer, and animal rescuer—or self-definition may be focused on a more limited number of identities (Deaux, 1996). Research has shown that those who have a larger number of self-defining identities tend to be better prepared to deal with life changes and stress (Sarbin and Allen, 1968). They also tend to experience better health (Linville, 1985), and to feel more satisfied with their lives (Spreitzer, Snyder, and Larson, 1979) than do those who have only a few defining identities.

However, the very identities and roles a person is able to claim can also serve as constraints on his or her expression of other important aspects of self and identity (Stryker and Statham, 1985). That is, based upon the roles we are perceived to fill, the others around us have certain expectations about how we should behave, the opinions, attitudes, and qualities we should express, and the other kinds of identities we should claim for ourselves. Should an individual express self-qualities or identities that are at variance to those expectations, his or her peers and family members may be unwilling to accept or acknowledge them. Important others may even respond quite negatively. Anticipating or fearing such a response, an individual may not even attempt to express these aspects of self (Derlega, et al., 1993; Pennebaker, 1989).

Summary

Individuals then are often caught between the need to express important aspects of identity to others (e.g., Gollwitzer, 1986; Swann, 1990), and the simultaneous need to contain or protect information about the self (e.g., Pennebaker, 1989; Rubin, 1977). Because the opinions that the significant others hold of oneself are so vitally important to one's self-esteem, anxiety levels, and happiness (e.g., Baumeister and Leary, 1995), both of these motives are likely to be chronic over the life-term, and thus well-practiced and highly efficient (see Bargh, 1990). However, should a safe and nonthreatening avenue for self-disclosure become available, people will be motivated to take advantage of that opportunity. There are a number of qualities of electronic communication that make the Internet a prime avenue for such self-disclosure and identity-expression.

The Role of the Internet

Anonymity

A major difference between online and face-to-face interaction is that online communication provides individuals with a feeling of anonymity. Often, people can be completely anonymous on the Internet. Internet service providers such as AOL or Yahoo allow individuals to choose screen names for themselves to use in chat rooms or instant messaging that have little or no relationship to their real name or true identity. When meeting someone in a face-to-face situation, it is very rare to develop intimacy with that person, while still retaining anonymity. However, on the Internet, such feelings can emerge between individuals who are completely anonymous to one another, ultimately leading to the development of close relationships (e.g., Parks and Floyd, 1995; McKenna, Green, and Gleason, 2002; Walther, 1996).

An issue that is closely tied to that of anonymity is the issue of identifiability. In our face-to-face lives we frequently, and often repeatedly, interact with others (e.g., the clerk at our local drugstore, the woman who goes to our laundromat the same day of the week as we do) to whom we do not reveal personal information, such as our names, occupations, hometown, and so forth. However, despite the relative anonymity we have with these people, they may still be able to easily recognize us in a different setting. Occasionally, we do engage in what Zick Rubin (1976) called the "strangers on a train" phenomenon. That is, we may share the most intimate details of our lives, details our closest friends may not even know, with perfect strangers. We feel safe making such disclosures to complete strangers whom we expect to never see again.

In contrast, even when people interact openly (i.e., using their true names, providing information about their profession) on the Internet, they often still feel relatively anonymous (McKenna and Bargh, 2000). Due to this feeling of anonymity, they often engage in a "strangers on the Internet" phenomenon, disclosing personal, intimate information to others whom they may well encounter online again. These disclosures can thus become the groundwork for a continuing and close relationship. Additionally, the ability to interact anonymously allows people to join groups and explore aspects of self on the Internet that they might otherwise keep hidden in their existing relationships (e.g., McKenna and Bargh, 1998; McKenna et al., 2002).

Removal of Gating Features

Physical appearance and mannerisms play an essential role, not only in impression formation, but also in determining whom we will approach and, and even with whom we will develop friendships and romantic relationships (e.g., Hatfield and Sprecher, 1986). We tend to use physically available features to immediately categorize others (e.g., their ethnicity, attractiveness, age; Bargh, 1989; Brewer, 1988). For example, research on impressions at the zero-acquaintance level has shown that there is extremely high consensus among participants in their initial impressions of others, across a wide variety of personality measurements, based only on physical appearance (e.g., Allbright, Kenny, and Malloy, 1988). In addition, research has shown that it is rather difficult to get past first impressions (e.g., Fiske and Taylor, 1991) because people tend to selectively focus on information that confirms rather than disconfirms their initial judgment, in when they interact with people again (e.g., Higgins and Bargh, 1987).

Thus, those features that are most readily perceived, such as physical appearance (attractiveness), an apparent stigma (e.g., stuttering), or apparent shyness or social anxiety often serve as gates in our face-to-face interactions. These gates often open to those who are physically attractive and outgoing, but close when we encounter the less socially skilled or physically attractive, keeping these individuals out of our social and romantic circles.

When interactions with new online acquaintances take place in newsgroups, instant messengers, chatrooms, and so forth online, such gating features are not usually immediately apparent and thus do not become a barrier to potential relationships. Instead, impressions are formed on very different criteria. Rather than basing impressions on superficial features, such as attractiveness, the opinions expressed and the information about the self that is revealed become the basis of first impressions. However, to the extent that such gating features are in evidence initially (for example, online dating services such as Match.com provide member profiles with an accompanying picture) then the same biases that operate in our face-to-face lives will come into play and we are likely to similarly bypass or reject out of hand from the outset potentially satisfactory and mutually profitable relationships.

Control

In online interactions, individuals are able to control interactions in a way that is not possible in face-to-face or telephone communication. In face-to-face and telephone interactions one is expected to respond immediately and "off the cuff." However, immediate response is not expected in online communication. People realize that typing a reply can take time, especially since some individuals are better typists than others. Pauses that may seem unnaturally long in speech can go unnoticed in an online instant message. Immediate replies to e-mails are not expected because we know that it often takes time for people to check their e-mail and find the time to write a response. The opportunity to delay response provides individuals with the chance to edit their message before sending it and it gives them more time to think about what they are going to say. This removes the pressure to respond immediately and allows for a more thoughtful response.

In addition, in person and telephone conversation, norms require people to communicate in short bursts, rather than long speeches. This can inhibit the degree to which people can express themselves. However, online, long e-mails or instant messages are perfectly acceptable. Interaction partners therefore have more time to plan what they will say, they can type as much or as little as they want in a single reply, and they can edit responses before sending them. All of these factors give individuals greater control over how they present themselves and their ideas and opinions to others than generally occurs in face-to-face or telephone exchanges.

Connecting to Similar Others

A final unique aspect of the Internet is the ease with which people can find and connect with similar others there. Even if we are aware of groups in the community that share our interests, we may not have the time or means to attend those get-togethers. Online, people can participate in interest groups at times that are most convenient for them, thus allowing interpersonal and group connections to be made. The Internet can be particularly useful for locating others who share very specialized interests (such as candle making), who are experiencing similar health or emotional difficulties, or who share aspects of identity that are socially sanctioned and thus are often not readily identifiable in one's physical community.

Summary

The unique qualities of computer-mediated communication discussed above can produce different outcomes than those that occur in traditional interaction settings. However, it is not the case that these qualities produce "main effects" on the user. Rather, the particular aspects of the Internet interaction situation will interact with the goals, motivations, and personal characteristics of the individuals involved to produce effects on psychological and interpersonal outcomes (McKenna and Bargh, 2000; Spears, Postmes, Lea, and Wolbert, 2002). For instance, anonymity has been shown to produce anti-normative behavior online; it has also been shown to produce even stronger normative effects online than in face-to-face situations (e.g., Spears, et al., 2002). Yet other studies have shown that being identifiable rather than anonymous increases online participants' group-normative behavior (e.g., Douglas and McGarty, 2001). While on the face of it these findings appear at odds, these differential outcomes are readily explained when one takes into account the way in which anonymity is interacting with other situational factors.

Social Identity Processes Online

Social interaction and group functioning on the Internet follow many of the same rules that govern socializing and group dynamics in traditional, face-to-face venues. Whether interactions take place in person or electronically, group processes and effects will evolve in much the same way (Spears, et al., 2002). Theoretical models that were developed based on research on face-to-face groups, such as social identity theory, have been tested and shown to also apply to online behavior. Below we briefly discuss the facets of social identification processes that appear to be particularly important to our understanding of how social processes unfold online.

The Role of Participation

Kay Deaux and her colleagues have shown that simply identifying with an identity-relevant group is not enough for benefits such as increased self-esteem to accrue. Rather, the amount that an individual participates or is involved in the identity-relevant group is an important mediator of the benefits of identification. For instance, in their studies of ethnic identification (Ethier and Deaux, 1994), motherhood (Ethier, 1995), and deafness (Bat-Chava, 1994) no overall relationship between the respective identifications and self-esteem were found. Increases in self-esteem occurred only for those whom were actively involved in the respective groups. McKenna and Bargh (1998) tested Deaux's (1996) model of social identity in online settings and found that the same process unfolds over the Internet. What sets the Internet apart in this instance is that the benefits of belonging can now be expanded to populations that otherwise would have had no opportunity to participate in identity-relevant groups.

The Crucial Role of Self-Disclosure

Mutual self-disclosure is a critical component for the formation of close interpersonal bonds and the establishment of a sense of belonging and acceptance. We have a strong need to feel that we are accepted and valued for who we are inside (e.g., Swann, 1990) and not just for how we look, our obvious abilities and accomplishments, the social roles we fulfill, and so forth. In other words, we strive to connect with others with whom we can share not only our outer accomplishments but also the important qualities of our inner selves.

However, there are many reasons why an individual may be constrained in the expression of important inner-self qualities and thus have his or her need for belonging inadequately met in everyday life. Turkle (1995) was the first to argue that the Internet constitutes a unique opportunity for self-expression. As we have argued, people are motivated to use the Internet to express those aspects of self that they cannot often or easily express to others in traditional interaction settings. Indeed, laboratory studies by Bargh et al., (2002) have shown that the qualities of the Internet communication experience quickly bring forth the activation and expression of such important, but generally unexpressed, inner self-aspects for the average person—at least when communicating with new acquaintances. In contrast, when participants in these studies interacted in a face-to-face setting, these inner qualities were inhibited and the self-qualities that the participant easily and generally expresses to others became more accessible.

Identity Salience

In both face-to-face groups and groups that form and function over the Internet, the degree to which the group identity is salient within a given context and the degree to which given members have incorporated the group into his or her self-concept are important mediators of the effects of group membership. Qualities of the Internet, such as anonymity, have been shown to interact with identity salience to produce different outcomes from those that often occur in face-to-face environments. For instance, Spears, Lea, and Lee (1990) found that when members of online groups interacted under anonymous conditions and group salience was high, normative behavior increased in those groups as compared to groups in which members were anonymous but the salience of the group was low. Intermediate levels of conformity were observed for participants interacting under nonanonymous conditions, regardless of the degree of group salience.

Incorporating Relationships into the Self

Recent research into the relational nature of the self (e.g., Andersen and Chen, 2002) has shown that conceptions of self include not only a "me" but also a "we" component. That is, one also tends to incorporate one's important relationships (along with one's important group identities, e.g., Deaux, 1996; Tajfel and Turner, 1986) into one's sense of self. Only relationships of high personal significance tend to be incorporated into the self in this way; in these studies, control stimuli related to another experimental participant's significant other produce no such activation-of-self effects.

One might expect then, that should an individual form a relationship online in which he or she is able to express important inner aspects of self that go unexpressed within other, existing relationships, that this new relationship would become highly important to the individual. This new relationship, with its relational association to aspects of the inner or true self, should also tend to be incorporated into one's sense of self. Indeed, this does appear to be the case, as is discussed in more detail later.

Making Important Identities and
Relationships a Social Reality

When individuals acquire a new aspect of identity, they tend to be highly motivated to share this identity with others in order to have it socially validated. As Wicklund and Gollwitzer (1986) have shown, group memberships do not become psychologically real until the individual is able to make them a social reality. That is, the individual needs to have others notice and acknowledge his or her membership in the group. In the same way, when we form important new personal relationships we tend to tell our friends and family members about him or her and to often introduce and attempt to integrate this new person into our existing social circle.

Consequences of Social Identification Online

Increased Self-Acceptance

McKenna and Bargh (1998) studied Internet users involved in electronic newsgroups catering to marginalized aspects of identity. One study focused on those who have marginalized sexual proclivities (e.g., homosexuality) and a second provided a replication with stigmatized ideological beliefs (e.g., believers in government conspiracies). We hypothesized that active participation in identity-relevant electronic groups would result in the same benefits for these individuals as has been found for group membership and identification in traditional face-to-face groups (e.g., Deaux, 1996; Ethier and Deaux, 1994). Specifically, to the extent that participation in these groups leads to stronger group identification, the individual should come to accept the marginalized identity as part of, rather than distinct from, the self-concept.

We found that active participation in the online groups did allow these individuals to reap the self-related benefits of joining a group of similar others. Moreover, because these groups dealt with stigmatized identities, for most participants this was the first time and the only way possible for them to find similarly-minded others. Participation in the groups allowed these individuals to disclose a long-secret yet important part of their identity, and in return gain emotional and motivational support from their fellow group members (Archer, 1987; Derlega et al., 1993; Jones et al., 1984). Participation in the online group resulted in increased feelings of acceptance of one's marginalized identity.

McKenna, Green, and Smith (2001) replicated this finding for those with normative, mainstream aspects of sexuality. In this study, participants taking part in groups devoted to the expression of mainstream aspects of sexuality were surveyed. Participants who were barred from expressing or acting upon their sexual needs in their everyday lives, and who turned to the Internet to explore these issues in a safe and non-threatening environment, also benefited from increased self-acceptance of their sexuality.

Decreased Loneliness, Estrangement, and Isolation

In the studies discussed above (McKenna and Bargh, 1998; McKenna et al., 2001) active participation in identity-relevant online groups also led to decreased feelings of being "different" from others. These participants reported feeling less estranged from society at large and less isolated and alone than did those members who did not take an active part in the group.

Online participation in groups and interacting online with members of one's existing social circle also appears to decrease feelings of loneliness and isolation for the average person. For instance, Howard, Rainie, and Jones (2001) concluded from their large random-sample survey that the Internet enables people to keep in touch with family and friends and to extend their social networks. The researchers note, "A sizeable majority of those who email relatives say it increases the level of communication between family members ... these survey results suggest that online tools are more likely to extend social contact than detract from it" (p. 399).

A number of other national surveys and longitudinal studies have found that Internet users actually have the larger social networks (e.g., DiMaggio, Hargittai, Neuman, and Robinson, 2001). For instance, a longitudinal study by Kraut et al. (2002) found that, for the average participant, using the Internet more led to larger increases in their local and distant social circles and to increasing the amount of face-to-face contact with family and friends. These participants also experienced a reduction in feelings of loneliness and depression. Similarly, in a longitudinal study of Internet newsgroup participants, McKenna et al. (2002) found significant decreases in feelings of social anxiety and loneliness for their participants over a two-year period of time. Importantly, feeling that one is able to express more of one's true self online was also associated with decreased feelings of loneliness.

Increased Social Support

A related consequence of increasing one's social network is often that of increased social support. While feeling that one has a supportive social network is important for all of us, it can be particularly so for those dealing with stressful and traumatic life events. As Pennebaker (1997) and others have shown, those around an individual who is dealing with such a painful or stressful event often, implicitly or explicitly, place a ban on discussing the issue far too soon. Thus, as for those with stigmatized aspects of identity, the Internet provides the opportunity for individuals in such situations to connect with similar others, to share the feelings and fears they feel they must hold back from members of their existing social network, and to reap the associated benefits.

A study of online support provision and seeking by those with grave illnesses (Davison, Pennebaker, and Dickerson, 2000), found that people used Internet support groups particularly for embarrassing, stigmatized illnesses such as AIDS, alcoholism, and prostate cancer, because of the relative anonymity of the online community. The authors point out that these patients feel anxiety and uncertainty and are thus highly motivated by social comparison needs to seek out others with the same illness. When the illness is an embarrassing, disfiguring, or otherwise stigmatized one, they prefer to do this online because of the anonymity afforded by Internet groups.

Those dealing with common and socially accepted health issues also benefit from seeking additional support online. For instance, Barrera and colleagues (2002), conducted a study with diabetics, assigning some participants to participate in Internet support groups for diabetes and others to use the Internet only as a means of gathering information about their illness (and to thus rely on their existing social networks for support). They found that those who participated in the online groups reported feeling that they had received more support than did those who relied solely on their offline social network. Among older adults, greater participation in community support web sites for the elderly, such as SeniorNet, was associated with lower perceived life stress (Wright, 2000). Similarly, participation in an online support group for the hearing impaired was particularly beneficial for participants with little "real world" support (Cummings, Sproull, and Kiesler, 2002).

Formation of Close, Lasting Relationships

To the extent that an individual does use the Internet to express and disclose important aspects of self with others, these online relationships should become identity important. This should be particularly the case when the aspects of self one is expressing are those that one is generally unable to express within one's face-to-face social circle. Mental representations of external social entities (such as groups) through which a person defines his identity tend to become incorporated into one's self-concept (see Spears, et al., 1992). Because the self is relational in nature, one's self tends to become "entangled" or defined in large part in terms of important interpersonal relationships as well (e.g., Baldwin, 1997; Chen and Andersen, 1999).

Confirming this prediction are the results of a longitudinal study

(McKenna et al., 2002) conducted with nearly 600 participants who take part in quite mainstream electronic groups (e.g., groups devoted to discussions of computer programming, pet care, history, parenting). Those individuals who reported feeling that they were better able to express or "locate" their true self on the Internet than in face-to-face settings were more likely to have forged close online relationships. Many of these participants had developed quite intimate online relationships indeed. Those who felt that their "real self" resides on the Internet, compared to those who didn't, were significantly more likely to have become engaged to, or have an affair with, someone they met on the Internet.

Those who felt that their true self was better expressed online than offline also reported that their online relationships developed intimacy more quickly than did their face-to-face relationships. It may well be the faster disclosure of important qualities of one's inner self in these online interactions that drives these relationships to form more quickly. Consistent with this logic, laboratory studies (Bargh et al., 2002; McKenna et al., 2002) have shown that people tend to like one another more if they first become acquainted through the Internet than if they first meet in person, at least when it comes to members of the opposite sex.

Relationships that begin online can also be durable. A follow-up was done to see how the relationships reported by the 600 newsgroup users had fared after two years. McKenna et al. (2002) found that the majority of these participants' online relationships were enduring two years later. Indeed, 75 percent of the relationships were ongoing, with the majority being characterized as having grown closer and stronger over the intervening years. The stability of these friendships and romantic relationships compares favorably to relationships that form and develop in traditional face-to-face settings.

Coming Out and Coming Together

As with important group identities and personal relationships that are forged in traditional settings, people are motivated to make their important online memberships and relationships into a social reality. That is, they are not content to only express these important aspects of self in the virtual realm. Rather, they tend to tell others in their social circles about their important online group memberships and they bring important online relationships into their everyday lives.

In the study of relationships that form and develop over the Internet, McKenna et al., (2002) found that those who felt better able to express important aspects of their inner self on the Internet were also more likely than others to have brought their online relationships into their non-Internet life. They did this by meeting the other person face-to-face, talking with them on the telephone, and exchanging letters. At the time of the first phase of the study, more than 50 percent of participants had taken the step of meeting their closest online friend in person. By the time of the follow-up two years later, slightly more than 70 percent had done so.

Perhaps one of the most surprising findings, and one that demonstrates the powerful self-transformational effect that participation in an identity-relevant group on the Internet can have, concerns those with socially sanctioned identities. McKenna and Bargh (1998) found that, as a direct result of group membership and participation, fully 50 percent of individuals with stigmatized (sexual and ideological) identities took the step of revealing this identity for the first time to non–Internet family members and friends. The average age of participants in these two studies was 37 years and so these individuals had kept the stigmatized identity a closely held, embarrassing secret for their entire adult lives. It is thus remarkable that involvement in these electronic groups for an average of less than two years caused these participants to "come out" to family and friends. They were not content to only express this important aspect of self in the virtual realm, but rather were motivated to integrate this new-found identity and self-acceptance into their everyday social sphere.

A Word of Caution

Thus far in this chapter we have focused on the positive aspects of finding a sense of belonging and connectedness to others through the Internet. It is important to keep in mind, however, that there can be pitfalls as well as pluses. For instance, armed with newfound feelings of self-acceptance gained from belonging to an identity-relevant group on the Internet, an individual with a stigmatized identity may "come out" to family and friends, only to be met with the very rejection he or she had feared. Such self-disclosure may result in the relationship being changed or even ended (e.g., Kelly and McKillop, 1996), and the rejection may leave the individual with feelings of more isolation and less self-worth than he or she experienced before finding the identity-transforming group.

Because mainstream society does not, by definition, value marginalized identities it will place a negative value on any mechanism that encourages their expression. Thus whether the demonstrated effects of increasing an individual's marginalized identity, providing social support and validation of beliefs, and the encouragement of real-life behavior is considered a positive outcome will depend on one's valuation of the marginalized identity in question. Certainly in the event that this process results in acts of violence and harm against an innocent victim, it will be unequivocally viewed as a bad thing. Consider, for instance, an individual with a latent interest in pedophilia who finds others with a similar interest on the Internet and, through the identity demarginalization process, comes to feel that not only are such desires acceptable but is motivated to act upon those desires in the real world. While we do not have direct evidence that such would be the case, results from the studies by McKenna and Bargh (1998) and McKenna et al. (2001) suggest that it well may be. Of particular relevance is the finding that the more an individual expresses a hidden, albeit thoroughly mainstream, sexual fantasy with others over the Internet, the stronger the desire and inclination becomes to act out that fantasy with a physical partner (McKenna et al., 2001).

Finding one's soul mate online may also prove to be a mixed bag of positives and negatives. For instance, if one is currently involved in a steady or married relationship with someone else, that someone else will certainly end up feeling hurt and betrayed. Further, while society's view of Internet-initiated relationships has certainly changed over the past few years from one of disapproval and skepticism to one that is more accepting, this change may lead to difficulties and disappointments. In the last year, for instance, 40 million Americans visited online dating sites in an effort to find the perfect romantic partner (Harmon, 2003). If one views the Internet as "the answer" to finding compatibility and comes up short, it may prove to be a serious blow to one's self-esteem.

Ironically, the more the Internet has become embraced as a means of connecting with others on a romantic level, the more people are relying on traditional criteria for possible mate-selection, albeit now utilized over the Internet. They are increasingly eschewing many of the interaction qualities that originally accompanied electronic communication and that have been shown to promote one's chances of finding one's soul mate, such as initially interacting with physical information about the partner being absent or joining interest groups that may allow a relationship to naturally develop. To date, studies of successful online relationship formation and development (e.g., McKenna et al., 2002; Parks and Floyd, 1995) have examined relationships that developed naturally as a result of taking part in an interest group and that began with physical information about the other initially absent. Importantly, many of those who forged satisfying and durable romantic relationships noted that, had they initially come into contact with their partner in a situation where physical features were in evidence, they most likely would not have approached the other or pursued the relationship to the point where they could discover that they were, in fact, a good match (McKenna and Bargh, 1998). This finding is in line with numerous studies on the influence of physical attractiveness on relationship formation (e.g., Hatfield and Sprecher, 1986). Increasingly, however, people are approaching potential partners online, just as they do offline, based primarily on the physical attractiveness of the other, rather than on interest match or engaging personality characteristics. Thus, it may well be the case that, as we make our Internet experiences more closely approximate "real life," we may well be discarding some of the very factors that made online interactions unique and profitable to begin with.

Conclusion

It is clear that the Internet can be a useful tool for bringing people together and enabling them to meet important needs for belonging and acceptance that are otherwise inadequately being met in their lives. The unique qualities of electronic communication can facilitate the sharing of identity-important aspects of self that one may not be able to readily express in traditional interaction venues and with existing members of one's social circle. People are often motivated to express and explore important facets of self online because of the lack of a real-world opportunity to do so. However, what occurs in the virtual domain can have real consequences in the everyday sphere as well. In other words, what happens in the one sphere can affect behavior in the other.

Forming identity-important bonds with others, whether over the Internet or in other venues, has many psychological and social benefits. Increased feelings of self-esteem and self-acceptance are major benefits, as is the reduction in stress that often accompanies such gains (e.g., Jones et al., 1984). As Pennebaker (1989) has shown, being able to bring hidden or hard-to-disclose identities and emotions into the open, even anonymously, significantly improves one's physical, as well as emotional, health. Strengthening existing bonds and forging new ones reduces feelings of loneliness and isolation. And the important new relationships and identities that develop over the Internet are quite likely to be integrated into and acted upon in one's face-to-face life. The way in which people use the Internet, however, along with their motivations and goals will do much to determine what the outcomes will be.

References

Allbright, L., Kenny, D. A., and Malloy, T. E., (1988). Consensus in personality judgments at zero acquaintance. *Journal of Personality and Social Psychology*, 55, 387–395.

Andersen, S. M., and Chen, S. (2002). The relational self: An interpersonal social-cognitive theory. *Psychological Review*, 109, 619–645.

Archer, R. L. (1987). Commentary: Self-disclosure, a very useful behavior. In V. L. Derlega and J. H. Berg (eds.), *Self-disclosure: Theory, research, and therapy* (pp. 329–342). New York: Plenum.

Baldwin, M. W. (1997). Relational schemas as a source of if-then self-inference procedures. *Review of General Psychology*, 1, 326–335.

Bargh, J. A. (1989). Conditional automaticity: Varieties of automatic influence in social perception and cognition. In J. S. Uleman and J. A. Bargh (eds.), *Unintended thought* (pp. 3–51). New York: Guilford.

_____ (1990). Auto-motives: Preconscious determinants of social interaction. In E. T. Higgins and R. M. Sorrentino (eds.), *Handbook of motivation and cognition: Foundations of social behavior*, Vol. 2 (pp. 93–130). New York: Guilford.

_____, McKenna, K. Y. A., and Fitzsimons, G. M. (2002). Can you see the real me? Activation and expression of the "true self" on the Internet. *Journal of Social Issues*, 58(1), 33–48.

Barrera, M., Jr., Glasgow, R. E., McKay, H. G., Boles, S. M., and Feil, E. G. (2002). Do Internet based support interventions change perceptions of social support? An experimental trial of approaches for supporting diabetes self-management. *American Journal of Community Psychology*, 30, 637–654.

Bat-Chava, Y. (1994). Group identification and self-esteem of deaf adults. *Personality and Social Psychology Bulletin*, 20, 494–502.

Baumeister, R. F. and Leary, M. R. (1995). The need to belong: Desire for interpersonal attachments as a fundamental human motivation. *Psychological Bulletin*, 117(3), 497–529.

Brewer, M. B. (1988). A dual process model of impression formation. In T. K. Srull and R. S. Wyer, Jr. (eds.), *A dual process model of impression formation. Advances in social cognition*, Vol. 1 (pp. 1–36). Hillsdale, NJ: Erlbaum.

_____ (1991). The social self: On being the same and different at the same time. *Personality and Social Psychology Bulletin*, 17, 475–482.

Chen, S., and Andersen, S. M. (1999). Relationships from the past in the present: Significant-other representations and transference in interpersonal life. *Advances in Experimental Social Psychology*, 31, 123–190.

Cummings, J., Sproull, L., and Kiesler, S. (2002). Beyond hearing: Where real world and online support meet. *Group Dynamics: Theory, Research, and Practice*, 6, 78–88.

Dakof, G. A., and Taylor, S. E. (1990). Victims' perceptions of social support: What is helpful from whom? *Journal of Personality and Social Psychology*, 58, 80–89.

Davison, K. P., Pennebaker, J. W., and Dickerson, S. S. (2000). Who talks? The social psychology of illness support groups. *American Psychologist*, 55, 205–217.

Deaux, K. (1996). Social identification. In E. T. Higgins and A. W. Kruglanski (eds.), *Social psychology: Handbook of basic principles* (pp. 777–798). New York: Guilford Press.

Derlega, V. L., and Chaikin, A. L. (1977). Privacy and self-disclosure in social relationships. *Journal of Social Issues*. 33(3), 102–115.

Derlega, V. L., Metts, S., Petronio, S., and Margulis, S. T. (1993). *Self-disclosure*. London: Sage.

DiMaggio, P., Hargittai, E., Neuman, W. R., and Robinson, J. P. (2001). Social implications of the internet. *Annual Review of Sociology*, 27, 307–36.

Douglas, K. M., and McGarty, J. (2001). Identifiability and self-representation: Computer mediated communication and intergroup interaction. *British Journal of Social Psychology*, 40, 399–416.

Ethier, K. A. (1995). *Becoming a mother: Identity acquisition during the transition to parenthood*. Unpublished doctoral dissertation, City University of New York.

_____, and Deaux, K. (1994). Negotiating social identity when contexts change: Maintaining identification and responding to threat. *Journal of Personality and Social Psychology*, 67, 271–282.

Fiske, S. T., and Taylor, S. E. (1991). *Social cognition* (2nd ed.). New York: Scott, Foresman.

Frable, D. E. S. (1993). Being and feeling unique: Statistical deviance and psychological marginality. *Journal of Personality*, 61, 85–110.

Gollwitzer, P. M. (1986). Striving for specific identities: The social reality of self symbolizing. In R. Baumeister (ed.), *Public self and private self* (pp. 143–159). New York: Springer.

Harmon, A. (June, 29, 2003). Online dating sheds its stigma as losers.com. *The New York Times*, A1.

Hatfield, E., and Sprecher, S. (1986). *Mirror, mirror: The importance of looks in everyday life*. Albany: State University of New York Press.

Helmrath, T. A., and Steinitz, E. M. (1978). Death of an infant: Parental grieving and the failure of social support. *Journal of Family Practice*, 66, 785–790.

Henderson, L., and Zimbardo, P. G., (1999). Commentary on Part III: Developmental outcomes and clinical perspectives. In L. A. Schmidt and J. Schulkin (eds.), *Extreme fear, shyness, and social phobia: Origins and outcome* (pp. 294–305). New York: Oxford University Press.

Higgins, E. T., and Bargh, J. A. (1987). Self-discrepancy theory. *Psychological Review*, 94, 1120–1134.

Hogg, M. A., and Abrams, D. (1993). Towards a single-process uncertainty-reduction model of social motivation in groups. In M. A. Hogg and D. Abrams (eds.), *Group motivation: Social psychological perspectives* (pp. 173–190). London: Harvester Wheatsheaf.

Homey, K. (1946). *The neurotic personality of our time*. New York: Norton.

Howard, P. E. N., Rainie, L., and Jones, S. (2001). Days and nights on the Internet. *American Behavioral Scientist*, 45, 383–404.

Jones, E. E., Farina, A., Hastorf, A. H., Markus, H., Miller, D. T., and Scott, R. A. (1984). *Social stigma: The psychology of marked relationships*. San Francisco: Freeman.

Kelly, A. E., and McKillop, K. J. (1996). The consequences of revealing personal secrets. *Psychological Bulletin*, 120, 450–465.

Kraut, R., Kiesler, S., Boneva, B., Cummings, J., Helgeson, V., and Crawford, A. (2002). Internet paradox revisited. *Journal of Social Issues*, 58, 49–74.

Kraut, R. E., Patterson, M., Lundmark, V., Kiesler, S., Mukhopadhyay, T., and Scherlis, W. (1998). Internet paradox: A social technology that reduces social involvement and psychological well-being? *American Psychologist*, 53, 1017–1032.

Leary, M. R. (1983). Socially based anxiety: A review of measures. In Tardy (ed.), *A Handbook for the study of communication*, pp. 365–384. Norwood, NJ: Ablex.

_____, and Atherton, S. C. (1986). Self-efficacy, social anxiety, and inhibition in interpersonal encounters. *Journal of Social and Clinical Psychology*, 4, 256–267.

Lehman, D. R., and Hemphill, K. J. (1990). Recipients' perceptions of support attempts and attributions for support attempts that fail. *Journal of Social and Personal Relationships*, 7, 563–574.

Lepore, S. J. (1997). Social-environmental influences on the chronic stress process. In B. H. Gottlied (ed.), *Coping with chronic stress: The Plenum series on stress and coping* (pp. 133–160). New York: Plenum.

_____, and Helgeson, V. S. (1998). Social constraints, intrusive thoughts, and mental health after prostate cancer. *Journal of Social and Clinical Psychology*, 17, 89–106.

Lepore, S. J., Silver, R. C., Wortman C. B., and Wayment, H. A. (1996). Social constraints, intrusive thoughts, and depressive symptoms among bereaved mothers. *Journal of Personality and Social Psychology*, 70, 271–282.

Linville, W. (1985). Self-complexity and affective extremity: Don't put all of your eggs in one cognitive basket. *Social Cognition*, 3, 94–120.

McKenna, K. Y. A., and Bargh, J. A. (1998). Coming out in the age of the Internet: Identity Demarginalization through virtual group participation. *Journal of Personality and Social Psychology*, 75(3), 681–694.

_____, and _____ (1999). Causes and consequences of social interaction on the Internet: A conceptual framework. *Media Psychology*, 1, 249–269.

_____, and _____ (2000). Plan 9 from Cyberspace: The implications of the Internet for personality and social psychology. *Personality and Social Psychology Review*, 4, 57–75.

McKenna, K. Y. A., Green, A. S., and Gleason, M. E. J. (2002). Relationship formation on the Internet: What's the big attraction? *Journal of Social Issues*, 58, 9–31.

McKenna, K. Y. A., Green, A., and Smith, P. K. (2001). Setting the sexual self free: The consequences of Online sexual expression. *Journal of Sex Research*, 38, 302–312.

Parks, M. R. and Floyd, K. (1995). Making friends in cyberspace. *Journal of Communication*, 46, 80–97.

Pennebaker, J. W. (1989). Confession, inhibition, and disease. In L. Berkowitz (ed.), *Advances in experimental social psychology* (Vol. 22, pp. 211–244). New York: Academic Press.

_____ (1997). *Opening Up: The Healing Power of Expressing Emotion.* New York: Guilford.

_____ (1997). Writing about emotional experiences as a therapeutic process. *Psychological Science*, 8, 162–166.

_____, and Harber, K. D. (1993). A social stage model of collective coping: The Persian Gulf War and other natural disasters. *Journal of Social Issues*, 49, 125–145.

Rimé, B., Mesquita, B., Philippot, P., and Boca, S. (1991). Beyond the emotional event: Six studies on the social sharing of emotion. *Cognition and Emotion*, 5, 435–465.

Rogers, C. (1951). *Client-centered therapy.* Boston: Houghton-Mifflin.

Rubin, Z. (1975). Disclosing oneself to a stranger: Reciprocity and its limits. *Journal of Experimental Social Psychology*, 11, 233–260.

Sarbin, T., and Allen, V. L. (1968). Increasing participation in a natural group setting: A preliminary report. *Psychological Record*, 18, 1–7.

Sedikides, C. (1993). Assessment, enhancement, and verification determinants of the self-evaluation process. *Journal of Personality and Social Psychology*, 65, 317–338.

Smyth, J. M. (1998). Written emotional expression: Effect sizes, outcome types, and moderating variables. *Journal of Consulting and Clinical*, 66, 174–184.

Spears, R., Lea, M. and Lee, S. (1990). De-individuation and group polarisation in computer mediated communication. *British Journal of Social Psychology*, 29, 121–134.

Spears, R., Postmes, T., Lea, M., and Wolbert, A. (2002). When are net effects gross products? The power of influence and the influence of power in computer-mediated communication. *Journal of Social Issues*, 58, 91–107.

Spreitzer, E., Snyder, E. E., and Larson, D. (1979). Multiple roles and psychological well-being. *Sociological Focus*, 12, 141–148.

Stryker, S., and Statham, A. (1985). Symbolic interaction and role theory. In G. Lindzey and E. Aronson (eds.), *Handbook of social psychology* (Volume 1, pp. 311–378). New York: Random House.

Swann, W. B., Jr. (1990). To be known or to be adored? The interplay of self-enhancement and self-verification. In E. T. Higgins and R. M. Sorrentino (eds.), *Handbook of motivation and cognition* (Vol. 2, pp. 408–448). New York: Guilford.

Tajfel, H., and Turner, J. C. (1986). The social identity theory of intergroup behavior. In S. Worchel and W. G. Austin (eds.), *Psychology of intergroup relations* (pp. 7–24). Chicago: Nelson-Hall.

Turkle, S. (1995). *Life on the screen: Identity in the age of the Internet.* New York: Simon and Schuster.

Walther, J. B. (1996). Computer-mediated communication: impersonal, interpersonal, and hyperpersonal interaction. *Communication Research, 23,* 3–43.

Wicklund, R. A., and Gollwitzer, P. M. (1982). *Symbolic self-completion.* Hillsdale, NJ: Erlbaum.

Wright, K. (2000). Computer-mediated social support, older adults, and coping. *Journal of Communication, 50,* 100–118.

7

Decision Making and Group Dynamics in the Virtual Office

Rodney J. Vogl, Chanda Simkin, *and* Sandra D. Nicks

In today's workforce, conference calls, team sites, e-mails, instant messaging, and discussion boards are beginning to replace face-to-face communication (Greenlee, 2003). This reduction in personal contact has even gotten to a point where many people within a company can work closely with someone for years and have little to no face-to-face contact with that person. The virtual office, also called the virtual workplace or telecommuting, is defined as a work environment in which employees work cooperatively and remotely from different locations using a computer network. In this way, employees are commuting to work through telephone or other telecommunications equipment rather than by car or mass transit (Alverson, 1998). Ultimately, the virtual office allows people to work from home and in offices away from the corporate headquarters.

Companies all over the world are rapidly moving toward becoming a totally virtual environment using virtual offices. The electronic workplace is said to be the workplace of the future. Today, about 10 percent of the workforce telecommutes (Alverson, 1998). A recent study by Bell Atlantic estimated that 2 million companies nationwide support some kind of telecommuting program (Alverson, 1998). Also, two-thirds of Fortune 500 companies employ teleworkers (Cascio, 2000).

Much of this movement toward the virtual office extends from the changes occurring in society and the world. The most obvious change is technology. Today's business leaders have a simple choice. They can quickly learn how to use online collaboration technology or they can lose their share of the market to their technologically superior competitors. Those who choose to learn new technologies increase their chances of staying competitive. In today's fast-paced business world it takes months, not years, to experience loss in the competitive edge if companies cannot keep up with the changing technology (Greenlee, 2003). In essence, e-mail has replaced the telephone, e-learning has replaced instructor-led training, and e-meetings have outdated in-office conference room meetings.

Benefits of the Virtual Office

Economic Benefits

Companies moving toward the virtual office have good reason to do so. One enticing benefit to companies is the cost effectiveness of the virtual office. The virtual office has been shown to reduce costs in a variety of areas. For example, by eliminating the physical offices of employees and setting them up in virtual offices, companies have been able to save money in real estate by not having to pay for housing space for the employees. Corporations (such as IBM) have been able to save 40 to 60 percent annually by setting up many of their employees virtually. Similarly, Northern Telecom estimates that the savings gained from not having to house an employee in a typical 64 square foot space is $2,000 per person per year (Cascio, 2000).

Not only have virtual offices proven to reduce costs, but they have also been known to increase profit and customer satisfaction. Upon moving its salespeople to virtual workplace arrangements, Hewlett Packard doubled its revenue per salesperson (Alverson, 1998; Cascio, 2000). Another benefit of the virtual office is overall improved customer service. According to Cascio (2000), consultants at Anderson Consulting spent 25 percent more time face-to-face with customers when they did not have permanent offices.

The final economic benefit of using the virtual office is that it allows easier access to global markets. By placing employees in virtual offices all over the world, corporations learn more about a variety of cultures. To attempt to understand a culture is to gain an understanding of the needs and desires of its people. Once a corporation begins to understand a culture, the company could customize its products and services to better match the people's needs. Thus, using virtual offices provides companies with a competitive edge by expanding their markets (Cascio, 2000).

Environmental Benefits

Another important benefit of virtual offices comes through environmental conservation. The headquarters of Georgia Power conducted a study on the benefits of the virtual office on the environment. Georgia Power has cut annual commuting mileage by 993,000 miles by having 13 percent of their workers telecommute. The Georgia Power study also found that automobile emissions have been reduced by almost 35,000 pounds. Similarly, the U.S. Government also conducted a study on the environmental benefits of telecommuting. It was found that if 20,000 federal workers could telecommute just one day a week it would save over 2 million commuting miles per week; 102,000 gallons of gasoline per week; and 81,600 pounds of carbon dioxide emissions each week (Alverson, 1998; Cascio, 2000).

Psychological Benefits

Although the economic and environmental benefits may be enticing, the psychological benefits of the virtual office also increase its attractiveness. As mentioned previously, the virtual office eliminates the need for the employees to physically commute to the office every workday, thus, telecommuting saves time. Also, employers do not have to constantly deal with employees' tardiness or excuses for early departure from the workplace. The elimination of commuting to the office each workday also reduces aggravation. The employees report for work in a pleasant mood more often because they have not had to deal with the frustrations of traffic.

All of the psychological elements also add into the psychological benefit of employee satisfaction. Employees working in a virtual office report a stronger work-life balance. They are able to spend more time at home because they are spending less time in their cars. Also, they are able to get more work done without the distractions that occur in an office, therefore, they work less after hours. Another element of employee satisfaction that extends from the virtual office is that employees are able to have more flexible work schedules leading to a more productive use of limited cognitive resources such as attention. In essence, employees can start their workday when they feel most alert. They work more efficiently and produce a higher quality product because they are not worried about the constant pressure of time constraints.

All of these psychological components ultimately lead to the psychological benefit of increased productivity. Internal IBM studies show gains of 15 to 40 percent in their employees work. U.S. West reported that the productivity of their employees increased, some by as much as 40 percent when allowing their employees to work from virtual offices (Cascio, 2000). Employees working in a virtual office have reported that their increased productivity has stemmed from their enhanced comfort while working from home (e.g., being in their natural environment, being able to wear comfortable clothes). Finally, virtual offices increase productivity because companies can make use of asynchronous meetings. These asynchronous meetings allow an employee to post a topic for discussion on the computer and instead of expecting people to respond within an hour-long meeting, that employee can allow people to offer feedback over an extended period (e.g., a week). The employees, who may differ from one another in personality, have more opportunities to respond, which improves the quality of the group's output.

The last psychological benefit of the virtual office is that it eliminates some of the drawbacks of face-to-face interaction such as nonverbal cues. People feel less pressure to conform to a decision or less intimidation to present an idea when they do not experience the nonverbal gestures associated with rejection. For example, an employee has an idea he would like to suggest to the rest of the group but as he starts talking he sees a few people roll their eyes. The employee will be less likely in the future to propose an idea, even though his ideas may have merit. Another drawback of face-to-face interaction that is reduced by the virtual office is the occurrence of discrimination. An employer will be less likely to reject an idea or not hire a person based on physical appearance if the employer cannot see the other person. Similarly, a person working from a virtual office would not be promoted based on physical appearance if the decision makers have never seen him or her.

Disadvantages of the Virtual Office

Economic Disadvantages

Despite its many benefits, the virtual office does have its drawbacks. Despite the savings over time, one disadvantage to the virtual office is setup costs. To set up a virtual office from an individual's home is an additional cost of $3,000 to $5,000 to that of setting up a cubicle in an office (Cascio, 2000). In addition, employers should expect an additional $1,000 in upgrades and computer-office supplies every year (Cascio, 2000). Virtual offices also have additional requirements to those needed in the traditional office space. For example, all forms or materials used by employees in a virtual office would need to be available online in order to be downloaded and printed from remote locations (i.e., materials cannot be passed along from employee to employee). Also, well-indexed, automated central files need to be accessible from remote locations as well as easily accessible product and customer databases. Finally, the last setup and maintenance disadvantage of the virtual office is that companies must use flawless technology or their technical support staff need to be available around the clock. Companies must have people staffed to address technical issues at any time of the day due to varying time zones across the nation and around the world.

The disadvantages of the virtual office also include the loss of cost efficiencies. In a traditional office, multiple users can share/access expensive equipment or services, thus maximizing the cost efficiency. The company loses cost efficiency if they have to distribute equipment across locations. For example, the ability to obtain up-to-the-second stock quotes for brokers is very expensive. The costs of the hardware and software to receive the stock quotes is $1,200 per month for the first installation and $200 per month to install each additional system in the same location, therefore it is the most cost efficient to keep all of the workers in one location (Cascio, 2000). In essence, if the employees are working from virtual offices, the cost would be $1,200 per employee. The expenses needed to maintain a virtual office could put a company on a "technology treadmill."

Cultural Disadvantages

Cultural issues may also become a disadvantage to the employees of the virtual office. The potential exists for clashes between both business and national cultures. For example, Japanese business practices involve the Japanese representatives getting to know their counterparts on a personal level (i.e., what is the person's sense of honor, integrity, and connection to family) before they discuss the business deal. So, Japanese businesspeople may have problems conducting business deals via the computer because they lose that personal connection to their counterpart. Cultures may also place different levels of importance on punctuality (Triandis, 1981). For example, business executives from Latin America who report late for an online business meeting may be puzzled by the negative reactions of their North American counterparts. Ultimately, if the members of international virtual teams do not understand one another's cultures, then their technological advantage is useless and their competitive advantage is worthless (Cascio, 2000).

Psychological Disadvantages

In contrast to the psychological benefits of the virtual office, there are also psychological disadvantages. Employees working from a virtual office may have increased chances of experiencing feelings of isolation. Without some level of social interaction with supervisors and coworkers, employees will feel isolated and uninformed. The employees indicate that they do not have the crucial social contact and communication with the decision makers that will make or break their career. This lack of personal contact can also lead to another psychological disadvantage: lack of trust. In order for the virtual workplace to be successful, workers must trust that their coworkers will fulfill their obligations and behave in a predictable manner. In one study, a significant decline in trust was found in virtual teams and was related to reneging on obligations (Piccoli and Ives, 2003). According to Cascio (2000), lack of trust can undermine any technological advances, training programs, or selection of personnel.

Group cohesion may also be reduced in virtual teams. Group cohesion is defined as the attraction members have toward the group and the extent to which they desire to remain part of the group. Cohesive groups are more likely to exhibit more positive interpersonal and task-related communication interactions than less cohesive groups (Evans and Dion, 1991; Hogg, 1992; Lott and Lott, 1965). Prior studies have shown that group cohesiveness is strongly related to improved group performance (Langfred, 1998; Mullen and Copper, 1994). In the virtual group, the reduction in both personal and task-related communication may contribute to the group members' feelings of isolation. Studies are mixed on the findings of whether or not group cohesion is lessened in non-face-to-face groups. Olaniran (1996) found no significant difference on group satisfaction ratings between face-to-face and computer-mediated groups. Similarly, Berry (2002) found that both virtual teams and face-to-face teams had similar ratings of group cohesion; however, the virtual team members were more likely to indicate a desire to change teams than those on face-to-face teams. In a study that compared groups that communicated with a mixed-mode (combination face-to-face interaction and computer-mediated interaction) with a group that strictly used computers, the members of the mixed-mode groups rated their groups higher in cohesiveness, the ability to manage conflict, and in overall satisfaction as compared to the computer-mediated groups (Ocker and Morand, 2002).

Another psychological disadvantage that occurs with the virtual office is the loss of nonverbal cues. The virtual office can accentuate miscommunication if companies do not counteract the loss of nonverbal cues. For example, the loss of nonverbal cues may lead to inferences that could lead people astray. Therefore, people need to use precise wording and be explicit when interacting with employees via the computer. Also, telecommuters will not be able to point or use hand gestures that aid communication and clarify complicated issues, therefore, it may take longer to convey a message.

Another disadvantage to the virtual office, which is also found in the traditional office, is the occurrence of groupthink. According to Janis (1972, 1982), groupthink is a mode of thinking that occurs when desire for harmony in a decision-making group overrides appraisal of alternatives. Janis (1982) identified several symptoms of groupthink (see Janis, 1982 for a complete listing). For example, one symptom of groupthink is the pressure to conform. People want to maintain group harmony, therefore the desire for harmony leads to a suppression of opposing views. Groupthink most often occurs during decision making about nonroutine, crucial issues that affect large numbers of people, such as the types of decisions made by business executives and government officials (Janis, 1989; t'Hart, 1990). The occurrence of groupthink may result in poor decisions because decision makers may not have considered the alternatives. Much research has been done on groupthink (see Esser, 1998 for a review); however, little research has examined groupthink in groups making their decisions via computer.

Two factors of the virtual office that may reduce the occurrence of groupthink are the mode of communication and the levels of cohesiveness. Changing the mode of communication (computer-based vs. face-to-face interaction) may change the group dynamics. For example, decision makers may feel less pressure to conform while responding via computer because they are not picking up on the nonverbal cues of the other members of the group. In addition, a decrease in group cohesion, especially social-emotional cohesion, will reduce the likelihood of groupthink occurring in non-face-to-face groups (Bernthal and Insko, 1993).

Are Better Decisions Made Online?
An Empirical Study

Due to the increased implementation of the virtual office, a study was conducted to determine if better group decisions were made via computer in comparison to interacting face-to-face. The purpose of the experiment was to determine whether the findings from previous research on group dynamics would generalize to a situation where the group members are not meeting face-to-face.

The present study also strived to examine whether the decisions made online would be more efficient than the decisions made face-to-face. Some previous research assessing the quality of group decisions made either online or face-to-face has found no difference between the two modes of communication (e.g., Hiltz, Johnson, and Turoff, 1986; Hollingshead, 1996a). However, it is important to note that in a second study, Hollingshead (1996b) found that the face-to-face groups made better decisions than the computer-mediated groups when they were instructed to rank order their decision alternatives. Also, Straus and McGrath (1994) found that face-to-face groups made better decisions on judgment tasks where the goal involves reaching a consensus decision. Similarly, Hedlund, Ilgen, and Hollenbeck (1998) found that their face-to-face teams had significantly higher decision accuracy than their computer-mediated teams. It is possible that groups that interact via computer make better decisions than the groups that interact face-to-face because the face-to-face groups receive nonverbal cues, such as facial expressions, that influence their decisions. Conversely, the "computer" groups would not be subjected to these nonverbal cues, thus, be less likely to conform.

Hypotheses

It was hypothesized that groups should make better decisions than individuals. Groups should make better decisions because the logical arguments (i.e., central route to persuasion; see Petty and Caccioppo, 1986) made during the group discussion should reinforce the beliefs and ideas of those who had already generated the "correct" responses and stimulate thinking in the individuals that overlooked the item. Our second hypothesis was that the groups that interact via computer would make better decisions than the groups that interact face-to-face because the latter group would respond to irrelevant cues (e.g., facial expressions) that may influence their decisions. In addition, we hypothesized that less groupthink would occur in the computer groups than the face-to-face groups. We thought that decision makers might feel less pressure to conform (and other symptoms of groupthink) while responding via computer because they are not picking up on the nonverbal cues of the other members of the group. Thus, the computer groups would experience less groupthink than the face-to-face groups. Finally, based upon previous research (e.g., Hiltz, et al., 1986), it was hypothesized that leaders would be more likely to be elected or self-appointed in the groups that were face-to-face.

Method

One hundred thirty-six undergraduates at a small, private university in the Midsouth volunteered to be in the experiment. The majority of the participants were Caucasian between the ages of 18 and 22 years old. Approximately two-thirds of the participants were female.

The groups discussed *The Lake St. Clair Incident* (Canfield, 1988). In this problem-solving task, the members of the group had to rank order a series of items (e.g., life jackets, sweaters, flashlights) as to the importance of their survival value. The Lake St. Clair incident was used because it allowed examination of different decision-making processes. First, each participant made his or her own decisions independently (i.e., autocratic decision making). Next, all the members of the team tried to work toward a common solution (i.e., consensual decision making). During this study, half of the groups interacted via computer using Yahoo Messenger. Thus, four computers were needed to present the scenario to the four group members. A fifth computer was used by the experimenter to monitor and record the group's interaction. The other half of the groups interacted face-to-face. The face-to-face groups also had their interactions recorded. A videotape of both the computer and face-to-face sessions was made to examine whether nonverbal cues affected the interaction. After the problem-solving task, participants then completed a Leadership/Teamwork questionnaire so that the occurrence of groupthink and the emergence of leaders could also be examined.

The experiment was divided into four phases. During the first phase, the small groups of four participants had 10 minutes to make independent rankings regarding the items on the Lake St. Clair Incident. The second phase of the experiment involved the participants consulting (either face-to-face or via computer) with the other members of their group for 35 minutes. During this phase, the group attempted to reach a consensus decision (i.e., a solution that every group member could accept) for their "team" ranking. The third phase involved the participants making a second set of individual rankings for three minutes. In essence, would their individual rankings be influenced by their consultation with the group? Lastly, participants had seven minutes to complete the Leadership/Teamwork questionnaire.

Results

Accuracy of Decisions and Decision Times. The accuracy of the rankings was determined by comparing the participant's/team's rankings with those of Coast Guard experts. The accuracy score is a sum of the deviations of the participant's rankings from the expert's rankings. No significant difference was found between individual ($M = 55.14$) and team ratings ($M = 56.91$) on decision-making ability, $F(2, 64) = 1.49$, $p = .23$, $MSE = 26.63$. In addition, no significant difference was found between computer groups and face-to-face groups on decision-making ability, $F(1, 32) < 1$. However, a significant difference was found between computer groups and face-to-face groups on decision-making time, $F(1, 31) = 19.88$, $p < .001$, $MSE = 67.10$. It is evident that the computer groups took significantly longer to reach consensus ($M = 33.96$ minutes) than the face-to-face groups ($M = 21.24$ minutes).

Emergence of Leadership. We found that 52 percent of the participants in the face-to-face groups believed that a leader emerged in their group compared to only 34 percent of participants in the computer groups. Similarly, Hiltz, et al. (1986) found that a dominant member was more likely to emerge in the face-to-face groups than in the computer-mediated groups. We identified 25 leaders and 111 nonleaders. In order to be classified as a leader, at least two of the four members of the group had to identify the participant as a leader. In addition, no more than two leaders could be identified per group.

Groupthink. The first aspect of group dynamics that was studied was the occurrence of groupthink. Results indicated that groupthink occurred in both the computer and face-to-face groups ($M = 14.24$), $t(33) = 32.54$, $p < .001$ (note that the minimum score is 6 indicating an absence of groupthink). No significant differences were found between computer groups and face-to-face groups on groupthink, $F(1, 32) < 1$. It is important to note that significant differences were found between leaders ($M = 12.92$) and nonleaders ($M = 14.55$) on groupthink, $F(1, 132) = 4.44$, $p = .04$, $MSE = 21.80$. The leaders may have been less perceptive to the occurrence of groupthink. Previous research has shown that promotional leadership (where a leader promotes one idea early on instead of encouraging the generation of different ideas) is positively related to the occurrence of groupthink (Flowers, 1977; described in McCauley, 1989).

Trust. A second element of group dynamics that was studied was feeling an atmosphere of trust. A nonsignificant difference was found between computer groups ($M = 4.01$) and face-to-face groups ($M = 4.38$) on feeling trust, $F(1, 32) = 2.68$, $p = .111$, $MSE = .43$. However, a marginally significant Leader x Grouptype interaction was found on management of trust, $F(1, 131) = 3.19$, $p = .076$, $MSE = 4.51$. Management of trust refers to a person's perceived trustworthiness (the willingness to take a position and avoid shifting positions). The leaders in the computer groups thought that they were better at management of trust than the nonleaders (Figure

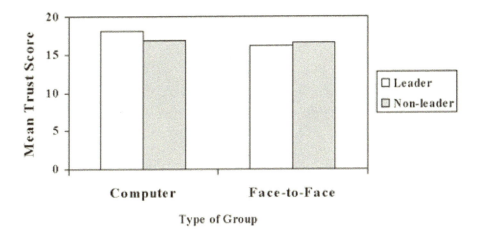

Figure 7.1. Mean score (out of 20 possible) on the Management of Trust scale for the team members for both the computer and face-to-face groups.

7.2). However, the leaders in the face-to-face groups perceived themselves as being less capable of managing trust than the nonleaders. The computer groups also believed that they were better at managing trust than face-to-face groups, $F(1, 131) = 4.62$, $p = .033$, $MSE = 4.51$.

Treat Each Other with Respect. Whether or not the participants felt they treated each other with respect was also studied. A marginally significant difference was found between computer groups ($M = 4.32$) and face-to-face groups ($M = 4.71$) on treating each other with respect, $F(1, 32) = 3.09$, $p = .088$, $MSE = .428$. In addition, a marginally significant Leader x Grouptype interaction was found regarding treating each other with respect, $F(1, 132) = 3.35$, $p = .07$, $MSE = 2.06$. As can be seen in Figure 7.3, the leaders in the computer groups were more likely than the nonleaders to perceive that the group members treated each other with respect. However, the leaders and nonleaders in the face-to-face groups were equally likely to perceive that the group members treated each other with respect. In general, the leaders were more likely than the nonleaders to believe that the members of the group treated each other with respect, $F(1, 132) = 3.00$, $p = .085$, $MSE = 2.06$. In essence, the nonleaders in the computer group were the people least likely to feel that members of their team were treating each other with respect.

Group Cohesion and Other Aspects of Group Dynamics. The next factor of group dynamics that was examined was group cohesion. A marginally significant difference was found between computer groups ($M = 24.97$) and face-to-face groups ($M = 26.88$) on group cohesion, $F(1, 32)$

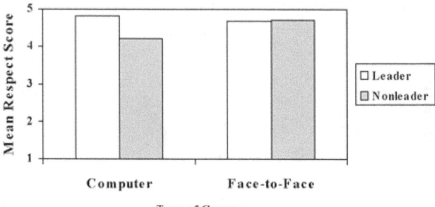

Figure 7.2. Mean score on the degree to which the participants felt that their team members treated each other with respect. The means are presented for the team members of the computer and face-to-face groups.

= 3.35, p = .076, MSE = 9.26. Significant positive correlations were found between group cohesion and the following factors: how well the teams worked together, $r(34)$ = .84, p < .001; group unity, r (34) = .74, p < .001; and team enjoyment, $r(34)$ = .65, p < .001. Significant differences were found between the computer groups (M = 3.38) and the face-to-face groups (M = 4.47) in terms of how well the groups worked together, $F(1, 32)$ = 8.96, p = .005, MSE = .33. In addition, significant differences were found between computer groups (M = 3.69) and face-to-face groups (M = 4.22) on how unified the groups were, $F(1, 32)$ = 7.14, p = .012, MSE = .33. Thus, the face-to-face groups felt more unified and believed they worked well together.

There were several elements of group dynamics that were studied, but no significant differences were found between the computer groups and face-to-face groups. For example, a nonsignificant difference was found between computer groups (M = 4.30) and face-to-face groups (M = 4.54) on allowing one another freedom and responsibility to make decisions that affected their individual work, $F(1, 32)$ = 2.58, p = .118, MSE = .231. Also, a nonsignificant difference was found between computer groups (M = 4.32) and face-to-face groups (M = 4.60) on cooperating with one another to get the work accomplished, $F(1, 32)$ = 2.16, p = .152, MSE = .308. Finally, no significant differences were found between computer groups and face-to-face groups on how well they enjoyed working on the team, $F(1, 32)$ < 1. Although the differences are non-significant, it should be noted that members of face-to-face groups rated their groups higher on each of these aspects of group dynamics.

Disadvantages of Virtual Teams

The findings of our study indicate that there are some disadvantages of virtual teams. We had hypothesized that the groups that interacted via computer would make better decisions than the groups that interacted face-to-face. We thought that the face-to-face groups would receive nonverbal cues, such as facial expressions, that might influence their decisions and promote conformity to the group. We suggested that the computer groups would not be subjected to these nonverbal cues and therefore would be less likely to conform (i.e., better decisions would be made online). However, similar to previous research examining decision accuracy (e.g., Hiltz, et al., 1986; Hollingshead, 1996a), no differences were found between the face-to-face and the computer groups regarding the accuracy of their decisions (i.e., better decisions were not made online). One reason why face-to-face and computer groups made equally less accurate decisions was that groupthink occurred in both types of groups. Also, it is possible that individuals (especially the leaders of the group) may have lead the group astray. Further analyses and future research could examine these possibilities in more detail.

Another disadvantage to virtual teams is that it takes longer to make decisions online. In fact, groups that make their decisions online take approximately 4 to 10 times longer to reach a decision compared to groups who meet face-to-face (Dubrovsky, Kiesler, and Sethna, 1991; Hiltz, et al., 1986; Siegel, Dubrovsky, Kiesler, and McGuire, 1986). One reason for this loss of time efficiency is due to a loss of nonverbal cues when communicating via computer. Individuals interacting via computer cannot point, use hand gestures, or read facial cues as aids to comprehension of a message; therefore, the communication process is slowed. Also, individuals communicating via computer must be specific in their use of wording to ensure that their message is clearly stated, thus, lowering the likelihood of confusion or misinterpretation (Robb, 2002). Another reason why it takes longer to make decisions online is because the lack of nonverbal cues may lead to inferences that could lead people astray. For example, Chapanis, Ochsman, Parrish, and Weeks (1972) found that pairs of people solving a problem face-to-face solved it 14 percent more quickly than pairs discussing the same problem over a telephone line. It should be noted that aside from taking longer, computer-mediated groups also have more difficulty reaching consensus than face-to-face groups (Dubrovsky, Kiesler, and Sethna, 1991; Siegel, Dubrovsky, Kiesler, and McGuire, 1986).

Another disadvantage of the virtual office is the lack of trust that can occur among team members. A lack of trust may occur due to the lack of physical interaction (i.e., the loss of verbal and nonverbal cues) among the team members. Also, the lack of synergies that occur in face-to-face communication can also cause a lack of trust (i.e., people cannot see the facial expressions of others that reinforce that the team is in agreement and everyone is head-gelling together). Cascio (2000) points out that in order for teams to be effective, workers must trust that their coworkers will fulfill their obligations and behave in a predictable manner.

Cascio cites an empirical study on trust in which 29 global virtual teams communicated strictly by e-mail for six weeks. Cascio discusses the characteristics of teams high in trust. Teams that were high in trust began their interactions with a series of social messages before working on a task. The individuals on "high-trust" teams also introduced themselves to each other and they provided some personal background to the other members of their team. The teams that were high in trust also set clear roles for each team member that enabled all team members to identify with one another. In addition, all of the "high-trust" team members displayed positive attitudes by consistently showing eagerness, enthusiasm, and an intense action orientation. Conversely, low-trust teams were less productive than high-trust teams. Cascio (2000) concludes from the study that initial messages in a virtual environment need to be handled well. Also, the tone of all communication should be kept positive and upbeat, because one pessimist has the potential to undermine the trust in the whole team. Finally, the lack of trust in a virtual team affects the overall productivity of the team.

Additional disadvantages of virtual teams involve low morale among team members and the loss of group unity. The interactions of virtual teams may result in a loss of group cohesion and therefore people do not feel like they are part of a team. One aspect of group cohesion concerns whether or not the team members treat each other with respect. It was found that computer-mediated groups felt that they treated each other with less respect than the face-to-face groups. Previous research has found that online interactions create less inhibitions and thus lead to more frequent expression of personal opinions, the expression of personal insults, and profanity (Dubrovsky, et al., 1991; Siegel, et al., 1986; Weisband, 1992).

Predictions and Applications

The movement toward the virtual office appears to be gaining momentum. In 2000, 40 million employees worldwide telecommuted to work. Estimates for 2003 were that more than 137 million workers globally were expected to work from a virtual office at least on a part-time basis (Cascio, 2000). As economic pressures continue, there will be constant striving to save on costs. Also, there will always be the element of competitive advantage in which companies will fight to stay ahead of the competitors. For example, Cascio (2000) reports that virtual teams located all over the globe can work around the clock on products in order to stay ahead of their competitors. Cascio provides the example of Veriphone who uses a "relay race" to keep ahead of the competition. In the relay race, the software engineers at Veriphone's headquarters in Dallas, Texas, work a full day on a project and then post their work on the company's Intranet. A team of company engineers in Hawaii take up the project and post their results for a team in Bombay, India. After the team from Bombay spends their workday on the project, they post their work for the team back at the headquarters in Dallas who are just coming in to start the next workday. One can see how corporations can stay ahead of the competition when projects receive attention 24 hours a day. Finally, there will continue to be technological advances that will only make the virtual office seem that much more appealing.

The concept of the virtual office is making its way onto college campuses. Many colleges and universities have been attempting to expand their markets by offering courses via computer (i.e., distance education). A list of many institutions offering on-line courses may be found at the American Distance Education Consortium <http://www.adec.edu/virtual.html>. For example, one of the largest universities in the world is the Open University, located in the United Kingdom, which has a large part of its curriculum available online. The Open University has over 200,000 students. Approximately 150,000 students are online. In fact, about 26,000 students are studying their courses outside of the United Kingdom (Open University, 2003). Therefore, people from all over the world can take college courses from this university. Other universities are following suit in that they have been encouraged to develop online courses to increase enrollment. Some of the advantages of using the Internet to deliver distance learning have included: potential to reach a global market, time and location flexibility, quick development time for courses (in comparison to CD-ROMs or videotapes), relative ease of updating course content, and usually lower development and operating costs (Bates, 1995; Eastmond,

1995; Wulf, 1996). The role of the virtual university will continue to play a tremendous part in distance education. In order for virtual universities to be both productive and profitable, both students and educators must be made aware of the advantages and disadvantages of learning using virtual environments.

In addition to universities making use of the virtual office for education and training purposes, businesses may also have a lot to gain by using technology-assisted training. Companies are moving to technology-assisted training because of the tremendous savings. For example, MCI WorldCom slashed approximately $3 million in travel, facility, and labor costs over a year by offering 20 percent of its classes over the World Wide Web (Greengard, 1999).

Unfortunately, businesses have a lot to lose if they do not take advantage of technological advances. Businesses are under tremendous economic pressures to lower their costs and increase their productivity. As mentioned previously, the virtual office allows businesses to lower their costs (e.g., reduce office space/real estate costs) while increasing worker productivity (i.e., through distraction-free virtual offices without the aggravation associated with commuting) and opening up new global markets. In addition, many businesses are feeling the pressure to stay ahead of their competitors. As mentioned previously, Cascio (2000) suggests that virtual teams located all over the globe can work around the clock on products in order to stay ahead of their competitors. One method of keeping ahead of competition involves the relay race. In the relay race, workers in one office work a full day on a project and then post their work on the company's Intranet so that a virtual team in another part of the world can continue the project.

Conclusions

It is clear that there are many benefits to the virtual office. Companies receive many economic benefits such as lowering costs and increasing profits and customer satisfaction. Companies are also encouraged to move to the virtual office because it helps conserve environmental resources. The psychological benefits of the virtual office also add to its appeal. The elimination of commuting to the office each day reduces stress and leads to increased employee satisfaction and productivity (e.g., a stronger work-life balance, flexible schedules). It is important to note that the psychological benefits come to the individual, *not* the team.

Before a company decides to move all of its employees to a virtual office, the potential costs of such a move need to be considered. For example, virtual offices do require substantial set-up and maintenance costs (depending upon the products or services of the company). It is important to note that the maintenance costs include not only equipment and supplies but also technical support. Another disadvantage of the virtual office is the loss of cost efficiencies because employees are not able to share access to expensive pieces of equipment. Perhaps the greatest disadvantages of the virtual office come from the psychological effect of the virtual office on virtual teams. It was found that virtual teams take longer to make decisions online (possibly due to a loss of nonverbal cues when using the computer). Also, virtual teams must be specific in their word usage to reduce the likelihood of misinterpretation. Finally, the virtual office may promote a lack of trust among team members (due to the loss of verbal and nonverbal cues) thus, affecting the overall productivity of the team. The current findings, taken together with the findings of McKenna and her colleagues (McKenna and Green, 2002; see also, McKenna and Seidman, chapter 6 this volume), suggest that the social rules that govern relationships are different in virtual spaces. Therefore, even though the virtual office may have psychological benefits to the individual, there are substantial psychological costs to the virtual team.

References

Alverson, M. (1998). Welcome to the "virtual workplace." *Women in Business*, 50 (6), 20–24.

Bates, A. W. (1995). *Technology, open learning, and distance education.* London: Routledge.

Bernthal, P. R., and Insko, C. A. (1993). Cohesiveness without groupthink. *Group and Organization Management*, 18 (1), 66–88.

Berry, R. W. (2002). The efficacy of electronic communication in the business school: Marketing students' perceptions of virtual teams. *Marketing Education Review*, 12, 73–78.

Canfield, A. A. (1988). *The Lake St. Clair incident.* Los Angeles, CA: Western Psychological Services.

Cascio, W. F. (2000). Managing a virtual workplace. *Academy of Management Executive*, 14 (3), 81–90.

Chapanis, A., Ochsman, R. B., Parrish, R. N., and Weeks, G. D. (1972). Studies in interactive communication: I. The effects of four communication modes on the behavior of teams during cooperative problem-solving. *Human Factors*, 14(6), 487–509.

Dubrovsky, V. J., Kiesler, S., and Sethna, B. N. (1991). The equalization phenomenon: Status effects in computer-mediated and face-to-face decision making groups. *Human-Computer Interaction*, 6, 119–146.

Eastmond, D. V. (1995). *Alone but together: Adult distance study through computer conferencing.* Cresskill, NJ: Hampton Press.

Esser, J. K. (1998). Alive and well after 25 years. A review of groupthink research. *Organizational Behavior and Human Decision Processes*, 73 (2/3), 116–142.

Evans, C. R., and Dion, K. L. (1991). Group cohesion and performance: A meta-analysis. *Small Group Behavior*, 22, 203–216.

Flowers, M. L. (1997). A laboratory test of some of the implications of Janis's groupthink hypothesis. *Journal of Personality and Social Psychology*, 35, 888–896.

Greengard, S. (1999). Web-based training yields maximum returns. *Workforce*, 78(2), 95–96.

Greenlee, D. (2003). Getting together in cyberspace. E-meeting of the minds: The new virtual workplace. Visited May 27, 2003. <http://www.webtalkguys.com/article-virtualoffice.shtml.>

Hedlund, J., Ilgen, D. R., and Hollenbeck, J. R. (1998). Decision accuracy in computer-mediated versus face-to-face decision-making teams. *Organizational Behavior and Human Decision Processes*, 76, 30–47.

Hiltz, S. R., Johnson, K., and Turoff, M. (1986). Experiments in group decision making: Communication processes and outcomes in face-to-face versus computerized conferences. *Human Communication Research*, 13, 225–252.

Hogg, M. A. (1992). *The social psychology of group cohesiveness: From attraction to social identity.* New York: New York University Press.

Hollingshead, A. B. (1996a). Information suppression and status persistence in group decision making: The effects of communication media. *Human Communication Research*, 23, 193–219.

_____ (1996b). The rank-order effect in group decision making. *Organizational Behavior and Human decision Processes*, 68, 181–193.

Janis, I. L. (1972). *Victims of groupthink: A psychological study of foreign-policy decision and fiascoes.* Boston: Houghton Mifflin.

_____ (1982). *Groupthink: Psychological studies of policy decisions and fiascoes.* Boston: Houghton Mifflin.

_____ (1989). *Crucial decisions: Leadership in policymaking and crisis management.* New York: Free Press.

Langfred, C. W. (1998). Is cohesiveness a double-edged sword? An investigation of the effects of cohesiveness on performance. *Small Group Research*, 29, 124–143.

Lott, A. J., and Lott, B. E. (1965). Group cohesiveness as interpersonal attraction. *Psychological Bulletin*, 64, 259–309.

McCauley, C. (1989). The nature of social influence in groupthink: Compliance and internalization. *Journal of Personality and Social Psychology*, 57, 250–260.

McKenna, K. Y. A., and Green, A. S. (2002). Virtual group dynamics. *Group Dynamics: Theory, Research and Practice*, 6, 116–127.

Mullen, B., and Copper, C. (1994). The relation between group cohesiveness and performance: An integration. *Psychological Bulletin*, 115, 210–227.

Ocker, R. J., and Morand, D. (2002). Exploring the mediating effect of group development on satisfaction in virtual and mixed-mode environments. *E-Service Journal*, 1(3), 25–41.

Olaniran, B. A. (1996). A model of group satisfaction in computer-mediated communication and face-to-face meetings. *Behaviour and information technology*, 15, 24–36.

Open University (2003). About us. Retrieved October 4, 2003, from http://www.open.ac.uk/about/

Petty, R. E., and Cacioppo, J. T. (1986). *Communication and persuasion: Central and peripheral routes to attitude change.* New York: Springer-Verlag.

Piccoli, G., and Ives, B. (2003). Trust and the unintended effects of behavior control in virtual teams. *MIS Quarterly*, 27, 365–395.

Robb, D. (2002). Virtual workplace. *HR Magazine*, 47 (6), 105–109.

Siegel, J., Dubrovsky, V. J., Kiesler, S., and McGuire, T. W. (1986). Group processes in computer-mediated communication. *Organizational Behavior and Human Decision Processes*, 37, 157–187.

Straus, S. G., and McGrath, J. E. (1994). Does the medium matter? The interaction of task type and technology on group performance and member reactions. *Journal of Applied Psychology*, 79, 87–97.

t'Hart, P. (1990). *Group think in government.: A study of small groups and policy failure*. Amsterdam: Swets and Zeitlinger.

Triandis, H. C. (1981). *Some dimensions of intercultural variation and their implications for interpersonal behavior*. Paper presented at the American Psychological Association convention.

Weisband, S. P. (1992). Group discussion and first advocacy effects in computer-mediated and face-to-face decision making groups. *Organizational Behavior and Human Decision Processes*, 53, 352–380.

Wulf, K. (1996). Training via the Internet: Where are we? *Training and Development*, 50(5), 50–55.

8

What We Remember from Television and Movies: Using Autobiographical Memory to Study Media

RICHARD JACKSON HARRIS, JENNIFER M.
BONDS-RAACKE, *and* ELIZABETH T. CADY

Over their lifetimes, all people interact with technology in many different ways. Of the many forms of technology, perhaps the most important in terms of their influence on the thoughts, attitudes, and behaviors of humans are the media. Although it is tempting to think of television, radio, movies, print media, and computer-mediated communications as exerting direct and uniform influence on people who are passive receptacles, in truth each person actively processes the information and constructs his or her own meaning. In this way, an individual's knowledge can change to reflect the information provided by the media experience, while giving rise to a variety of potential interpretations of the experience.

Much research has been performed with the goal of identifying the effects of media consumption on viewers (see overview in Harris, 2004). For example, studies on the effects of watching violence in the media have identified and examined several effects. One such effect is *modeling*, in which a person who watches media violence will subsequently behave more violently themselves (Bandura, 2002). This can occur either through observational learning, when the viewer performs a behavior similar to that on screen, or through disinhibition, when the viewer lowers his or her inhibitions toward performing a previously known violent act.

Another documented effect of viewing media violence is *desensitization*, in which one's sensitivity and arousal to violence lessens. This leads people to tolerate more violence, both in the media and in life. A third observed effect is *cultivation*, in which people who watch media violence tend to believe that the real world is like the dangerous world portrayed in the media (Gerbner, Gross, Morgan, Signorielli, and Shanahan, 2002). Finally, watching violence in the media often induces *fear*, as viewers feel emotions similar to those experienced by the characters on the screen (Cantor, 1998, 2002).

Using Autobiographical Memory
to Study Media

One method of studying the effects of media draws on participants' autobiographical memory of their experiences watching TV and movies. Autobiographical memory involves the recall of the events of one's life, and like many media events, it is highly personal and affect-laden. Although this method does not allow for direct measure of participants' reactions to media, it does provide a way to investigate effects on a long-term basis, and as such provides a complement to more traditional methodologies, which assess participants' reaction to a film clip. Although infrequently used to study media, autobiographical memory has been a very active research area since around 1980 (for varying perspectives, see Conway and Pleydell-Pearce, 2000; D. C. Rubin, 1996; Thompson, et al., 1998).

In the autobiographical memory paradigm, participants (usually college students) complete anonymous questionnaires in which they recall a media event seen at some point in their lives. After describing the event and the experience of watching it, participants answer questions about it. These questions occur in a variety of formats, including Likert-scale ratings, multiple-choice questions, open-ended questions, or checking off applicable options from a list of choices. In some studies, the participants also completed a personality or attitude scale, measuring such dimensions as gender role attitudes (Spence and Helmreich, 1978), sensation-seeking (Zuckerman, 1994), empathy (Davis, Hull, Young, and Warren, 1987), or attitudes toward homosexuals (Herek, 1988).

Advantages

This paradigm affords several advantages. First, since the participant usually has chosen the event and watched it in its entirety with a normal level of attention in an actual social setting, there is a high level of ecological validity. Since the experiences recalled are almost universal among college students, this sample is both convenient and highly appropriate.

Second, since the questionnaire asks the participants to recall their prior experiences watching media, there is no exposure to antisocial stimuli during the experiment. This avoids possible ethical problems associated with presenting violent or sexual media but still allows the assessment of effects of viewing such media. Third, despite the procedural differences from other methods of studying media effects, the results from autobiographical memory studies are quite consistent with those using other methodologies and thus offer converging evidence with other lines of research. Fourth, this method also allows the indirect study of long-term effects. Although such effects are not directly observed, asking people about their memories of the aftermath of viewing can tap into possible consequences that can be investigated more systematically in other ways.

Finally, the paradigm offers the ability to test several theoretical frameworks describing the relationship people have with the media. One of these is Rubin's (2002), which uses a gratifications paradigm, and focuses on how people use media and what they obtain from this use. Another testable model is Zillmann and Weaver's (1996) gender role socialization model, developed to describe how men and women learn differently from media exemplars about how to behave watching a violent movie. A third theory is Bandura's (2002) social cognitive theory, which focuses on the modeling of behavior seen in the movie or TV show. Finally, this paradigm allows examination of Gerbner et al.'s (2002) cultivation theory, which predicts that heavy viewers believe that the real world is more like what is shown in the media than light viewers do.

Limitations

Despite these advantages, however, the autobiographical memory paradigm does have its limitations. First, because completing the questionnaires requires retrospection, there exists the possibility of memory loss and distortion in participants' memories. However, testing with dating couples has shown that the memories of both partners closely coincide and the memories provided by participants are in general very rich, thus suggesting that memory loss and bias are not critical concerns (Harris, et al, 2004, study 2). Related to this, since the participants recall their own memories for the experiments, verification of the accuracy of these memories cannot occur. However, this research is less concerned with the actual content of the media event than with memory for the experience of consuming it. Also, the major comparisons of interest are typically based on other variables, such as gender, age, or type of event recalled. Therefore, the way in which the participants recall their memories and how those memories affect their attitudes and behavior are the main variables of interest, not how factually accurate these memories are.

Applications

This paradigm has been used to investigate several different types of memories, including those for frightening movies seen in childhood or on a date and romantic movies seen on a date. In addition, participants' memories for soap operas, televised sporting events that they either enjoyed or did not enjoy, TV and film portrayals of smoking, gay and lesbian characters, media therapists, and memories elicited by songs have been examined. We now turn to briefly examine these various studies conducted in our laboratory and present some sample findings. These are just a few of the results obtained from each of these studies and are offered here to illustrate the type of data that can be obtained using the autobiographical memory paradigm. This methodology produces very rich data sets whose complexity is not fully addressed here. Table 8.1 summarizes some of the major results from this research program.

Memory for Frightening and Romantic Movies

Three of our studies used autobiographical memory to study the experience of recalling a frightening or romantic movie the participants had previously seen. The first study (Hoekstra, et al., 1999) asked 338 college students to recall seeing a movie in their childhood or teen years that had seriously frightened them. Every single participant could readily remember such an experience and describe it in detail, even though it had occurred an average of nine years earlier, when the participant was around 10. In almost half the cases, the film had been viewed in a group and the choice to see it had been a group decision. Using a list of possible effects with instructions to check off all that applied, substantial percentages of people remembered experiencing specific effects, including generalized fear (63 percent), specific fears (30 percent), wild imagination (46 percent), fear of sleeping alone (25 percent), needing to sleep with the light on (21 percent), insomnia (20 percent), and nightmares (22 percent). Very consistent results were found in a similar study by Harrison and Cantor (1999).

TABLE 1. SUMMARY OF SELECTIVE RESULTS FROM
AUTOBIOGRAPHICAL MEMORY FOR MEDIA STUDIES

Participants Recalled	Selected Results	Implications
Frightening movie seen as child or teen watching (Hoekstra, et al., 1999)	1. 63 percent recalled generalized fear 2. 30 percent recalled specific fear 3. 46 percent recalled wild imagination 4. 25 percent recalled fear of sleeping alone 5. 21 percent recalled needing nightlight 6. 20 percent recalled insomnia 7. 22 percent recalled nightmares	1. Shows some uses and gratifications for frightening movies 2. Shows universality of being scared by media at a young age
Frightening movie seen on a date (Harris, et al., 2000)	1. Recalled similar effects as in in Hoekstra, et al. (1999) 2. 46 percent of men, 80 percent of women scared 3. Men more amused, aroused, surprised by date's reaction 4. Women more jumpy, disgusted, screaming, holding date, hiding eyes	1. Identifies some uses and gratifications for watching frightening movies on dates 2. Some support for gender-role socialization
Romantic movie seen on a date (Harris, et al., 2004)	1. Accurate in estimating how much date liked movie, but estimated "most men" would like the movie much less 2. Chose themselves to play in a romantic scene, but men also chose more sex scenes than women 3. Women underestimated how often date chose romantic scene	1. Relied on gender stereotypes to rate "most men" liking 2. Shows some uses and gratifications for watching romantic movies on dates
Soap operas (Bonds-Raacke and Hrenchir, unpublished)	1. Watch 29 hours per month 2. Watch to see what happens or for drama and suspense 3. Heavy viewers more likely visit web page, schedule around soaps, watch for daily pleasure, talk to others about soaps, watch for favorite characters 4. Light viewers more likely to watch because "nothing else on," not tell others, be embarrassed by watching, and be bothered by slow plot	1. Soap opera viewing is fulfilling personal needs 2. Support for cultivation theory
Sporting events enjoyed or not enjoyed on TV in four different social circumstances (Bonds-Raacke and Harris, submitted)	1. Men more likely amused or entertained, clap or cheer, laugh, increase heart rate, feel anxiety 2. Women more likely feel bored, do concurrent tasks, fall asleep, think event was stupid	1. Support for uses and gratifications theory 2. Watching and enjoying event depends on many factors

Participants Recalled	*Selected Results*	*Implications*
	3. Uses and gratifications differ depending on social circumstance 4. Uses and gratifications differ depending whether event enjoyed	3. Social context of watching sports very important
Tobacco use by TV or film characters (Cady, et al., in preparation)	1. Male smoking characters rated tougher, more rebellious, preparing for action 2. Female smoking characters rated more glamorous and attractive to men 3. Behaviors perceived with different frequencies in life, movies, and TV 4. Smokers/non-smokers perceive different frequencies of smoking	1. Media upholds the image of smoking as enhancing gender stereotypes 2. Media does not portray an accurate image of smoking frequency 3. Individual differences influence perceptions of media images
Popular music from different lifetime eras (Cady, et al., submitted)	1. Memories from high school and college more vivid and emotional than from earlier lifetime periods 2. Early childhood and grade school memories more pleasant than those from later life periods 3. Felt more brought back to moment of high school memories than to early childhood or middle school memories 4. Hearing song did not elicit more vivid or emotional memories than lyrics or title	1. Music universally an effective cue for eliciting autobiographical memories from different times of life. 2. Viewing a song title can induce a representation of song
Mental health professionals in media (Martin, et al., unpublished)	1. Most recalled a psychologist or psychiatrist, but misidentified their occupation 2. Most recalled male characters 3. Characters rated positively	1. Mental health professionals viewed in a generally positive light 2. Media don't differentiate different types of therapists
Homosexual characters portrayed positively or negatively on TV or film (Bonds-Raacke, et al., under review)	1. Majority participants recalled a few very salient characters 2. Recalling a positive portrayal led to less negative attitudes towards gay men	1. Support for Drench Hypothesis 2. Positive portrayals may prime attitudes

Two other studies asked college students to remember the experience of watching either a frightening movie (Harris et al., 2000) or a romantic movie (Harris et al., 2004) on a date. Again, the experiences were almost universal (98.7 percent), although there were some interesting differences between the two movie genres. For example, although the most common way (40–60 percent of cases) to choose both types of films was a joint decision, men were somewhat more likely to have chosen the violent movie and women the romantic movie. These same preferences were reflected in ratings of how much they liked each movie, although to a lesser degree women also liked the violent movies and men the romantic movies. When asked how much they thought their date had liked the romantic movie, both men and women were highly accurate in estimating their partner's liking; however, when asked how much "most men" would like that movie (or romantic movies in general), both men and women rated the liking much lower, thus falling back on gender stereotypes when rating these nonspecific "most men."

Although the violent movie was seen with a group or with only the couple about 40 percent of the time each, the romantic movie was viewed by only the couple 70 percent of the time. Men and women remembered the same effects of the scary movie that people had reported experiencing as a child in the earlier study, although most of them were more often reported by women than by men. Almost half (46 percent) of the men and 80 percent of the women reported themselves being "somewhat" or "very" scared by the film, but only about half of each wanted their dates to *think* they were scared. Sex was a very strong predictor of being scared and remembering negative reactions, stronger than measures of gender-role attitudes. Some components of dispositional empathy were weak, though significant, predictors of liking. When asked about concurrent behaviors and reactions, men more often than women reported themselves amused, sexually aroused, and surprised by their date's reactions, while women more often than men reported themselves as having been jumpy, disgusted, screaming, holding onto their date, and hiding their eyes.

A final type of measure was developed specifically for the romantic movies study. Participants were asked to think of a scene in the movie they had seen in which they would like to "stand in" for the same-sexed lead. They were also asked to pick a scene they would like to see their date stand in for, and pick a scene they thought their date would choose for himself or herself. The scenes were then content-analyzed into different types of scenes, of which the three most common were romance, intimate conversation, and sex. Everyone's first choice for themselves and their date was a romantic scene, which was the only type of scene present in all the films (given that the target film for the study was defined as "romantic movies"). Men were far more likely than women (21 percent vs. 3 percent) to choose a sex scene for themselves but both greatly overestimated how often the date would choose such a scene (women guessed men would choose sex 36 percent of the time and men guessed women would choose it 21 percent). Women greatly underestimated how often men would choose a romantic scene (guess of 23 percent vs. actual 40 percent).

These studies of memory for watching violent or romantic films show that both are socially useful and provide some uses and gratifications, although these differed for the two types of films and often differed for men and women. There was some support for Zillmann and Weaver's (1996) model of differential gender-role socialization with film, although our participants did not differ by sex as strongly as theirs.

Memories for Soap Operas

Autobiographical memory can also be used to investigate people's memories for viewing specific types of television genres; two that have been studied with this paradigm are soap operas and sporting events. The genre of soap operas is worth attention because cultivation theory research has documented that extensive, repeated exposure to any medium will begin to shape worldviews and social reality (Gerbner et al., 2002). Portrayals seen on soap operas are therefore important because effects of such images could influence as many as 30 million adults and 3.5 million adolescents (Greenberg and Busselle, 1996). Thus, "heavy" viewers of soap operas could potentially think and behave differently from "light" viewers.

In a study to examine this, Bonds-Raacke and Hrenchir (unpublished) had soap opera viewers complete a questionnaire assessing: (1) what soaps they watch (e.g., *Days of Our Lives*); (2) how often they watch (e.g., twice a week); and (3) appeals for viewing (e.g., escape from reality). Finally, participants indicated if they had ever visited a soap opera's web page or scheduled their day (including classes) around soaps, and to what extent they agreed with statements including "Watching soaps is a daily pleasure for me," and "I am embarrassed by the fact that I watch soaps."

On the average, this sample of soap opera viewers indicated that they watched 29 hours of soaps per month (7.25 hours per week), 70 percent at the scheduled hour and 42 percent by themselves. The most common appeals for viewing were: "To see what happens" (90 percent), and "The drama and suspense involved" (69 percent). In comparison to light viewers, heavy viewers were more likely to: visit a soap's webpage, schedule their day around soap operas, watch for a daily pleasure, enjoy talking to others about the soaps, see their favorite characters, see what happens, and watch the drama and suspense. In comparison to heavy viewers, light viewers were more likely to: watch because nothing else was on TV, feel embarrassed by watching, not tell others they watch, and be bothered by the slow moving plot.

The sheer number of hours that participants watched soap operas was remarkable and seems to indicate this behavior is fulfilling personal needs. Results also supported cultivation theory by demonstrating that differences existed between heavy and light viewers. Specifically, differences were found in those participants who viewed more hours per month (i.e., heavy viewers) and those who watched fewer hours per month (i.e., light viewers). Future research should focus on examining the heavy viewing population to better understand their appeals for viewing and gratifications obtained from viewing.

Memories for Televised Sporting Events

The genre of sporting events has also been investigated using autobiographical memory. Bonds-Raacke and Harris (under review) examined gender differences in behaviors and cognitions and uses and gratifications for sporting events that were either enjoyed or not enjoyed. Participants recalled four different sporting events that they had enjoyed watching on television, one in each of four different social situations (with family; with group of friends; with date, boyfriend/girlfriend or spouse; and by themselves) and four different sporting events that they had not enjoyed watching in the same four social situations. For each sporting event, participants checked off options they had experienced from a list of possible concurrent behaviors and cognitions and uses and gratifications for viewing.

Gender differences existed in concurrent behaviors and cognitions. Specifically, men were more likely to report that they were amused and entertained, clapped and cheered, felt their heartbeat increase, laughed with pleasure, and felt a general anxiety. Women, on the other hand, were more likely to report that they were bored, did household tasks while watching, fell asleep, and thought the sporting event was stupid.

Differences in uses and gratifications existed as a function of social circumstances of viewing for enjoyed sporting events. Results indicated that those watching with family checked the following uses and gratifications significantly more often than in at least one other social circumstance of viewing: "rituals," "root for favorite team/player," "entertainment," "thrill in victory," "something to talk about," "pride in team," and "commercials." Those watching with friends checked the following uses and gratifications significantly more often than in at least one other social circumstance of viewing: "escape," "reason to drink alcohol," "something to do with others," "something to talk about," "root for favorite team/player," and "root against certain team/player." Viewing with significant others resulted in the following uses and gratifications being checked significantly more often than in at least one other social circumstance of viewing: "pass time," "something to do with others," "something to talk about," and "nothing else on television." Finally, watching alone resulted in the following uses and gratifications being checked significantly more often than in at least one other social circumstance of viewing: "escape," "relaxation," "pass time," "diversion from daily routines," and "nothing else on television."

Differences in failed uses and gratifications also existed, based on social circumstances of viewing for the sporting events that were watched but not enjoyed. Specifically, watching with family resulted in the uses and gratifications of feeling bored and not interested in team/player being checked significantly more often than in at least one other social circumstance. Watching with friends resulted in the use and gratification of being drunk being checked significantly more often than in at least one other social circumstance of viewing. In addition, those watching with a date or significant other checked the following uses and gratifications significantly more often than in at least one other social circumstance of viewing: "was bored," "not interested in team/player," and "game was too violent." Finally, those watching alone checked that they were bored and that there were too many commercials significantly more often than in at least one other social circumstance.

These results support the uses and gratifications framework by demonstrating the reciprocal relationship that viewers have with the media. Moreover, uses and gratifications for enjoyed and not enjoyed events vary depending on social circumstance of viewing and sex of the viewer. Specifically, viewers do not always watch sporting events for the same reasons, nor do they obtain the same gratifications from each event. Why viewers watch and whether or not they enjoy the event is dependent on many factors.

Memories of Tobacco Use in Media

Another line of autobiographical memory media research has looked at memories for specific kinds of behaviors rather than a specific genre of programming. As an example of this type of study, Cady, Harris, Berger et al.(in preparation) had participants recall their memories of viewing smoking in media, both in print advertisements and by movie and TV characters. In addition, participants rated their perception of how often smoking occurred (1) on television, (2) in film, and (3) in real life. Participants were divided based on their smoking status into smokers, former smokers, and those who had never smoked.

In one question, participants were asked to think of a positive image of smoking as portrayed by a movie or TV character and rate the positive aspects of those characters. Female characters who smoked were rated as looking more glamorous and more attractive to the opposite sex, suggesting that the characters perpetuated a media image of beautiful women smoking to attract men. On the other hand, male characters who smoked were rated as having a tough "real man" image to a greater extent than female characters were seen to have a "real woman" image. Male characters were also seen to more strongly have a rebel image and as preparing for a fight or other action more than female characters who smoked. These findings suggest that the media uphold the image of smoking enhancing masculinity.

In addition, participants rated their perceptions of the frequency of smoking in certain settings differently on TV, in film, and in real life. For example, smoking after dinner and attempts to stop smoking were seen as occurring more frequently in life than in TV or film. On the other hand, smoking to relieve stress and smoking while drinking alcohol were seen as being less frequent on TV than in film or life. Conversely, smoking after sex was seen as least frequent in life, next most frequent on TV, and most frequent in film. In addition, smoking to look cool was seen as being more frequent in film than on TV or in life. These results show that perceived frequency of smoking in media does not mirror its perceived frequency in real life.

Moreover, smokers perceived the frequency of these behaviors differently from nonsmokers. For example, while former smokers and those who have never smoked perceived no significant differences in the frequency of smoking after dinner in real life and in film, smokers perceived significantly more smoking after dinner in life than in film. This pattern also held for the perception of smoking to relieve stress, in that smokers saw significant differences in this behavior between TV, film, and life, while nonsmokers perceived a significant difference only between TV and film. On the other hand, smokers and former smokers saw a similar pattern of attempts to stop smoking on TV and in life, while those who have never smoked saw significantly more attempts to stop in life than in either of the media categories and significantly more attempts to stop smoking on TV than in film. Finally, nonsmokers perceived significant differences between TV, film, and life for the behavior of smoking after sex, with the frequency of this behavior being seen as highest in film and lowest in life, while smokers saw this behavior most frequently in film but with similar frequency in life and on TV. These results indicate that a person's own habits and behavior may influence his or her perceptions of that behavior in media characters, as well as its frequency in real life.

Popular Music as Cues to Autobiographical Memories

Another way that media can affect memory is in serving as a cue to retrieve autobiographical information. One type of medium that is particularly powerful in this regard is music, which can serve as a particular potent cue to retrieve personal memories.

In a study by Cady, Harris, and Knappenberger (under review), college students ages 18 to 23 were shown lists of five to eight songs, determined from pilot research to have been very popular during particular lifetime eras in the participants' lives; they were asked to choose the song from each list with the strongest positive memory attached to it. Five lists of songs were used, one each from early childhood, grade school, middle school, high school, and college. Participants in the auditory group then heard a minute of the chosen song prior to filling out the questionnaire. Participants in the lyrics condition saw and read the typed lyrics for one minute. Participants in the picture condition saw a picture of the album cover (and artist if not shown on the cover). Participants in the control condition began filling out the questionnaire immediately after choosing the song. Each participant chose one song from each of the five lifetime eras, allowing for comparisons both between conditions and across lifetime eras within participants. The questionnaire gathered ratings of the song and the associated memory on a variety of dimensions.

Almost all of the participants were able to complete all five music questionnaires, with less than 1 percent of the questionnaires not completed, indicating that songs almost universally elicited autobiographical memories from five different lifetime periods. Results showed that memories from high school and college were more vivid, specific, and emotional than memories from earlier lifetime eras. The vividness and specificity of the memories gradually increased from early childhood through college. The means for the emotionality of the memories were lower for early childhood, grade school, and middle school and higher for high school and college.

However, the memories chosen from early childhood and grade school were more pleasant than those from later lifetime eras. In addition, the memories from high school caused the participants to feel more "brought back to the moment" than memories from early childhood and middle school. These relationships held across the conditions, and participants were able to "hear" the song in their heads equally well, regardless of whether they had heard the song, read the lyrics, seen the album cover, or seen only the title of the song. These results show that music can be an effective cue for autobiographical memories going back many years.

Memories for Particular Types of Media Characters

The final type of study discussed assesses autobiographical memory for particular types of characters in the media. Although there are numerous content analyses available documenting the numbers of various types of people on television (Harris, 2004), they do not necessarily directly translate into impact on the audience. Some shows and characters and some movies are seen by many millions of people over many years, with the characters becoming popular culture icons in their own right. Many other shows and characters are seen by few and quickly fade from memory. The autobiographical memory paradigm, by asking participants to come up with an example of a certain type of character, taps more directly into the most memorable, and thus probably most influential, from the possible set of exemplars. This view is consistent with Greenberg's (1988) Drench Hypothesis, which posits that a few very popular characters (e.g., Bill Cosby, Jerry Seinfeld, Ross/Joey/Chandler/Monica/Rachel/Phoebe) will have a disproportionate influence on the audience, while many other more seldom seen persons have far less influence.

This type of study can have one of two purposes. First, it can be used to describe a prevailing media image of a certain type of person. Second, it can be used to test the impact of a character on social attitudes more generally, assessing a type of priming effect. One study with each of these purposes will be described, starting with a study of the media image of mental health professionals. This will be followed by a study of a priming effect from thinking about a homosexual character on attitudes toward gays and lesbians.

Media Image of Mental Health Care Professionals

Examining memories for media experiences can provide information on perceptions of professions; the particular group examined here is mental health professionals. Individuals' perceptions of mental health professionals (therapists) are important because various representations of mental health professionals in the media might easily influence a potential client's decision whether or not to seek therapy. In an experiment to examine attitudes toward media depictions of mental health care professionals, Martin, Bonds-Raacke, and Barlett (unpublished) asked participants to: (1) recall a media character who fit the description of a psychologist, psychiatrist, counselor, marriage-family therapist, religious counselor, or other helping professional; (2) rate their perceptions of the character on various personality dimensions; and (3) indicate the attire of the character and the physical setting.

The majority of participants recalled a character that they indicated was a psychiatrist or psychologist. Two of the most frequently recalled characters were Dr. Frasier Crane and Dr. Sean Maguire (from the 1997 film *Good Will Hunting*). However, only 16 percent of participants correctly identified Frasier Crane's occupation, and 50 percent correctly identified Sean Maguire's occupation. This may reflect that participants do not know the difference between psychologists and psychiatrists, or that the characters were not clearly identified by profession in the show. It is also interesting to note that over 90 percent of the characters recalled were males, in contrast to a much closer even gender split in those professions.

Results for character ratings on various dimensions were generally positive, with the characters rated as responsible, serious, and a good role model, with few differences in ratings between psychologists and psychiatrist. The most recalled settings included both the client and the professional sitting upright in chairs, or the client lying down on a couch. For the attire, the therapist generally wore either business clothing or casual clothing. Results from this research give the psychological community reason to be pleased in looking at the perceptions of mental health professionals in the media, while knowing that there is some improvement to be made. Future research should look at positive and negative images of mental health professionals and the willingness of the public to seek help.

Social Priming Effect from Remembering a Homosexual Media Character

As an example of how media characters can affect social attitudes, consider a study demonstrating how memories of media characters can influence attitudes toward gay men and lesbians (Bonds-Raacke, Cady, Schlegel, Harris, and Firebaugh, submitted). This particular study asked participants to think about either (1) a positive homosexual media character (i.e., media character who is "presented in such a way that many people would tend to admire and or like this person"); (2) a negative homosexual media character (i.e., character who is "presented is such a way that many people would dislike and or have little respect for this person"); or (3) an unmarried media character, with no mention made of sexual orientation (control group). After answering some questions about their character and rating that person on several personality scales, participants completed Herek's (1988) 40-item Attitudes toward Lesbians and Gays (ATLG) scale. Results showed that those recalling a positive portrayal later showed a more positive attitude toward gay men than those recalling a negative or neutral portrayal, and women overall had a more positive attitude than men toward both gay men and lesbians. Such findings illustrate the importance of positive role models in the media as potential primes of social attitudes.

These results were consistent with Greenberg's (1988) Drench Hypothesis, in that a few highly salient characters such as Ellen Morgan, Will Truman, and Jack McFarland were recalled by the majority of participants. These results suggest the potentially enormous influence that a few positive role model media characters appearing on very popular shows can have on attitudes toward a social group. It may be that the show *Will and Grace*, with its huge audiences, is doing more to improve attitudes toward gay men than any amount of explicit social teaching in schools, families, churches, and elsewhere.

General Discussion

Autobiographical memory for media characters and programming can be a very useful complement to existing research on media effects using more traditional paradigms. It is useful in addressing certain aspects of media experience, particularly the following:

Social Dimensions of Media Consumption

Media are often consumed in a social setting, and that setting greatly colors the experience of viewing, what we remember from it, and its subsequent effects. Bonds-Raacke and Harris' study of sporting events, for example, showed considerable differences in uses and gratifications, depending on whether the event was viewed alone or with family, friends, or significant other. Harris et al.'s (2000, 2004) studies of seeing frightening or romantic movies on a date showed uses and gratifications closely tied into the gender roles of the dating situation. Cady, Harris, and Knappenberger's study using music to cue autobiographical memory also indicated a social component in that a majority of the memories chosen across lifetime eras were related to friends or family. With autobiographical memory, information about these social dimensions can be easily gathered.

Indirect Measures of Effects

Although retrospective memory cannot directly assess effects, people's perceptions of effects they have experienced can be enlightening. Consistent with the Drench Hypothesis, the most popular, and thus presumably most influential, portrayals will be the ones most easily recalled. The rich detail that participants are able to recall from the experience is striking, as is the similarity of memory in couples watching a film together. The types and degrees of effects recalled are quite consistent with media effects research using other methodologies, thus offering converging evidence for consistent effects.

Contributions to Attitude and Stereotype Literature

Autobiographical memory can help to describe the nature of the prevailing stereotype of certain social groups. It can also be a way to assess the role of media on attitude change. The demonstration of a priming effect from thinking about a positive gay or lesbian character is an example. Comparisons of stereotypes with reality can be examined, as in the study of portrayals of mental health professionals. The romantic movies study found that people sometimes judged others individually (self and one's date), while at other times relying on gender stereotypes (generalized others).

Individual Differences

For example, in the study of tobacco use in the media, the results showed that smokers and nonsmokers saw different patterns of smoking behavior in the media. In several studies, men and women responded differently to the same media stimuli. Individual differences may also be assessed psychometrically, as in the cases of the movies studies where empathy and sensation seeking were shown to be significant predictions of reactions to frightening movies. This focus on individual differences can contribute to a better understanding of how people consume the media in different ways.

Future Research and Concluding Remarks

Research using and extending the autobiographical memory paradigm has a bright future. Some research in progress directly extends the work discussed above. For example, one study will further examine the results from the tobacco study by having participants view a clip from a movie where characters either smoke or do not smoke, and rate the characters on several dimensions, as well as providing information on their own smoking behaviors. Responses will be compared based on the clip shown and the smoking status of the participants. A similar study is looking at reactions to particular clips with no cues to sexual orientation but where some participants are told that a certain character is gay.

Many possible directions of future research exist, such as comparing the uses and gratifications framework to others to determine which paradigm best explains viewing consumption and resulting behaviors and cognitions. In addition, it is worth exploring what other prosocial issues that media can address in an attempt to change viewers' attitudes in a more positive direction. Also, the study of music can be extended to older adults to determine whether they show the same patterns of recall. These techniques could be combined with neuroscience studies to determine patterns of activation that lead to these types of memory. Finally, a new direction for media research is proposed where the focus is not on viewing behaviors, attitudes, or effects, but research that focuses on media memories themselves including how and where memories for media experiences are stored in long-term memory.

Research using the autobiographical memory paradigm to recall memories for media experiences has resulted in a line of research that is broad in scope and rich in data. This research has made contributions to the literature on social dimensions of media consumption, indirect measures of media effects, and attitude and stereotypes. In addition, the findings help to better understand how the media consumer interacts with not only particular media, but also how the viewers' behaviors and social circumstances of viewing can potentially influence subsequent attitudes and perceptions.

References

Bandura, A. (2002). Social cognitive theory of mass communication. In J. Bryant and D. Zillmann (eds.), *Media effects: Advances in theory and research* (2nd ed), (pp. 121–153). Mahwah, NJ: Erlbaum.

Bonds-Raacke, J. M., Cady, E. T., Schlegel, R., Harris, R. J., and Firebaugh, L. C. (submitted). Remembering gay/lesbian characters: Can Ellen and Will improve attitudes toward homosexuals?

Bonds-Raacke, J. M., and Harris, R. J. (submitted). Autobiographical memories of televised sporting events watched in different social settings.

Bonds-Raacke, J. M., and Hrenchir, C. (2002). Watching soap operas. Unpublished manuscript.

Cady, E. T., Harris, R. J., Berger, J. M., Hermesch, J., and Barlett, C. P. (in preparation). Images of tobacco use in the media.

Cady, E. T., Harris, R. J., and Knappenberger, J. B. (submitted). Using music to cue autobiographical memory of different lifetime periods.

Cantor, J. (1998). *"Mommy, I'm scared": How TV and movies frighten children and what we can do to protect them.* San Diego, CA: Harcourt Brace.

_____ (2002). Fright reactions to mass media. In J. Bryant and D. Zillmann (eds.), *Media effects* (pp. 287–306). Mahwah, NJ: Erlbaum.

Conway, M. A., and Pleydell-Pearce, C. W. (2000). The construction of autobiographical memories in the self system. *Psychological Review,* 107, 261–288.

Davis, M. H., Hull, J. G., Young, R. D., and Warren, G. G. (1987). Emotional reactions to dramatic film stimuli: The influence of cognitive and emotional empathy. *Journal of Personality and Social Psychology,* 52, 126–133.

Gerbner, G., Gross, L., Morgan, M., Signorielli, N., and Shanahan, J. (2002). Growing up with television: Cultivation processes. In J. Bryant and D. Zillmann (eds.), *Media effects: Advances in theory and research.* (2nd ed., pp. 43–67). Mahwah, NJ: Erlbaum.

Greenberg, B. S. (1988). Some uncommon television images and the Drench Hypothesis. In S. Oskamp (ed.), *Television as a social issue* (pp. 88–102). Newbury Park, CA: Sage.

Greenberg, B. S., and Busselle, R. W. (1996). Soap operas and sexual activity: A decade later. *Journal of Communication,* 46, 153–160.

Harris, R. J. (2004). *A cognitive psychology of mass communication* (4th ed.). Mahwah, NJ: Erlbaum.

_____, Hoekstra, S. J., Scott, C. L., Sanborn, F. W., Karafa, J. A., and Brandenburg, J. D. (2000). Young men's and women's different autobiographical memories of the experience of seeing frightening movies on a date. *Media Psychology,* 2, 245–268.

Harris, R. J., Hoekstra, S. J., Scott, C. L., Sanborn, F. W., Dodds, L. A., and Brandenburg, J. D. (in press). Autobiographical memories of the experience of seeing romantic movies on a date: Romance is not just for women. *Media Psychology.*

Harrison, K., and Cantor, J. (1999). Tales from the screen: Enduring fright reactions to scary media. *Media Psychology,* 1, 97–116.

Herek, G. M. (1988). Heterosexuals' attitudes toward lesbians and gay men: Correlates and gender differences. *Journal of Sex Research,* 25, 451–477.

Hoekstra, S. J., Harris, R. J., and Helmick, A. L. (1999). Autobiographical memories about the experience of seeing frightening movies in childhood. *Media Psychology,* 1, 117–140.

Martin, A. E., Bonds-Raacke, J. M., and Barlett, C. P. Portrayals of mental health professionals in media. Unpublished manuscript.

Rubin, A. M. (2002). The uses-and-gratifications perspective of media effects. In J.

Bryant and D. Zillmann (eds.), *Media effects: Advances in theory and research* (2nd ed.). Mahwah, NJ: Erlbaum.

Rubin, D. C. (ed.) (1996). *Remembering our past: Studies in autobiographical memory.* Cambridge, U.K.: Cambridge University Press.

Spence, J. T., and Helmreich, R. L. (1978) *Masculinity and femininity: Their psychological dimensions, correlates, and antecedents.* Austin, TX: University of Texas Press.

Thompson, C. P., Herrmann, D. J., Bruce, D., Read, J. D., Payne, D. G., and Toglia, M. P. (eds.). (1998). *Autobiographical memory: Theoretical and applied perspectives.* Mahwah, NJ: Erlbaum.

Zillmann, D., and Weaver, J. B. (1996). Gender-socialization theory of reactions to horror. In J. B. Weaver and R. Tamborini (eds.), *Horror films: Current research on audience preferences and reactions.* (pp. 81–101). Mahwah, NJ: Erlbaum.

Zuckerman, M. (1994). *Behavioral expressions and psychobiological bases of sensation seeking.* New York: Cambridge University Press.

9

Minorities as Marginalized Heroes and Prominent Villains in the Mass Media: Music, News, Sports, Television, and Movies

JEFFREY A. GIBBONS, CHERYL TAYLOR, *and* JANET PHILLIPS

Gordon Allport (1954) stated that stereotyping is an adaptive and effective means of processing information; individuals can formulate beliefs about groups and avoid processing information on an individual basis. Unfortunately, images of gender and race in the mass media foster the development of negative individual and societal stereotypes. The literature suggests that women and African Americans in the media are marginalized if they are positive characters, and they are promoted if they are negative characters. Conversely, the majority (i.e., white males) are marginalized if they are negative characters and promoted if they are positive characters.

This chapter will demonstrate the basis for these gender and racial stereotypes across five types of mass media: music, news, sports, television, and movies.

Gender Stereotypes

Virginia Woolf (1929) eloquently summed up gender stereotypes in the mass media when she stated: "If a woman had no existence save in the fiction written by men, one would imagine her a person… Very various; heroic and mean; splendid and sordid; infinitely beautiful and hideous in the extreme" (p. 43). This quote describes the positive and negative stereotypes for women that appear in the media and influence society. For example, Cobb, Boettcher, and Taylor (2001) argued that hostile and benevolent sexism stem directly from gender stereotypes. Hostile sexism is negative and suggests that women are temptresses, career women, or feminists. Benevolent sexism is considered to be positive, and it is akin to chivalry where women are homemakers, wives, and mothers, who are generally considered to be in need of a man's protection. Benevolent sexism is a prevalent gender stereotype shown in the media, where male characters are dominant and female characters are subordinate. In various areas of the media (i.e., music, news, sports, television, and movies), women are marginalized if they are portrayed as positive characters and promoted if they are negative characters, whereas the converse is true for men in the media.

Music

Inappropriate gender stereotypes consistently marginalize positive women in the music media. One such 'positive' characteristic is beauty. Women are simply portrayed as decorative objects in music, having physical attributes rather than having musical abilities (e.g., Cobb et al., 2001; Signorielli, McLeod, and Healy, 1994). In music videos, women are condescended to and given menial roles, where they are merely portrayed as objects. Although beauty is perceived to be a positive characteristic, music media has marginalized beautiful women as subservient to dominant male figures. Barol (1985) summed up this portrayal of women in the music media:

> All too often—especially as supporting characters in the videos of male singers—they're played as bimbos. Dressed in fishnet and leather, they drape themselves over car hoods, snarl like tigers, undress in silhouette behind window shades. Most rock videos give free reign to the cheesiest imagery of women as playthings [p. 54].

In contrast to women who are marginalized, notable women in the music industry are perceived negatively. For example, Madonna was considered to be a rebel in the music industry because, as a female protagonist, she purposely violated the societal and patriarchal class structure. As a credit to her notoriety, a recent poll conducted by the British Broadcasting Corporation (BBC) named Madonna as the greatest woman in music, even surpassing such legends as Billie Holiday and Aretha Franklin (BBC News, 2002).

Just as the negative women in the music industry are promoted, positive men are also promoted. Johnny Cash was a man who epitomized the hard-working man and the struggles of daily life, and thus, he was highly respected in the music industry. Cash was nominated for a MTV Video Music Award in six categories for his cover of the Nine Inch Nails song *Hurt*, a song about the fight with drug addiction. Even though Cash did not win the award, the winner (Justin Timberlake) stated that Cash deserved to win the award. Throughout Cash's life, he played in concerts in several countries, and his fans loved him (Smolowe and Dougherty, 2003). Cash was portrayed as a positive man in the music industry, and he was heavily promoted as such.

The music media, on the other hand, marginalizes negative male artists by down playing controversial songs and lyrics. Eminem (2000, track 2) states in the song *Kill You* that women are "vile venomous volatile bitches." Although he is a controversial musician, infamous for his violent and angry lyrics, he consistently wins music awards such as Grammys and American Music Awards (Allen, 2001).

Though one could argue that lyrics, songs, and music videos are simply an art form depicting fictional gender stereotypes and that they have no effect on personal stereotypes, research has shown that gender stereotypes broadcast by the music media influence individuals' thoughts. For example, St. Lawrence and Joyner (1991) revealed that sexually violent heavy metal rock music caused men to have more stereotypic and negative attitudes toward women. Similarly, Hansen and Hansen (1988) discovered that music videos portraying gender stereotypes actually increased individuals' stereotypes of other people. Therefore, music and music videos have the potential to influence societal views and continue to marginalize positive women and portray powerful women negatively.

News

Technological advances have created an increasingly smaller world as journalism attempts to stay current with the latest news and trends. However, journalism and newscasting have typically been considered male occupations, such that newscasts without men receive low ratings from viewing audiences (Sanders and Rock, 1988). Moreover, news anchors have typically been men, and prime time anchors, such as Walter Cronkite and Peter Jennings, have become household names. Male news anchors may project and represent credibility and reliability, presenting serious news from around the world. Whereas male anchors reported stories on politics, natural disasters, and sports, the few female anchors studied in the literature reported health and human-interest stories (Cann and Mohr, 2001). The fact that men dominate the local and national evening news marginalizes women in the news media.

Although men take the spotlight in the media as news anchors, the converse is true for stories depicting onerous behavior. That is, the negative actions of men are marginalized, or downplayed, by the media. For example, President Bill Clinton was involved in unscrupulous sexual behavior with a White House intern, Monica Lewinsky. Yet, the media focused on Clinton's popularity, and marginalized his indiscretions with Lewinsky to such a degree that Clinton's ratings in the polls skyrocketed. In February 1999, his approval rating stood at a staggering 68 percent (Miller, 2001).

In contrast to marginalizing negative male behavior, the news media portrays women negatively. For example, Marilyn Quayle, wife of former Vice President Dan Quayle, holds a law degree, has practiced law, and was the primary advisor to her husband's political campaigns. However, she was portrayed negatively by the media in stark contrast to first ladies who remained silent behind the scenes. The media suggested that Mrs. Quayle was "a bossy and aggressive woman" (Gold and Speicher, 1996, p. 97). This media portrayal promoted her negatively as cold and impersonal, and it marginalized her accomplishments. However, the press portrayed her in a more positive light when she acted more traditionally and publicly cried over her mother's death (Gold and Speicher, 1996). Clearly, the media portrays political men and women differently, downplaying the negative actions of men and promoting women negatively.

In addition to prime-time television news, male dominance and classical gender stereotypes are also commonplace in the lighter side of the news, known as the comic strip. Comic strips reflect societal values and beliefs, and they present gender stereotypes, which displays the marginalization of positive women. For example, research has shown that the satire in comic strips reinforces the sexism found in American society (Brabant and Mooney, 1986, 1997; Mooney and Brabant, 1987). Female characters in comic strips are presented in passive or servitudinal roles, whereas male characters are portrayed as dominant (Spiegelman, Terwilliger, and Fearing, 1953). In fact, Spiegelman et al. (1953) stated that "the world of the comic strip is a man's world" (p. 203).

Although one might argue that comic strips and their characters have evolved over time, researchers have recently shown that comics have not changed (Brabant and Mooney, 1986, 1997; Mooney and Brabant, 1987). For example, Blondie is a clever woman married to Dagwood, and she has two teenage children. Blondie is still portrayed in a traditional, stereotypical role, even though Blondie is the proprietor of her own catering business. She primarily remains in the home environment, which marginalizes her abilities as a businesswoman. Like Blondie, most comic strip women are often seen wearing aprons or doing "women's work," whereas male characters are frequently involved in leisure activities, such as reading a book (Mooney and Brabant, 1987).

According to Mooney and Brabant (1987), female comic strip characters seeking power or high status receive disapproval from individuals around them. For example, Sally Forth is portrayed as a powerful comic strip character capable of completing any task. However, Sally is also shown as hard, unfeminine, and mannish, which are considered negative female characteristics. Therefore, comic strips, like other forms of media, marginalize positive women, and they portray powerful women negatively. Conversely, the negative characteristics and actions of male comic strip characters are marginalized. For example, Hägar the Horrible, appearing in 1,900 papers worldwide, is a Viking with a "voracious appetite for pillaging and plundering" England and surrounding countries. Yet, despite his violence, Hägar is portrayed as a devoted husband, loving father, and family man (Browne, 2003). While comic strips are created with the purpose of entertainment, they perpetuate gender stereotypes (Brabant and Mooney, 1986, 1997). These gender stereotypes in the news promote positive men, marginalize positive women, promote negative women, and marginalize negative men.

Sports

In addition to music and news, sports are dominated by men and segregated by sex. According to Beal (1997), sports and its venues publicly showcase the perceived and assumed superiority of men. Sports, as a hegemonic masculine arena, have been used throughout history to revitalize male leadership (Beal, 1997; Koivula, 1999). For example, Messner (1998) stated that sport was a male-created domain providing "dramatic symbolic proof of the natural superiority of men over women" (p. 200). Messner also stated that football shows men as dominant and aggressive, while relegating women to act as supportive sex objects on the sidelines. Through visual productions, language, technology, and terminology, media has marginalized, trivialized, and sexualized women in sports (Kennedy, 2001; Koivula, 1999).

Sports commentators ensure the dominance of men by using language that marginalizes female athletes. For example, Koivula (1999) examined sports broadcasting in Sweden from September 1, 1995 to August 31, 1996 and found that male athletes were referred as "men" or "guys." Women, on the other hand, were most often referred to as "young ladies," or "girls." Some commentators even used the terms *babe, broad, chick,* and *dame* to describe female athletes. Koivula also illustrated that dominant athletes and male athletes are usually referred to by their surnames, showing respect, whereas subordinate athletes and female athletes are called by their first names, showing disrespect. In fact, female athletes were four times more likely to be mentioned by their first name than male athletes, and male athletes were twice as likely to be mentioned by their last name than female athletes. Therefore, the language used by the sports media promotes male athletes and marginalizes female athletes.

The media also treat negative men and women in sports differently. For example, Tonya Harding has never been a favorite in ice skating fans' eyes because she was athletic instead of graceful on the ice. However, when Harding was involved in a brutal attack (a blow to the knee) on her top rival for Olympic gold, the graceful Nancy Kerrigan, just nine weeks before the 1994 Winter Olympics, Harding became a pariah in the skating world (Kindred, 1994). Sports reporters even expressed dismay when Harding stated that she hoped Kerrigan would be back from her injuries so that Harding could beat her in the upcoming Olympic games. Kindred (1994) stated that Harding was "graceless even for a pool-shootin', trash-talkin' mama" and a "certified villain" (p. 8). Because of her involvement in the attack on Kerrigan, Harding was permanently banned from competing in amateur figure skating competitions.

On the other hand, negative male athletes have not faced the same negative portrayals by the media. Pete Rose, former player and manager for the Cincinnati Reds, spent time in jail for filing false tax returns and was suspended for 30 days for shoving an umpire (*Pete Rose,* n.d.). Even though Pete Rose was banned from major league baseball and Baseball's Hall of Fame for gambling on baseball, the media and fans alike petition every year for the removal of his ban, stating that Rose was an excellent player and coach, and, consequently, deserved an immortal place in baseball's history. This dichotomy between Harding and Rose shows that sports media promote the negativity of female athletes and marginalize the negativity of male athletes.

Television

Music, news, and sports all portray gender stereotypes that marginalize or diminish women on television. Television is a primary venue for events that transcends language and literacy barriers. Additionally, television has become a primary means of socialization, cultivating common universal viewpoints and values as well as common perceptions and ideologies for gender roles. According to Bagdikian (1987), television has "become the authority at any given moment for what is true and what is false, what is reality and what is fantasy, what is important and what is trivial" (p. xviii). Along with the other media, television marginalizes positive female characters and promotes negative female characters (Signorielli, 1989).

Female television characters are significantly more likely than male characters to be involved in a romantic relationship, supporting the traditional notion that women need a man. One typical example of a positive, yet marginalized female character is Rebecca Howe from the television series *Cheers*. She was beautiful and feminine, and she dreamed of marrying a knight in shining armor, thus showing that a woman needs a man if she is to be successful and fulfilled in life. In contrast, Carla Tortelli, the waitress on *Cheers*, was portrayed as lacking warmth, charm, and feminine ideals. Her unladylike, sexually promiscuous behavior was in sharp contrast to the behavior of Rebecca Howe's character (Craig, 1993). Carla was a powerful nontraditional woman feared by other characters. These female characters are not uncommon on television, which is unsettling because television helps viewers delineate reality from fantasy. As a result of watching television, viewers should believe that "good" women derive their identity from men.

The positive and negative portrayals of male characters on television contradict the portrayals of women in the same medium. Men are typically portrayed as being more powerful and potent overall than women, and they also have occupations with higher prestige and better pay than women (Signorielli, 1989; Signorielli and Kahlenberg, 2001). Tim Taylor of *Home Improvement* is a classic example of a positive male character who teaches his sons to behave "like a man" (Olson and Douglas, 1997). Positive men are also promoted in situation comedies and prime-time dramas on television as heroic, strong, masculine, and athletic (Craig, 1993; Cuklanz, 2000). Examples of these positive male characters include Sam Malone of *Cheers* and Wood Newton of *Evening Shade*; both characters displayed a rugged athleticism characteristic of hemogonic masculinity (Craig, 1993). According to Cuklanz (2000), prime-time television is a vehicle for this hemogonic masculinity, where masculine men are portrayed as saviors or rescuers of women. Prime-time detectives (e.g., Baretta, Starsky and Hutch) are a classic example of this type of positive male character.

Unlike positive characters, the negative actions of male characters are downplayed on television sit-coms and dramas. For example, J. R. Ewing was immortalized on *Dallas* as the man who fans loved to hate. Even though J. R. was underhanded in his dealings with the competition in the oil industry and abusive to his wife, viewers adored him, and they were always willing to forgive his negative ways. In fact, 41 million households watched the episode of *Dallas*, where the question "Who shot J. R.?" was finally answered. Although the culprit was another one of his mistresses, who was pregnant with his child, J. R. was portrayed as the blameless victim (Manning, 2000). Therefore, television marginalizes positive women and portrays powerful women negatively, and the converse is true for male characters.

Movies

Much like the little screen (television), the big screen has allowed millions of Americans to escape the harsh realities of the world and to enter a world of fantasy for two or three hours. Film is a strong reflection of societal ideals, showing that art reflects life, and the converse is also true. Movies convey the same gender stereotypes as other forms of the media, such that the depictions on the big screen can maintain, or even propagate gender stereotypes. In the movies, men are portrayed and promoted as powerful and positive characters, whereas women are either marginalized as positive characters in traditional, subordinate roles, or they are portrayed as powerful characters with negative attributes (Bazzini, McIntosh, Smith, Cook, and Harris, 1997). Hedley (1994) argued that movies typically reinforce the gender stereotypes that men are powerful characters, who maintain their power with relative ease. Examples include Mel Gibson movies where he plays powerful men (e.g., William Wallace in *Braveheart*, Martin Riggs in the *Lethal Weapon* movies) who undergo torturous events and yet emerge victorious, even if the victory is posthumously awarded as in the movie *Braveheart* (J. A. Brown, 2002).

The cinematic ideology of the powerful man is consistently portrayed in contemporary times. For example, *The Man from Snowy River* is a tale of a young man who comes of age in Australia. Jim Craig must fight to earn status as a man by tests of adaptability, physical strength, and sheer determination. Throughout the movie, Jim is portrayed as an individual, who obtains the status of a legend and hero. In his victory, Jim claims his inheritance and the love of Jessica, the landowner's daughter (Miller, 1982). In this transference of power from her father to her future husband, Jessica is portrayed as a conventional object to be passed from one generation to the next, and thus reaffirming patriarchal authority and rewarding powerful male heroes with the love of a good (i.e., faithful and devoted) woman.

As in other forms of media, the negativity of male characters is downplayed, or marginalized. For example, Hannibal Lecter, known for his cannibalistic behavior, escaped from prison and lived a life of luxury in Florence, Italy in the movie *Hannibal*. Throughout the movie, characters are interested in his capture for various reasons (i.e., revenge and incarceration). Cannibalism has extremely negative connotations, but Hannibal's behavior was marginalized because he was charming and sophisticated. In fact, the audience actually hopes that he can escape from the law (Scott, 2001). Although extreme, this example is in no way uncharacteristic of negative male behavior portrayed in the media.

Cobb et al. (2001) argued that benevolent sexism, which affirms the patriarchal notion that women need to be protected and saved, is clearly present in movies, especially ones with fairy-tale themes. *Pretty Woman* (Marshall, 1990) is an example of this modern-day fairy tale. Vivian, played by Julia Roberts, is a prostitute hired by Edward Lewis, a successful and wealthy businessman. Edward, representing the prince in Cinderella, is actually the hero of the story, who comes from a privileged background and has considerable financial power, while Vivian hails from a poor, underprivileged childhood. The gender stereotypes observed in this film include a male hero with status and a woman as dependent, beautiful, feminine, excessively positive, and most of all, available to fulfill a man's needs (Kelley, 1994).

In the movie *A Long Kiss Goodnight*, Charly Baltimore, played by Geena Davis, is an ex–CIA assassin who has lost her memory in a horrific accident. Throughout the movie, she valiantly rescues Mitch Henessey, played by Samuel L. Jackson, on several occasions. However, Charly is literally begging someone to save her and her child near the end of the movie. Mitch heroically rescues her and her daughter, showing that even a strong woman needs a man's assistance for salvation (Harlin, 1996). Even in recent movies such as the *Matrix* series, women still need men to save them. In both *The Matrix* and *The Matrix Reloaded*, Trinity, played by Carrie-Anne Moss, is a warrior fighting for the salvation of humankind. Although she is a seasoned fighter and seemingly independent, Trinity weakens by the films' end, and Neo must save her emotionally and physically (Wachowski and Wachowski, 1999, 2003).

In contrast to positive women, a new trend in movies shows psychotic women stalking male lead characters (J. Brown, 1990). These portrayals show that powerful women are dangerous. Kathy Bates in *Misery* is a classic example of a psychotic woman, Annie Wilkes, who is obsessed with James Caan's character, Paul Sheldon, to the point that she violently hobbles him in order to keep him under her power (Reiner, 1990). Similarly, Alex Forrest, played by Glenn Close in *Fatal Attraction*, is another example of a powerful, psychotic female character. Alex becomes obsessed with Dan Gallager, played by Michael Douglas, stalks him, and attempts to murder his wife, Beth (Lyne, 1987). Although Alex was violently killed at the finale, she is, without a doubt, completely unforgettable to movie audiences as a strong and negative character. Both Annie Wilkes and Alex Forrest were powerful, negative female characters who challenged the patriarchy. Only through defeat (i.e., death) could these powerful and negative characters be marginalized and the patriarchy maintained.

These positive and negative stereotypes become readily apparent when examining the American Film Institute's (AFI) release, in the summer of 2003, of their choices for the top 50 heroes and the 50 top villains in American movie history. In order to be considered for one of the top 50 positions in either category, the film had to meet strict criteria, including the definition of a hero and a villain. A hero was defined as a character who overcame difficult circumstances and also showed strong morality and courage. A villain was defined as a character that expressed extreme wickedness and selfishness, and also desired great power. Atticus Finch in *To Kill a Mockingbird* was the number one top hero for the AFI's "100 Years ... 100 Heroes and Villains" list. Other characters selected to this prestigious and memorable category were Rick Blaine in *Casablanca*, Rocky Balboa in *Rocky*, and George Bailey in *It's a Wonderful Life*. Interestingly, only two out of the top 10 heroes were women: Clarice Starling of *The Silence of the Lambs* and Ellen Ripley of *Aliens*. Conversely the top 10 villains' list showed six women out of the top 10. Characters selected for this distinction included the Wicked Witch of the West (*The Wizard of Oz*), Nurse Ratched (*One Flew over the Cuckoo's Nest*), and Alex Forrest (*Fatal Attraction*). Even the Queen in *Snow White and the Seven Dwarfs* made the top 10 villains list (American Film Institute, 2003).

Movies seem to perpetuate gender stereotypes, such that women are not remembered for their positive, heroic roles. Rather, women are remembered vividly for their negative, villainous roles to the extent that they significantly outnumber and outweigh their positive counterparts in the movies. Conversely, male characters are portrayed as heroes in movies or their actions are downplayed, dismissed, or ignored.

Racial Stereotypes

The study of media stereotypes and their impact on cognition extends to race as well as gender, because racial stereotypes in the media also influence viewers' perceptions (Grandy and Baron, 1998). Although Tucker (1997) argued that the differences between Caucasians and African Americans should be recognized and accepted rather than eliminated in order to fight racism, many Caucasians hold an assimilationist perspective. This perspective asserts that African Americans can be accepted into mainstream culture as equals to Caucasians if they are willing to abandon their cultural identity. In fact, Caucasian Americans consistently estimate fewer inequalities between themselves and African Americans than African Americans do, thereby supporting the assimilationist perspective (Grandy and Baron, 1998).

Busselle and Crandall (2002) stated that the assimilationist view is related to modern racism, where Caucasian Americans deny traditional racist beliefs that African Americans are less intelligent than Caucasians and that segregation is appropriate. Rather, modern racists argue that racism no longer exists, thereby negating the need for antipoverty or affirmative action programs. Malcolm X eloquently illustrated African Americans' oppression due to modern racism when he stated that, "as long as African Americans view[ed] themselves through White lenses, they would be unable to achieve their goals of equality" (quoted in Winn, 2001, p. 453). The media are one such "White lens" that reflects Caucasian American ideals, including modern racism, because Caucasians control the media (Berry, 1998; Busselle and Crandall, 2002; Coover, 2001; Mastro and Greenberg, 2000; Tucker, 1997). Although mass media socializes viewers to embrace modern racism, the public may only be partially aware of the differences between actual racial qualities and the media's portrayal of those races (Busselle and Crandall, 2002).

One consequence of modern racism is that African Americans are portrayed as unrealistic, marginalized, or secondary to Caucasian Americans in the media. Conversely, powerful African Americans, those individuals who exhibit leadership qualities or assertiveness, are portrayed with negative characteristics (Dixon and Linz, 2002; Rada, 2000; Richardson and Scott, 2002; Romer, Jamieson, and de Coteau, 1998). As with gender stereotypes, this theme may be found across the five categories of mass media (e.g., music, news, sports, television, and movies), which have been examined in the literature.

Music

African Americans have been responsible for creating several popular music genres including blues, jazz, rock and roll, and hip-hop music. All of these musical genres and their subgenres signaled sociocultural changes, such as blues and jazz in the 1920s, rock and roll in the 1950s and 1960s, and hip-hop in the 1980s and 1990s. Music achieves such drastic effects by helping people connect at a private and public level (McMichael, 1998). In fact, several researchers have argued that blues and jazz help listeners to understand, express, and own their emotions while connecting with other listeners who have similarly struggled to know themselves and share that knowledge (Bromell, 2000; C. Brown, 2002). Consequently, music, especially blues and jazz, has been a conduit for social and racial integration as Caucasian musicians embraced and mimicked the original musicians' innovations (Bromell, 2000).

As the musical innovators of rock and roll, African Americans assumed unusually powerful social positions during the musical birth of rock and roll in the 1950s, which was not acceptable to powerful Caucasian American pastors. In fact, Caucasian pastors and white elitists argued that rock and roll was evil (Emerson, 2002). Caucasian listeners seemed to initially heed their pastors' words, but they changed their perceptions as Caucasian American musicians adopted the music as their own and marginalized the contributions of African American musicians (Bromell, 2000; Center for Black Music Research, 2002; O'Connor, Brooks-Gunn, and Graber, 2000).

Like the other genres, hip-hop originally left a negative impression on Caucasian Americans. However, a study by O'Connor et al. (2000) showed that both African American and Caucasian American girls prefer it. Gangsta rap continues to be perceived as an artistic expression of a realistically violent culture and a promoter of deviant behavior (Richardson and Scott, 2002). Caucasian Americans did not accept rap music until the rap artist, Eminem, brought it to them due to his crossover appeal.

The examples in this section illustrate that Caucasian Americans generally prefer to listen to Caucasian musicians and they have negative perceptions of African American music. Once a Caucasian American "brings" the music to the Caucasian masses, they embrace it as their own.

News

Much like music, racial stereotypes exist in the news media. News media portray Caucasian Americans as powerful and positive figures and report positive and effective programs to help underprivileged citizens such as African Americans living in poverty (Gilens, 2000). Therefore, news media promote Caucasian Americans as powerful figures and marginalize African Americans who are not involved in criminal activity. In fact, Romer et al. (1998) found that African Americans were rarely portrayed as victims of a crime or innocent onlookers of a crime. Rather, African Americans were predominantly shown as perpetuators of crimes, especially when Caucasian Americans were victimized. These portrayals showed African Americans as powerful and fearsome criminals. Further evidence demonstrates that news media promote the negative stereotypes of African Americans as violent criminals. Specifically, Romer et al. found that actual homicide rates in Philadelphia did not match news portrayals, which had inflated the frequency of African Americans depicted as criminals.

Such news portrayals misrepresent African Americans in pretrial publicity, increasing the hostility of viewers toward African Americans defendants (Dixon and Linz, 2002). This phenomenon was observed in the O. J. Simpson case, where Caucasian Americans considered the athlete guilty of murdering his wife before the trial had started, and their views remained constant across time (CNN.com, 1995). Pretrial portrayals by the media were powerful enough to change the portrayal of the once assimilated African American athlete into a hated criminal, even before evidence was presented. The O. J. Simpson case is an excellent example of modern racism, because arguments of racism against the athlete were marginalized due to his success and wealth (White, 1995). In contrast to O. J. Simpson, Rodney King was a citizen who was brutally beaten by Caucasian police officers, but the news media used his character and drug addictions to marginalize the crimes against him (Friedman, 1995). In other words, news media promote African Americans as guilty of accused crimes, whereas the criminal actions of Caucasian Americans are underestimated or ignored.

Sports

Although Caucasian Americans have dominated all areas of society for decades, African American athletes have recently started to dominate professional sports. The talents of African American athletes have placed Caucasian Americans at a disadvantage, which is a form of marginalization. Kusz (2001) reported on a 1997 *Sports Illustrated* cover story that portrayed Caucasian basketball players as victimized by the African Americans' prominence in the National Basketball Association (NBA). The author of the article explained that Caucasian Americans were bitter because African Americans had dominated and recreated the sport of basketball so that it centered on money and celebrity status. Kusz (2001) argued that basketball currently supports integration and equal opportunity, whereas the game had previously promoted segregation and false Caucasian supremacy. This *Sports Illustrated* cover story is not uncommon. Many sports stories attempt to undermine the talent, perseverance, and potential influence of African Americans in an effort to marginalize them and promote Caucasian American athletes (Busselle and Crandall, 2002; Kusz, 2001).

In addition to ludicrous proposals by Caucasian American sports writers, sports commentators use language to marginalize the ability of African Americans and promote the attributes of Caucasian Americans. According to McCarthy and Jones (1997), successful African American soccer athletes were described as natural athletes with effortless ability. Conversely, "hard work," "intellectual ability," and "effort" were terms used to illustrate the attributions of successful Caucasian American athletes. The media tried to make African Americans animallike, simple, beautiful, powerful, but mindless and in need of taming to console Caucasian American viewers (Kusz, 2001). McCarthy and Jones (1997) also found that half of commentators' total comments regarding African American athletes were negative.

Much like soccer, sports commentators use racist language when describing professional basketball players. Banet-Weiser (1999) found that the media highlighted negative characteristics for those African American athletes who were frequently presented in the media or were perceived as popular by sports audiences. Although the media acknowledge the popularity and dominance of African American basketball players, it also frequently highlights the "bad boy" behaviors, such as body piercings and tattoos, poor sportsmanship, as well as violence and aggression. In addition, the media frequently participate in racial blame by emphasizing a conglomeration of African American negative characteristics into one category that signifies "blackness and menace" (Banet-Weiser, 1999, p. 4).

Rather than realizing that current behavior problems described in the NBA may simply be the result of young, immature adolescents becoming instant millionaires, the media demonstrate modern racism by suggesting that African American athletes are naturally talented as well as natural thugs. The sports media suggest that Caucasian managers must domesticate their "untamed" African American players, which creates powerful images of Caucasian American managers (Banet-Weiser, 1999). Hoberman (1997) agrees that the media portray Caucasian Americans as mentors or father figures to helpless, underprivileged African Americans who are in need of white, middle-class values and domestication. Therefore, the media are able to marginalize African Americans as incapable of assimilating middle-class practices when the majority of African Americans actually reject Caucasian American values. Of course, the media label and promote these dissenters negatively for their unwillingness to conform to past traditions set by a different athletic cohort from another culture.

Television

The family was historically responsible for socializing children, which included instilling values, cultural regulations, and morals. However, television is fast becoming the predominant model of social learning for children. Television media may present African American characters in any way that they choose and viewers process these single examples as factual representations of the entire group (Berry, 1998; Busselle and Crandall, 2002; Coover, 2001; Signorielli and Kahlenberg, 2001). For example, viewers of African Americans acting negatively in one sitcom hold that same view for all African Americans. Consequently, television programming often projects subtle racial stereotypes, which includes modern racism for positive and negative portrayals of African American characters. Past research defined positive portrayals of African Americans as successful characters and negative portrayals of African Americans as unsuccessful characters (Berry, 1998; Busselle and Crandall, 2002; Coover, 2001; Signorielli and Kahlenberg, 2001; Tucker, 1997).

Television programs portray African Americans in unrealistic environments. *The Cosby Show* was a recurring example of assimilating African Americans into mainstream society (Berry, 1998; Coover, 2001). Tucker (1997) suggested that *The Cosby Show* portrayed African American characters living successfully among Caucasian middle-class standards and values, thereby ignoring the social and economic realities of the African American culture. Caucasian Americans accepted *The Cosby Show* and similar television portrayals of African Americans embracing Caucasian American values (Busselle and Crandall, 2002; Tucker 1997). Inadvertently, viewers were adopting an assimilation perspective as they enjoyed watching African Americans conforming to mainstream values. Indeed, Coover (2001) found that Caucasian Americans favored frequent and positive portrayals of African Americans because they affirmed their self-concepts as nonracists. Researchers have argued that an equal depiction of success only glorifies the assimilation of African Americans to Caucasian ideals (Berry, 1998; Busselle and Crandall, 2002; Coover, 2001; Tucker, 1997).

In contrast to successful portrayals, Signorielli and Kahlenberg (2001) evaluated prime-time television portrayals of African Americans in relation to their jobs. The findings suggested that race played a pivotal role in the occupations given to characters on television. For example, Caucasian American men were more likely to be portrayed as professionals than non–Caucasian American men and women. Although African Americans represent only one-fifth of the total characters on television, more than one-third of these characters could not be classified by an occupation or they were labeled as unemployed (Signorielli and Kahlenberg, 2001). Conversely, Caucasian Americans are depicted as successful professionals more frequently than African Americans (Mastro and Greenberg, 2000; Signorielli and Kahlenberg, 2001).

Whereas positive portrayals of African Americans on television marginalize African Americans by assimilating them into the Caucasian American culture, negative portrayals of African Americans on television promote negative stereotypes of joblessness. Therefore, television is another medium that marginalizes African Americans via assimilation and promotes negative images that may be generalized across contexts. The images of African Americans on television contradict the images of Caucasian Americans who are typically displayed as successful characters living in their own culture.

Movies

The film industry significantly influences the formation of ideologies and the acquisition of knowledge, probably more than any other form of mass medium (Winn, 2001). Hall (1981) explained that film media are a powerful source for racial ideas and an outlet where ideas are transformed and elaborated upon in order to satisfy the public's needs. Madison (1999) examined "anti-racist-white-hero" films, which exonerate "whiteness" and promote modern racism by presenting racism as a problem of the past. This common form of racism is achieved by displacing white supremacy geographically, historically, and also by defining white supremacy as a pathological hatred resulting in violence, wrongful imprisonment, and overt discrimination (Madison, 1999). Ironically, the "anti-racist-white-hero" films present the African American character positively on the surface, but a closer examination tells a different story.

Mississippi Burning and *Amistad* positively portrayed African Americans for their perseverance, courage, strength, and hope. However, the African American characters were still portrayed as secondary to their Caucasian American counterparts (Madison, 1999). *Mississippi Burning* was based on an actual event that took place during the Civil Rights Movement. The film depicted the African American characters as childlike, passive, victimized, weak, infantile, and in need of a strong, paternalistic Caucasian American hero to provide direction and ultimate victory. The white paternalistic ideology was reinforced in a scene where two Caucasian activists were in the front seat escorting Chaney, the African American activist. The physical placement of the characters suggested that the Caucasian activists were in charge. In reality, Chaney was the individual who made the decisions as to where his escorts would take him. These nonverbal elements of the film placed the Caucasians in the forefront of the scenes (Parker, 1988).

The second example, *Amistad,* was based on an actual slave ship rebellion, where the African leader of the rebellion, Cinque, demonstrated exemplary bravery and perseverance (Spielberg, 1998). However, in the movie Cinque held a secondary status to the Caucasian American characters, regardless of his positive portrayal (Madison, 1999). A quarter of the way through the movie, the audience had yet to hear translated dialogue of Cinque or the fellow slaves, who merely grunted and bickered in their native tongues. Furthermore, the only subtitles seen were for a Caucasian ship captain and his first mate (Spielberg, 1998), thus portraying Caucasians as important characters and marginalizing the actions of African characters. By extension, the portrayal marginalized many negative behaviors of the Caucasian characters, such as their vicious beatings, rapes, and murders of the African slaves (Madison, 1999).

John-Hall (2003) came to similar conclusions when he evaluated the prevalence of African American actors in *The Matrix: Reloaded.* With at least eight African American roles of significance, viewers reported hoping that a new standard had been set for diversity in science fiction. However, African American characters were continually undermined. Although the leader, Morpheus, was African American; the Messiah and Neo, the deliverer of humanity, were Caucasian Americans, thereby creating an undercurrent of white supremacy.

In contrast to marginalized positive portrayals, African American characters in movies such as *She's Gotta Have It* and *Shaft* have generally been powerful and negative. Manatu-Rupert (2000) identified African Americans as being objectified, oversexed, and promiscuous. In the film *She's Gotta Have It,* the main African American character, Nola, expressed her female sexuality as a source of power, yet her sexuality was portrayed negativity. Viewers believe early on that the film signified female independence. However, the film's sole purpose was a preoccupation with sexual vulgarity. Nola's character used sex as a way to seduce and control men, and, as a result, live independently of societal expectations and standards. Although powerful, Nola's actions were perceived negatively. Similarly, the movie *Shaft* illustrated a powerful African American who was perceived negatively by Caucasian viewers. Shaft was a strong, smart, competent, and confident character who was also portrayed as violent and promiscuous. Henry (2002) alluded to modern racism in these portrayals of African American characters, arguing that the powerful minority had to exhibit negative characteristics in order to maintain Caucasian American dominance. In other words, the same actions Caucasian viewers deem acceptable for Mel Gibson are not acceptable for characters played by Richard Roundtree.

Notable Exceptions: Positive Images in Mass Media

While the mass media can be generally criticized for reinforcing negative gender and racial stereotypes, there have been some notable exceptions. One of these exceptions was found in children's television programming. Jim Henson, the creative force behind television programs such as *The Muppet Show*, *Sesame Street* and *Fraggle Rock*, was extremely dedicated to presenting a diverse array of characters, who were represented in puppetry and by real life actors. These characters challenged conventional stereotypes without being overly "preachy" (e.g., Miss Piggy was a strong-willed female). The characters also openly wrestled with the problems of being a member of an out-group (e.g., Kermit the Frog's song "It's Not Easy Being Green").

Another exception was found in the science fiction phenomenon known as *Star Trek*. Gene Roddenberry, the creator and executive producer for the original *Star Trek* in the 1960s and the more recent *Star Trek—The Next Generation* of the 1980s and 1990s, pushed the envelope by creating a diverse cast comprised of intelligent minorities and strong female characters. Further, the episodes often dealt directly with issues of prejudice and racism. In an episode from the original series entitled "Let That Be Your Last Battlefield," two characters who represented the last of their kind, each of whom had their faces painted "half white" and "half black," expressed a deep hatred for each other that was clearly rooted in senseless racism.

Summary

Gender and racial stereotypes of marginalized heroes and notable villains have long existed, but the problem with these stereotypes is that they have not evolved with time, liberating minorities. Although stereotyping enables efficient information processing, stereotypes lead to discrimination and prejudice (Allport, 1954), which are easily perceived in music, news, sports, television, and movies. In these various forms of media, Caucasian men are promoted as powerful and successful individuals whose indiscretions are marginalized. In contrast, the negative actions of minorities are publicized and their positive and powerful actions are marginalized.

Women in music are treated as decorative objects (e.g., Cobb et al., 2001; Hedley, 1994; Signorielli et al., 1994) and African American music is loathed until it is assimilated into mainstream society (Bromell, 2000; Brown, 2002). In the news, positive women are allowed to report minor news or they are cast in minor roles (Brabant and Mooney, 1986, 1997; Sanders and Rock, 1988), whereas powerful women are cast with negative characteristics (Gold and Speicher, 1996; Mooney and Brabant, 1987). African Americans in the news are rarely portrayed as victims or innocent bystanders; they are cast as vicious criminals at an inflated rate and pretrial portrayals bias viewers' perceptions of them (Romer et al., 1998). Similarly, the negative language of sports commentators demeans women and African Americans, even when their performance is unquestionably impressive (Koivula, 1999; McCarthy and Jones, 1997). In television, minorities are given secondary roles, where they do not earn an income, because that role is left for Caucasian men (Signorielli, 1989). Alternatively, strong women and successful African Americans are portrayed in unrealistic roles (Craig, 1993; Tucker, 1997). Movies typically promote Caucasian men as powerful characters (Hedley, 1994), and they rarely cast women and African Americans in lead roles. In the rare instances that minorities are cast in lead roles, these characters are marginalized or promoted as behaving negatively (Bazzini et al., 1997; Cobb et al., 2001; Henry, 2002; Madison, 1999).

The overwhelming presence of negative gender stereotypes can be readily observed in the images found in music, news, sports, television, and movie media. According to Bazzini et al. (1997), popular media images reflect the attitudes and standards of a culture, and they project desired realities. These projections of marginalized positive minorities and promoted negative minorities coincide with the mass media's promotion of positive majority behavior and ignored majority indiscretions. Therefore, all Caucasian men may be created equal in the United States, but the media has treated women and African Americans like children who are seen (acknowledged) but not heard (marginalized), which has limited these individuals from coming a long way toward equality.

References

Allen, J. (2001). Eminem wins best rap album Grammy. *Entertainment*. Retrieved September 20, 2003, from www.cnn.com/2001/SHOWBIZ/Music/02/21/grammy. night.02

Allport, G. (1954). *The nature of prejudice*. Garden City, NY: Doubleday Anchor.

American Film Institute. (2003). *AFI's 100 years ... 100 heroes and villains*. Retrieved May 16, 2003, from http://www.afi.com/tv/handv.asp

Bagdikian, B. (1987). *The media monopoly*. Boston: Beacon Press.

Banet-Weiser, S. (1999). Hoop dreams: Professional basketball and the politics of race and gender. *Journal of Sport and Social Issues*, 23, 403–420.

Barol, B. (1985, March 4). Women in a video cage. *Newsweek*, 55, p. 54.

Bazzini, D. G., McIntosh, W. D., Smith, S. M., Cook, S., and Harris, C. (1997). The aging woman in popular film: Underrepresented, unattractive, unfriendly, and unintelligent. *Sex Roles*, 36, 531–543.

BBC News. (2002). *Madonna voted greatest female artist*. Retrieved July 9, 2003, from http://news.bbc.co.uk/2/low/entertainment

Beal, B. (1997). The Promise Keepers' use of sport in defining "Christlike" masculinity. *Journal of Sport and Social Issues*, 21, 274–284.

Berry, G. L., (1998). Black family life on television and the socialization of the African American child: Images of marginality. *Journal of Comparative Family Studies*, 29, 233–242.

Brabant, S., and Mooney, L. A. (1986). Sex role stereotyping in the Sunday comics: Ten years later. *Sex Roles*, 14, 141–148.

_____, and _____ (1997). Sex role stereotyping in the Sunday comics: A twenty year update. *Sex Roles*, 37, 269–281.

Bromell, N. (2000). "The blues and the veil": The cultural work of musical form in blues and '60s rock. *American Music*, 18, 193–222.

Brown, C. (2002). Golden gray and the talking book: Identity as a site of artful construction in Toni Morrison's *Jazz*. *African American Review*, 36, 629–642.

Brown, G. (1990, December 4). With fans like this.... *The Village Voice*, p. 21.

Brown, J. A. (2002). The tortures of Mel Gibson: Masochism and the sexy male body. *Men and Masculinities*, 5, 123–143.

Browne, C. (2003). About the characters. *Hägar the Horrible*. www.kingfeatures. com/features/comics/hagar/about.htm

Busselle, R., and Crandall, H. (2002). Television viewing and perceptions about race differences in socioeconomic success. *Journal of Broadcasting and Electronic Media*, 46, 265–279.

Cann, D. J., and Mohr, P. B. (2001). Journalist and source gender in Australian television news. *Journal of Broadcasting and Electronic Media*, 45, 162–174.

Center for Black Music Research. (2002). Hip-hop and other contemporary music. Retrieved July, 19, 2003 from http://www.cbmr.org/styles/hiphop.htm.

CNN.com (1995). *Simpson verdict opinion poll*. Retrieved online from http://www. cnn.com/US/OJ/daily/9510/10-04/poll/ojpoll1.html

Cobb, M. D., Boettcher, W., and Taylor, A. J. (2001). Exposure to misogynistic rap music and hostile and benevolent sexism: Does Eminem really promote gender stereotyping? Unpublished manuscript, North Carolina State University.

Coover, G. E. (2001). Television and social identity: Race representations "white" accommodation. *Journal of Broadcasting and Electronic Media*, 45, 413–431.

Craig, S. (1993). Selling masculinities, selling femininities: Multiple genders and the economics of television. *The Mid-Atlantic Almanack*, 2, 15–27.

Cuklanz, L. M. (2000). *Rape on prime time: Television, masculinity, and sexual violence.* Philadelphia: University of Pennsylvania Press.

Dixon, T. L., and Linz, D. (2002). Television news, prejudicial pretrial publicity, and the depiction of race. *Journal of Broadcasting and Electronic Media*, 46, 112–132.

Emerson, R. A. (2002). "Where my girls at?" Negotiating black womanhood in music videos. *Gender and Society*, 16, 115–135.

Eminem. (2000). Kill you. On *The Marshall Mathers LP* [CD]. New York: Interscope Records.

Friedman, S. S. (1995). Beyond white and other: Relationality and narratives of race in feminist discourse. *Journal of Women in Culture and Society*, 21, 1–49.

Gilens, M. (2000). The black poor and the "liberal press": With friends like these.... *Civil Rights Journal*, 1–14.

Gold, E. R., and Speicher, R. (1996). Marilyn Quayle meets the press: Marilyn loses. *The Southern Communication Journal*, 61(2), 93–103.

Grandy, Jr., O. H., and Baron, J. (1998). Inequality: It's all in the way you look at it. *Communication Research*, 25, 505–527.

Hall, S. (1981). The whites of their eyes: Racist ideologies and the media. In G. Bridges and R. Brunt (eds.), *Silver linings: Some strategies for the eighties* (pp. 28–52). London: Lawrence and Wishart.

Hansen, C. H., and Hansen, R. D. (1988). How rock music videos can change what is seen when boy meets girl: Priming stereotypic appraisal of social interactions. *Sex Roles*, 19, 287–316.

Harlin, K. (director). (1996). *The long kiss goodnight.* [Motion Picture]. Los Angeles: New Line Studios.

Hedley, M. (1994). The presentation of gendered conflict in popular movies: Affective stereotypes, cultural sentiments, and men's motivation. *Sex Roles*, 31, 721–740.

Henry, M. (2002). He is a bad mother *\$ percent@!#": Shaft and contemporary black masculinity. *Journal of Popular Film and Television*, 30, 114–119.

Hoberman, J. (1997). *Darwin's athletes: How sport has damaged Black America and preserved the myth of race.* Boston, MA: Houghton Mifflin/Mariner.

John-Hall, A. (2003, June 8). Diversity in "Matrix" breaks new ground. *The Daily Press*, p. I3.

Kalb, M. (2001). *One scandalous story: Clinton, Lewinsky, and thirteen days that tarnished American journalism.* New York: Free Press.

Kelley, K. (1994). A modern Cinderella. *Journal of American Culture*, 17, 87–93.

Kennedy, E. (2001). She wants to be a sledgehammer? Tennis femininities on British television. *Journal of Sport and Social Issues*, 25, 56–72.

Kindred, D. (1994). Life in an Olympic sport as cold as ice. *Sporting News*, 217(4), 8.

Koivula, N. (1999). Gender stereotyping in televised media sports coverage. *Sex Roles*, 41, 589–604.

Kusz, K. W. (2001). "I want to be the minority": The politics of youthful white masculinities in sport and popular culture in 1990's America. *Journal of Sport and Social Issues*, 25, 390–416.

Lyne, A. (director). (1987). *Fatal attraction.* [Motion Picture]. Los Angeles: Paramount.

Madison, K. J. (1999). Legitimation crisis and containment: The "anti-racist-white-hero" film. *Critical Studies in Mass Communication*, 16, 399–416.

Manatu-Rupert, N. (2002). The filmic conception of the black female. *Communication Quarterly*, 48, 45–51.

Manning, J. (2000). Who shot J. R.? Retrieved online October 10, 2003, from http://eightiesclub.tripod.com/id223.htm

Marshall, G. (director). (1990). *Pretty woman*. [Motion Picture]. Los Angeles: Touchstone.

Mastro, D. E., and Greenberg, B. S. (2000). The portrayal of racial minorities on prime time television. *The Journal of Broadcasting and Electronic Media*, 44, 690–703.

McCarthy, D., and Jones, R. L. (1997). Speed, aggression, strength, and tactical naiveté: The portrayal of the Black soccer player on television. *Journal of Sport and Social Issues*, 21, 348–362.

McMichael, R. K. (1998). "We insist—Freedom now!" Black moral authority, jazz, and changeable shape of witnesses. *American Music*, 16, 375–417.

Messner, M. A. (1988). Sports and male domination: The female athlete as contested ideological terrain. *Sociology of Sport Journal*, 5, 197–211.

Miller, G. (director). (1982). *The man from Snowy River*. [Motion Picture]. Los Angeles: Twentieth Century Fox.

Miller, T. (2001). The first penis impeached. In L. Berlant, and L. Duggan (Eds.), *Our Monica ourselves: The Clinton affair and the national interest*. (pp. 116–133). New York: New York University Press.

Mooney, L., and Brabant, S. (1987). Two martinis and a rested woman: "Liberation" in the Sunday comics. *Sex Roles*, 17, 409–420.

O'Connor, L. A., Brooks-Gunn, J., and Graber, J. (2002). Black and white girls' racial preferences in media and peer choices and the role of socialization for black girls. *Journal of Family Psychology*, 14, 510–521.

Olson, B., and Douglas, W. (1997). The family on television: Evaluation of gender roles in Situation comedy. *Sex Roles*, 36, 409–427.

Parker, A. (1988). *Mississippi burning*. [Motion Picture] Los Angeles: Orion Pictures.

"Pete Rose." (2003). *The story behind the stats*. Retrieved September 20, 2003, from www.baseballLibrary.com/baseballlibrary/ballplayers/R/Rose_Pete.stm

Rada, J. A. (2000). A new piece to the puzzle: Examining effects of television portrayals of African Americans. *Journal of Broadcasting and Electronic Media*, 44, 704–715.

Reiner, R. (director). (1990). *Misery*. [Motion Picture]. Los Angeles: Castle Rock Entertainment.

Richardson, J. W., and Scott, K. A. (2002). Rap music and its violent progeny: America's culture of violence in context. *The Journal of Negro Education*, 71, 175–192.

Romer, D., Jamieson, K. H., and de Coteau, N. J. (1998). The treatment of persons of color in local television news: Ethnic blame discourse or realistic group conflict? *Communication Research*, 25, 286–305.

St. Lawrence, J. S., and Joyner, D. J. (1991). The effects of sexually violent rock music on males' acceptance of violence against women. *Psychology of Women Quarterly*, 15, 49–63.

Sanders, M., and Rock, M. (1988). *Waiting for prime time: The women of television news*. Urbana, IL: University of Illinois Press.

Scott, R. (director). (2001). *Hannibal*. [Motion Picture]. Los Angeles: Universal Pictures.

Signorielli, N. (1989). Television and conceptions about sex roles: Maintaining conventionality and the status quo. *Sex Roles*, 21, 341–359.

_____, and Kahlenberg, S. (2001). Television's world of work in the nineties. *Journal of Broadcasting and Electronic Media*, 45, 4–22.

Signorielli, N., McLeod, D., and Healy, E., (1994). Gender stereotypes in MTV commercials: The beat goes on. *Journal of Broadcasting and Electronic Media*, 38, 91–100. Retrieved November 11, 2002 from http://proquest.umi.com

Smolowe, J., and Dougherty, S. (September 29, 2003). Fade to black. *People*, 60(13), 78–84.

Spiegelman, M., Terwilliger, C., and Fearing, F. (1953). The content of comics: Goals and means to goals of comic strip characters. *Journal of Social Psychology*, 37, 189–203.

Spielberg, S. (1998). *Amistad*. [Motion Picture]. Universal City, CA: Dreamworks.

Tucker, L. R. (1997). Was the revolution televised? Professional criticism about "The Cosby Show" and the essentialization of black cultural expression. *Journal of Broadcasting and Electronic Media*, 41, 90–108.

Wachowski, L., and Wachowski, A. (directors). (1999). *The Matrix*. Los Angeles: Warner Bros.

_____, and _____ (directors). (2003). *The Matrix: Reloaded*. Los Angeles: Warner Bros.

White, R. T. (1995). The economy of race and racism. *The Black Scholar*, 25, 1–3.

Winn, J. E. (2001). Challenges and compromises in Spike Lee's Malcolm X. *Critical Studies in Media Communication*, 18, 452–465.

Woolf, V. (1929). *A room of one's own*. San Diego, CA: Harcourt Brace.

10

Digital Dangers: Identity Theft and Cyberterrorism

STEPHEN TRUHON *and* W. RICHARD WALKER

As this text has repeatedly pointed out, the impact of technology is pervasive. Cognitive technology may affect classroom performance, distract us while driving, and reinforce gender and racial stereotypes in the form of characters in mass media. However, cognitive technologies can also be used as a means to promote criminal activities and terrorist agendas. At the beginning of a new century, identity theft and cyberterrorism represents two of the most destructive misuses of cognitive technologies. In this chapter, we will consider the scope of these threats and how researchers in cognitive technology might be able to limit the impact of these digital dangers.

Identity Theft

There has been a good deal of disagreement about what identity theft is. Legally, identity theft is said to occur when someone "knowingly transfers or uses, without lawful authority, a means of identification of another person with the intent to commit, or to aid or abet, any unlawful activity that constitutes a violation of Federal law, or that constitutes a felony under any applicable State or local law" (Identity Theft and Assumption Deterrence Act, 1998).

We would like to thank Rob Darner for comments made early in preparation of this manuscript.

The concept of identity theft is an old one. In the film *The Return of Martin Guerre* (Vigne, 1982), a soldier returns from the Hundred Years War after being gone for nine years. His wife accepts him while his neighbors are suspicious of him when he behaves in ways uncharacteristic of the man they knew. It is eventually revealed that he is an imposter. More recently, the film *Catch Me If You Can* (Spielberg and Parkes, 2002) tells the story of Frank Abagnale, Jr., who assumed the identities of a doctor, a lawyer, and an airline co-pilot before he was 18 years old. It is interesting to note that currently Mr. Abagnale (2001) is a consultant to prevent this kind of fraud.

What is new about identity theft is its relative ease and breadth. Formerly, one had to have some physical contact with the thief in order to have one's identity stolen. Currently, it occurs as result of an insider working at a bank, utility, or insurance company. As a result, someone across the country or even in another country could assume an individual's identity.

The Extent of the Problem

The Federal Trade Commission (FTC), which has been given oversight of this problem, says that identity theft is one of the fastest growing problems in this country. The General Accounting Office (2002, March) agrees with this assessment. The FTC (2002, 2003) reported that the number of cases in North Carolina jumped from 1,656 in 2001 to 3,383 in 2002; nationwide, the number in 2002 was 161,819. But these numbers represent the complaints made to the Federal Trade Commission: The actual number is probably much higher. In North Carolina, the estimate is 20, 000 (North Carolina, Department of Justice, n.d.), while the national estimate is 750,000 (Fischer, 2003).

Typical Occurrences

There is no single way that identity theft occurs. Usually, the identity thief obtains a copy of important information on an individual such as a Social Security number (SSN), driver's license number, or credit card number. The thief uses this information to set up additional accounts, including credit card, utility, and bank accounts. The thief then proceeds to ruin the original individual's credit by running up bills on these new accounts but refusing to pay, writing bad checks on the bank account, and declaring bankruptcy. While this information can be obtained online, most often low-tech approaches such as pickpocketing and mail interception are used (Ferrell, 2003). Still, high-tech approaches have probably contributed to the explosive growth in identity theft.

Responding to Identity Theft

Victims of identity theft do not usually know about it immediately. They become aware of the theft when they next balance their checkbook or apply for credit and are denied. This can occur months after the initial theft. Once identity theft is discovered, there are a number of steps that should be taken. First, the victim should contact the three major credit bureaus: Equifax (1.800.525.6285; *www.equifax.com*), Experian (1.888. 397.3742; *www.experian.com*), and TransUnion (1.800.680.7289; *www. transunion.com*). If the thief has taken over personal accounts (such as banking or insurance), they should also contact those institutions.

Second, victims should contact police departments, both in their local community as well as in locations where the identity theft has occurred. According to Linda Foley, Executive Director of the Identity Theft Resource Center:

> When you speak with law enforcement, you need to be concise. You need to have your case clearly summarized, have your evidence ready to go. Victims tend to ramble. They want to pull in all of the emotional distress that they have felt: "I've been victimized. This person did this to me. This person did that." Give them the facts in an orderly fashion, who you've spoken to, what you've done so far and give them the evidence that they need [Halden and Tacheny, 2003].

Third, victims should keep records of all contacts regarding the theft (phone calls, emails, and letters) with the police, creditors, and debt collectors. The FTC has an affidavit that can be downloaded from the Internet (*http://www.ftc.gov/bcp/conline/pubs/credit/affidavit.pdf*). This form makes it possible to have a common form to use when contacting various credit agencies. It is also useful to inform the FTC of the case for their statistical gathering purposes. Finally, it should be noted that identity victims can expect a lot of work. Estimates are that on the average victims spend 175 hours over two years and $1,000 to clear their names. It is estimated that 10 percent of cases are successfully prosecuted.

Government Response

Initially identity thefts were treated as instances of bank and mail fraud and prosecuted accordingly. By the early 1990s, states began to criminalize identity theft itself both to deal with the extent of the problem and to fill some gaps left by existing bank and mail fraud laws. Beginning in 1997, the United States Congress stepped in with proposals that led to the Identity Theft and Assumption Deterrence Act (1998). This act was passed by Congress and signed by President Clinton on October 30, 1998. The act took effect on January 1, 1999. There were three major provisions of this act (Matejkovic and Lahey, 2002): (1) victims of identity theft were considered primary victims (up to this time individuals so defrauded were considered secondary victims with the financial institutions considered primary victims); (2) identity theft was considered a federal crime, which allows identity theft victims to seek relief even if the thief has never visited the victim's residential state; and (3) identity theft itself was considered a crime even if no other crime were committed by the perpetrator. In addition, this act created the Identity Theft Data Clearinghouse database that the FTC uses to collect information on complaints of identity theft.

There have been recent proposals to strengthen individuals' protections against identity theft. The Bush administration has urged Congress to establish a single telephone number which consumers could use in the event of identity theft, and for the three major credit bureaus to provide a free credit report annually (Mayer, 2003). Meanwhile, in the House of Representatives, the Identity Theft and Financial Privacy Protection Act of 2003 (H.R. 2035, 2003) was proposed and is currently under consideration by the House Committee on Financial Services. Among its provisions is a requirement that receipts from credit card or debit charges be truncated to the last four digits of the account number.

Possible Solutions

In addition to the proposed congressional solutions, legal and financial experts have suggested other reforms. Matejkovic and Lahey (2002) have suggested tort laws be expanded so that individuals who have been defrauded can sue the perpetrators as well as make companies whose information is used for identity theft liable regardless of fault. (This is considered unlikely, because the trend in state and federal government is to restrict tort laws.) Another suggestion is that use of individuals' SSNs be curtailed so that they are no longer a primary means of identification (Thompson, 2002). Others (e.g., LoPicki, 2001) counter that, if the use of SSNs is banned, credit-reporting agencies will have to find another means of identification, which will produce another version of the same problem.

Others foresee solutions in newer technology. Biometric techniques exist which can verify an individual's identity. Fingerprints are probably the most commonly used, but other biometric techniques include handprints, iris scans, voice identification, and facial recognition devices. It should also be noted that biometrics include behavioral characteristics such as handwriting and body language. As part of the Military Construction Appropriations Act (2000), Congress authorized the United States Army to coordinate activities in the Department of Defense concerning biometric information. The Biometrics Management Office is working with the National Institute of Standards and Technology to standardize biometric protection profiles.

One problem with the use of biometrics is that most of these techniques require the individual to be physically present for identification to occur. (One exception is that voice identification could occur through a telephone.) An alternative is the use of smart cards, with a computer chip containing personal identifying information (including biometric information) are embedded in credit card sized cards. Smart cards can be use alone or combined with live biometric information (Marsh, 2003). Smart cards have met with some resistance in the United States because of fears that government or business will have too much information on everyone, not all of it essential (Ohr, 2003).

Identification Theory

Clarke (1994) has set forth three basic aspects of human identification. The first is knowledge-based identification, in which the individual is identified by information that only that individual would know (e.g., mother's maiden name). The second is token-based identification, in which the individual is identified by an object that only that individual would possess (e.g., driver's license). The third is biometric information, in which the individual is identified by unique physical characteristics which the individual possesses (e.g., fingerprints). Clarke uses this analysis to suggest how organizations can develop effective identification systems that are also acceptable to their employees and customers.

LoPicki (2001) has attempted to extend Clarke's approach by applying the process to the same individual at two different times: by providing a means of matching characteristics between identification data already existing and the individual, by matching the individual with the identification data, by layering the identification process (recognizing that a means of identifying an individual is based on another piece of identification), and finally by distinguishing between the use of the data to make a positive identification and its use to prevent impersonation. LoPicki's proposed system of identity theft prevention would be voluntary. In this system, a government agency (e.g., the Social Security Administration) would provide a means for guaranteeing identity of individuals. (There would also be procedures by which individuals could challenge this designation.) Once individuals are so identified, they could log into a secure website and provide the information by which they wish to be identified. When these individuals apply for credit, this information is matched with information available from the website.

Research

How can behavioral sciences contribute to the prevention of identity theft? One example is the work of Judith Collins and her colleagues in establishing an outreach group dealing with identity theft (Identity Theft: Partners in Prevention, n.d.). Part of their work involves advising organizations on procedures that they can employ to minimize identity theft. In addition, they are doing research on identity theft. Among their topics of research are: examination of the psychological factors (e.g., personality) of identity thieves, the sociology of the formation of identity theft rings, and how deficiencies in hormones and neurotransmitters can contribute to the development of identity thieves.

Other areas of research can focus on helping individuals avoid errors that lead to their identity being stolen. As Kahneman, Slovic, and Tversky (1982) have shown, human beings make use of heuristics and biases that can interfere with rational decision making. Identifying these faulty heuristics and alerting individuals to their possibility can be a first step in this process. Because so much of identity theft occurs via computer, programs can be written to remind users that certain actions increase the likelihood of identity theft.

Cyberterrorism

The events of September 11th, 2001, brought into sharp focus many of the security issues facing nation-states. While many of the concerns that were raised by these attacks are essentially "old" concerns (e.g., changes in security at sensitive locations such as airports), at least one new concern made its way into public consciousness: cyberterrorism (Arquilla and Ronfeldt, 2001; Denning, 2001). The fact that new technologies can be exploited by terrorists is of little surprise. The precise nature of such exploitation is a matter of debate. It is worth noting that the vast networks of data warehouses and information delivery systems that comprise the Internet are so complex that academics are creating mathematical formulas to determine exactly how these systems work (Barabasi, 2002). The complexity of the Internet is shared by other networked systems, such as the electric power grid that provides energy for North America. The largest blackout in U.S. history on August 14, 2003, is ascribed in the final report to "deficiencies in specific practices, equipment, and human decisions by various organizations that affected conditions and outcomes that afternoon ... deficiencies in corporate policies, lack of adherence to industry policies, inadequate management of reactive power and voltage" (http://reports.energy.gov/BlackoutFinal-Web.pdf). It is easy to conjecture that security at energy facilities may be similarly inefficient, and that their computer systems may be vulnerable to hackers.

These networked systems are appealing targets and tools for terrorists for many reasons. First, these systems are integral to the vitality of many nation-states and international corporations. Even a temporary or partial shutdown of these systems can have a significant financial and psychological impact. Second, because of the complexity of these systems, these systems provide multiple points of attack for parties interested in disrupting their operations. Third, because these networks are so vast, a single individual may launch attacks in relative anonymity. Fourth, the decentralized structure of these systems "fit" very well with the amorphous structure of many terrorist organizations. Groups such as al-Qaeda or the KKK are not single organizations. Instead, they are loose collections of groups and individuals that hold varying philosophies and goals. Thus, the same systems that allow these groups to interface can also be used as vehicles to carry out attacks. Fifth, because these systems are being increasingly used by users who are not computer experts (i.e., most users are not adept programmers or network managers), the user can become the unwitting accomplice of a cyberattack by opening infected e-mail or releasing sensitive information such as passwords to strangers.

Two Types of Cyberterrorism

While one could differentiate cyberattacks along several dimensions based upon various technical aspects of the attack (e.g., was a virus used or was it a worm?), it is perhaps more useful to think about how cyberattacks correlate with events in the real world outside of cyberspace. Some cyberattacks have direct and potentially life threatening consequences for the real world while other attacks are only indirectly related to events in the real world and are more typically viewed as "nuisance attacks."

The most alarming cyberattacks are the ones that are directly connected with events in the real world. Al-Qaeda used cyberspace to spread propaganda, recruit members, disrupt U.S. surveillance of its activities, and finance and plan the attacks of September 11th. The importance of cyberspace to the operation may never be fully realized; however, the seized computer of Zachiarias Moussouai would seem to indicate that Al-Qaeda's use of cyberspace enabled it to carry out the attacks in an efficient and clandestine fashion. Readers may be surprised to learn that September 11th was by no means the only successful case of using cyberspace to directly impact real world events. In fact, throughout the 1990s, several organizations successfully employed the techniques of cyberterrorism. Table 10.1, which was recreated from Arquilla and Ronfeldt's (2001) study of cyberterrorism, shows that of 10 major cyberterrorist campaigns conducted in the 1990s, eight were deemed successful. Perhaps the most televised of these campaigns took place in 1999 in what has become known as the *Battle of Seattle* against the World Trade Organization (de Armond, 2001). In this case, police forces were unable to deal with a piecemeal collection of protesters who coordinated their rallies via cell phones, instant-messaging systems, and the Internet. However, in this instance, the protests could be categorized in terms of First Amendment protected speech rather than terrorism in the Al-Qaeda category.

Thankfully, most cyberattacks are confined solely to cyberspace. These attacks typically disrupt or shut down servers, delete hard drives, and overwhelm e-mail and telephone systems. These attacks correlate indirectly with events in the real world. That is, the attacks cause problems

TABLE 1. PROMINENT CASES OF CYBERTERRORISM IN THE 1990S.

Campaign	Dates	Outcome
Greenpeace	1994	Limited Success
EZLN	1994–	Limited Success
Drug Cartels	1994–	Major Success
Chechnya I	1994–1996	Major Success
Burma	1996–	Failing?
ICBL	1998–	Limited Success
Battle of Seattle	1999	Major Success
East Timor	1999	Major Success
Chechnya II	1999–2000	Failure
Serb Opposition	2000	Major Success

Source: J. Arquilla and D. Ronfeldt, *Networks and Netwars*, MR-1382-OSD. Santa Monica, CA: RAND Corporation, 2001. Table Reconstructed with Permission.

for worker productivity and may cause widespread inconvenience for customers. That is not to say that these attacks inflict no damage. On the contrary, each attack is estimated to cost the U.S. economy an average of $100,000 in lost productivity and sales. Further, it is estimated that over 90 percent of these cyberattacks go either unreported or unnoticed. Another factor that makes these attacks so problematic is that because they do not coincide with other events, predicting their incidence is almost impossible.

Who Are Cyberterrorists?

In answering this question, one must first remember that cyberterrorism represents a unique type of terrorist act that can be carried out by anyone regardless of political or ethnic background. Again, it is useful to think about cyberterrorism in terms of a dichotomy. In this case, is the cyberattack the act of an organization or of a single individual? Cyberattacks that can be attributed to an organization are more likely to have a coherent foundation or at least an intelligible self-professed justification. Attacks by individuals are more random and often cannot be justified even by the attacker.

This point can be made by looking at the history of cyberterrorism, which goes back to the early 1990s. Early attacks could be easily classified as random and relatively harmless acts of vandalism. Some of these attacks might be considered acts of "civil disobedience," as the attacks were aimed at specific targets for specific reasons and caused little real harm (e.g., Arquilla and Ronfeldt, 2001 document attacks by Greenpeace). Other early attacks could be attributed to self-styled "hackers" or "hooligans" who used the new technological mediums to espouse confusing or contradictory ideologies. For instance, the late 1980s witnessed the adventures of "Captain Midnight" who hijacked a satellite signal for HBO to protest his purported right to "free TV." These individuals were usually competent programmers or technicians with a particular grudge against a company or government agency.

As the 1990s progressed, increased Internet traffic prompted the rise of more organized attacks sponsored by more determined organizations with stronger political agendas. Successful cybercampaigns were employed by the Zapatista (Mexico), various drug cartels in South America, and groups such as Al-Qaeda. Further, white supremacist groups, such as the Neo Nazis and White Aryan Resistance, have staked their claims in cyberspace in the form of web sites, bulletin boards, and chat rooms that espouse their philosophies and political aspirations.

The Worst Case Scenario and the Limits of Cyberterrorism

The worst case scenario would involve the use of coordinated cyber-attacks in conjunction with a simultaneous physical attack in the targeted real world. The beginnings of such a scenario would likely begin with "chatter"; increased volume of communication on networks and web sites frequented by suspected terrorist groups. Although such chatter seldom provides specific information regarding attacks, it is thought that increased communication is a predictor of imminent attacks. In the worst case scenario, such chatter would intensify and begin to overwhelm the systems that have been put in place to monitor such traffic (e.g., the web sites, communication networks, and even the human staff of intelligence agencies).

Once these networks were sufficiently distracted, a second wave of cyberattacks would be aimed at more general networks in a specific geographic region: Telecommunications and power supply grids. Even if the attacks had minimal impact, they would likely reduce the ability of such networks to handle significant amounts of information flow. At this point, the stage would be set for a physical attack in the targeted region. What makes the worst case scenario is that the attacks would likely unfold with a span of a few hours and would likely be undetected until significant portions of the targeted networks had been affected. In an environment in which the emergency responders, media, and government agencies are unable to field a coordinated response, even a minor attack could be transformed into a significant terrorist strike.

In various doomsday scenarios, it is important to emphasize the limits of cyberterrorism. The principle limitation of cyberterrorism is that, by itself, even the most devastating of attacks would do little real damage. Although it is easy to imagine that airplanes might crash, power grids might fail, and that widespread chaos might ensue, the reality is far more mundane. Consider the consequences of the northeastern blackout in late 2003, not, of course, caused by cyberterrorism. The event was an inconvenience, but it was not the trigger for a flash of widespread panic and violence.

The second limitation of cyberterrorism is the problem of the "technology treadmill" (Zanini and Edwards, 2001). For technology to be the most useful to any organization, the technology must be constantly updated and maintained, lest the technology becomes outdated. Functionally, this means that organizations must continually buy equipment, write software, and have access to trained technicians who can operate and maintain the technologies being utilized.

What Can Be Done to Fight Cyberterrorism

In many respects, the kinds of security measures that the individual would employ in combating identity theft would also be helpful against cyberterrorism. These measures involve limiting access to sensitive information, shredding documents, and updating passwords and virus protection programs. On a network level, security can be enhanced by the use of firewall systems and gating access portals to network data. In addition to these basic measures, we should begin identifying "soft targets" with significant amounts of overlap between physical and virtual reality. Mass transit systems, often heavily dependent upon sophisticated network systems, represent the most obvious example of overlap between these two realities. When considering these targets, the thinking should be aimed not at how a cyberattack might directly cause damage, but instead on how a cyberattack might worsen a physical attack on that target.

More fundamentally, the philosophies that serve as the underpinnings for cyberterrorism should be directly and continually challenged. Robert Sternberg (2003) proposed a psychological model of hate and discussed the implications of this model for terrorism. This model identifies propaganda as one of the chief instigating factors of terrorist movements. As the Internet is now being employed as a vehicle for terrorist organizations to spread propaganda and recruit new members, it seems reasonable that the Internet should be employed in efforts to counter these activities. There are ethical considerations which will accompany such efforts. Free speech activists would warn of censorship and the possibility that monitoring Internet activity could be seen as an invasion of privacy. These concerns do have legitimacy in the eyes of many; however, such concerns should be balanced with the clear and present danger of cyberterrorism.

Conclusion

Researchers in cognitive technology can provide a genuine service in deterring identity theft and cyberterrorism by considering two key questions. First, what kinds of data can be utilized to most accurately monitor the impact of these threats? In answering this question, researchers might consider creating profiles of online behavior for identity thieves, cyberterrorists, and their potential victims. This would help to identify any patterns that might exist in communication, web surfing, and data transfer to help better predict future criminal activity. Second, what kinds of safeguards can be put into place to minimize the impact of these threats? Many of these safeguards could be identified through basic research on cognitive and social processes. Cognitive psychologists might look at the impact of multipassword security systems on memory or how people evaluate security threats in a virtual environment compared to a real world environment. Social psychologists interested in influence might consider the impact of Internet based propaganda on attitudes or the effects of peer pressure in a virtual environment on behavior in the real world.

In sum, research into the problems of identity theft and cyberterrorism is greatly needed. While it is likely that these threats will never entirely be abolished, these threats can be more clearly defined so that preventative measures and meaningful responses can be implemented.

References

Abagnale, F. W. (2001). *The art of the steal: How to recognize and prevent fraud—America's #1 crime.* New York: Broadway.

Arquilla, J., and Ronfeldt, D. (2001). The advent of netwar. In J. Arquilla and D. Ronfeldt (eds.), *Networks and netwars: The future of terror, crime, and militancy* (pp 1–28) .Arlington, VA: RAND.

Barabasi, A. L. (2002). *Linked: How everything is connected to everything else and what it means for business, science, and everyday life.* New York: Plume.

Clarke, R. (1994). Human identification in information systems: Management challenges and public policy issues. *Information Technology and People,* 7(4), 6–37.

de Armond, P. (2001). Netwar in the emerald city: WTO protest strategy and tactics. In J. Arquilla and D. Ronfeldt (eds.), *Networks and netwars: The future of terror, crime, and militancy* (pp. 201–238). Arlington, VA: RAND.

Denning, D. E. (2001). Activism, hacktivism, and cyberterrorism: The internet as a tool for influencing foreign policy. In J. Arquilla and D. Ronfeldt (eds.), *Networks and netwars: The future of terror, crime, and militancy* (pp. 239-288). Arlington, VA: RAND.

Federal Trade Commission. (2002). *Figures and trends on Identity theft in North Carolina, 2001.*

_____ (2003). *Figures and trends on Identity theft in North Carolina, 2002.*

Ferrell, K. (2003, July 22). Identity theft soars, but it's still a low-tech crime. *InternetWeek.* http://www.Internetweek.com

Fischer, A. D. (2003, April 10). Identity theft tops white-collar crime boom, Better Business Bureau head says. *Arizona Daily Star,* p.

General Accounting Office (2002, March) *Identity theft: Prevalence and cost appear to be growing.* (GAO Publication No. GAO-02-363). Washington, DC: Author.

Halden, E. and Tacheny, M. (Producers). (2003). Losing your identity. (Television series episode No. 507). In *Right on the Money.* St. Paul/Minneapolis: TPT/Twin Cities Public Television.

Identity Theft and Assumption Deterrence Act, Pub. Law 105-318, 112 Stat. 3007, 18 U.S.C. § 1028 (1998).

Identity Theft and Financial Privacy Protection bill, H.R. 2035, 108th Cong. (2003).

Identity Theft: Partners in prevention (n.d.). Retrieved August 21, 2003, from http://www.cj.msu.edu/ percent7Eoutreach/identity/.

Kahneman, D., Slovic, P., and Tversky, A. (Eds.) (1982). *Judgment under uncertainty: Heuristics and biases.* New York: Cambridge University Press.

LoPicki, L. M. (2001). Human identification theory and the identity theft problem. *Texas Law Review,* 80, 89–135.

Marsh, D. (2003, March 20). Get smart. *EDN,* 48, p. 61.

Matejkovic, J. E., and Lahey, K. E. (2002). Identity theft: No help for consumers. *Financial Services Review,* 10, 221–235.

Mayer, C. E. (2003, July 1). Congress told to target identity theft: White House seeks tighter credit laws. *Washington Post,* p. E1.

Military Construction Appropriations Act of 2001. Pub. L. No. 106-246, § 112, 114 Stat. 511 (2000).

North Carolina Department of Justice (n.d.). Fact Sheet: Identity Theft. Retrieved June 13, 2003, from http://www.jus.state.nc.us/cp/IDFACTSHEET.pdf

Ohr, S. (2003, July 7). Cards conjure fears of 1984. *Electronic Engineering Times,* pp. 18–22.

Spielberg, S. (Producer/Director), and Parkes, W. F. (2002). *Catch me if you can* [Motion Picture]. United States: Dreamworks Pictures.

Sternberg, R. J. (2003). A duplex theory of hate development and application to terrorism, massacres, and genocide. *Review of General Psychology,* 7, 299–328.

Thompson, J. F. (2002, November/December). Identity, privacy, and information technology. *EDUCAUSE Review,* 37, pp. 64–65.

Vigne, D. (Producer/Director/Writer). (1982). *Le retour de Martin Guerre (The return of Martin Guerre)* [Motion Picture]. France: La Societé Français de Production Cinematographique, La Societé de Production des Films Marcel Dassault, France Region 3.

Zanini, M., and Edwards, S. J. A. (2001). The networking of terror in the information age. In J. Arquilla and D. Ronfeldt (eds.) *Networks and netwars: The future of terror, crime, and militancy.* Arlington, VA: RAND.

11

Cognitive Psychologists and Human-Technical Systems: Should We Choose the Red Pill?

Francis T. Durso *and* Catherine F. Hall

> Progress has never been a bargain. You have to pay for it. You can have a telephone, but you lose privacy and the charm of distance. You may conquer the air, but the birds will lose their wonder and the clouds will smell of gasoline.—*Spencer Tracy in* Inherit the Wind

On April 22, 2003, Mary Christian died at the age of 113. Mary was the oldest living American before her passing. She was born in 1889, just 10 years after Swan and Edison invented the light bulb. When Mary was young, people didn't drive automobiles or fly in planes. They couldn't listen to talkback radio or watch people get married on television. If Mary wanted to learn when the light bulb was invented, she'd have to find someone who knew the answer or go to a book, probably an encyclopedia, and look up something—maybe electric candle, or the inventors' names.

By the time Mary died, people could not only fly, they could fly faster than the speed of sound. Planes would come to have wingspans longer than the distance of the Wright brothers' first flight. She would have watched, via a box in her living room, men go to the moon. If Mary wanted to find

The authors would like to thank Keith Jones for comments on an earlier version of this chapter.

the name of the last man to walk on the moon, she could go to her own computer, type in "last walk on moon," and the computer in .30 seconds would spit back from a global computer network about 719,000 entries, the second of which would tell her that it was Gene Cernan and that he did it in Apollo 17 a little over 30 years ago.

Mary would have seen a great many changes. She would have witnessed Martha Graham's contraction give birth to modern dance and Pablo Picasso's painting of prostitutes seduce the world of art. She could have read *The Wasteland* or listened to that hep new Russian composer Stravinsky. She certainly would have heard of Einstein and maybe of the dice of quantum mechanics, although she was too big to be affected by quantum mechanics and too slow to be affected by relativity. But there were advances that did affect Mary, technological advances. Inventions would surround her.

In fact, Mary's later years saw some of the fastest growing technologies the 20th century had seen. The National Center for Policy Analysis, a conservative think tank, used as a metric the number of years it took a technology to reach 25 percent of the population (Cox and Alm, 1998), the growth of the Internet, mobile phone, and personal computer are remarkable. The personal computer was on the desks of a quarter of us in 16 years, the cell phone was companion to a fourth of us after 13 years, and it took a mere 7 years from the launch of the Internet (1991) until 1 out of every 4 of us was jacked-in. Compared to the telephone, the Internet has grown about five times as fast, and compared to electricity itself (which took 48 years to reach our quartile mark) the Internet spread at a virulent pace.

The rate of technological change is unlikely to abate. Mary will miss many future technological developments. If you're worried about people driving with a cell phone—and as Dave Strayer (chapter 4 this volume) indicates, you should be—imagine what it is like when grandma is driving her SUV using her GPS HUD to locate the nearest drive-through ATM? The rapidity of change promises to involve psychologists of all types, from our colleagues in the helping professions who will assist people with stress, loss of identity, helplessness, and other consequences of rapid change; to our colleagues in neuroscience who will find ways to exploit the new technologies to gain a better understanding of how the brain works.

We believe that cognitive psychologists especially, in all their manifestations should actively engage the technological issues, for both theoretical and practical reasons. Many of today's jobs are heavily cognitive. When Mary was a teenager, 51 percent of those gainfully employed were

TABLE 11.1. EMPLOYMENT PROJECTIONS (1998–2008)
OF THE 10 FASTEST GROWING OCCUPATIONS

Occupation	Percent change
Computer engineers	108
Computer support specialists	102
Systems analysts	94
Database administrators	77
Desktop publishing specialists	73
Paralegals and legal assistants	63
Personal care and home health aides	58
Medical assistants	58
Social and human service assistants	53
Physician assistants	48

unskilled or semiskilled workers (U.S. Census, 1945). Today (U.S. Census, 2000) the 10 fastest growing occupations all have cognitive components, often large cognitive components. Table 11.1 presents employment projections (from 1998 to 2008) of the 10 fastest growing occupations Thus, as occupations become cognitive it becomes important that researchers knowledgeable about human mental functions play a role.

In fact, the discipline of cognitive ergonomics concerns itself with cognitive factors of the workplace. Although a relatively young discipline, it is gaining prominence. Cognitive ergonomics plays a large role in the Human Factors and Ergonomics Society. The journal *Cognitive Technology* recently produced a special issue on cognitive ergonomics, and government and military funding for work in cognitive ergonomics is increasing. Although the discipline has attracted its share of investigators, attracting additional rigorous thinkers from among our basic-research colleagues and from among the nascent scholars in our classrooms will be critical to an increasingly technological society.

Assessing the Relative Values of Cognitive Technologies

An Example: Paper vs. Glass

In this chapter, we compare quite different cognitive technologies. On the one hand, we will talk about an ancient technology, paper; and, on the other, we will talk about modern computers and their glass displays. As a vehicle for understanding technology in heavily cognitive jobs, we will focus on the U.S. air traffic control system (ATC) and a debate that has been ongoing for over a decade and revolves around technologies and technological change.

The debate in ATC involves two technologies that, on the surface of things, couldn't be more different. One is a collection of 6⅜" × 1⅛" strips of paper and the other is a modern computerized system with a soupçon of artificial intelligence. The paper strips are one of the tools (radar and phone lines are others) that controllers use to keep aircraft separated by safe distances. Strips are records of the filed flight plan that controllers can manipulate and mark. They provide controllers with easy access to information that can be organized and reorganized and provide controllers with a structured output for note taking. The computerized glass system, on the other hand, will provide less information, require fewer inputs, and will predict future problems by extrapolating current flight information. Those interested in details of the debate and the reasons cited on either side are referred to Durso and Manning (2002). In the current chapter, we use the controversy in air traffic control simply as a backdrop against which to look at differences in technologies and the factors that influence the choice of the "right" or "better" technology. Throughout this discussion there will be a concern about the role of the cognitive psychologist as an arbiter of technology decisions in a world where the technology is interesting and the participants are interested.

Although the debate has many details that are of relevance only to the domain of air traffic control, the broader debate of paper versus computer is not restricted to air traffic control. In *The Myth of the Paperless Office*, for example, Sellen and Harper (2002) discuss a number of domains including crime reporting, chocolate manufacture, and even database management.

Technology-Centered vs. Human-Centered

For cognitive psychologists to work effectively with technology and with the operators who use it, understanding differences among views of technology is important. Broadly, we can identify two approaches to human-technical systems, the technology-centered view and the human-centered view. These different viewpoints lead to far-reaching differences in such issues as defining progress and attributing blame for errors.

Technology centered. Many people think that "good technology" can be assessed by looking at the technology itself. Computer programmers certainly believe that a good piece of software does more with less lines of code. Some have argued that to Americans "technological improvements are a primary basis for—and an accurate gauge of—progress" (Marx,

1987). The technocratic idea of progress, originally advocated by Daniel Webster in the 1840s, promoted the view that improved technology was evidence for and a good measure of general progress. Marx argues that, with the development of industrial capitalism, technological advancement was promoted by the economic gains associated with technology. Emerging industrial capitalists viewed technological improvements as indication of universal progress. The increase in economic productivity and the United States' rise to global power helped enforce this belief.

An urban legend captures the technophilia of this viewpoint. As the legend goes, when NASA attempted to solve the problem that pens would not write in the zero gravity of space, it spent considerable funds developing a new high technology, the space pen. How did the Soviets solve the same problem? They used a pencil. Although the urban legend serves as a succinct parable about technology, real world examples of our love of new technology are everywhere. A recent circular of a home furnishing retailer promoted new vacuum cleaners simply with the headline "New Technology."

In this technocentric view, failures of technology are, usually, failures of the operator. For example, in air traffic control for the year 1993, 99 percent of operational errors are attributed to "human error" (Durso, Truitt, Hackworth, Crutchfield, and Manning, 1998). Solutions to these errors, presumably, would involve better training and better selection procedures.

Human centered. The idea that increased knowledge in science and technology was a means to improving the human condition, emerged as the prevalent view of progress during the Enlightenment. From a period of political instability (the American and French revolutions), individuals such as Thomas Jefferson and Benjamin Franklin viewed progress as the benefits that technology and science could offer to society, and not that progress was the technology itself. Science and technology were a means to transform and improve humanity.

This view reemerges in reaction to the technocratic view of progress. The "counter-Enlightenment" or "romantic reaction" (Marx, 1987, p.8) to the technocratic view of progress was manifested in the works of writers such as Emerson, Thoreau, and Melville, who regarded increased industrialism as a departure from the idea of progress as intended to improve humanity, not just the economy.

Perhaps the best-known reaction against technology was Ned Ludd's movement, from which we get the word *Luddite*. This was a movement, not of technophobes, but of craftsmen, concerned about the production of a lower quality product and about being forced into lower wage factory jobs (Englander and Downing, 1998). Controllers who resist the elimination of paper strips also view themselves as skilled craftsmen who could be relegated to lower status positions while a lower quality product (i.e., lower safety) is produced. A few suspect the goal of the new technology is to replace them altogether.

The human-centered view also affects how accidents and faults are attributed. Cognitive ergonomists realize that making the simple attribution of "human error" is usually misleading. To understand error requires understanding the system, including the human, in which the error takes place (e.g., Woods and Cook, 1999). Unlike the technocentric view of performance, modern social scientists look at the fit with the human operator. Movements in human factors and computer science that speak of user-centered or human-centered are efforts to bring recognition to the problem. Good technologies get the job done, and we should appreciate that this is more likely when it fits with the human operator. Good technology is usable technology. Good technology fits within the system just as the appropriate operator fits within the system.

Most of those involved in the ATC debate view progress in the human-centered, Franklin sense, but again there are two sides to the issue. Today, air travel in the United States is incredibly safe. Since 1983, ATC has been identified as a primary or contributory cause in only 27 accidents in the United States. In addition, a lot less than half of one percent of the flight segments are even involved in an operational error (i.e., two en route aircraft coming within five miles of each other.) Safety is so close to ceiling, any further progress may be unrealistic.

However, societal progress may be possible without improving safety. Of course, no one wants safety to decline, but the new system may improve efficiency while not impacting safety. More planes, shorter delays, more direct flights, and so on are possible outcomes of replacing the low-tech paper strips with a high-tech alternative. In the next sections, we consider four gross differences among technologies. Each difference highlights an important contrast that appears in many real world decisions about technology.

Replacing Low Tech with High Tech

Imagine a survey in which we ask people to list the differences between computers and paper. Perhaps the first dimension that people would mention is that the computer is high tech and paper is not. Part of what they might mean by high tech is that computers are complicated, intricate devices, whereas paper is not. They might mean that computers are new, cutting-edge, whereas paper has been around a while. They might mean that computers are more efficient, more automated than some low-tech alternative. They might mean that they don't understand how the computer works, and only partially understand how to work the computer. Of course, new technologies are always more difficult to understand than their old-tech predecessors. However, this seems especially true with modern technologies. Pool (2003) argued that modern technologies are more complicated in both their consequences and their operation. For example, the impact of CFCs is global in both its benefits and its unintended consequences. "The plow, the cotton gin, even the lightbulb—these are simple devices. No matter how much they are changed and improved, it is still easy to understand their functions and capabilities" (Pool, 2003, p.15). No one, on the other hand, understands all of Windows and no team can anticipate all the consequences of a 21st century technology.

Unlike the powerful, complicated, new, high-tech computer, paper is simple, old, and familiar. Perhaps, because of these characteristics, some of our fictional respondents would not have thought of paper as technology at all. In fact, an increasing amount of information has become digitized, paper has become symbolic of old-fashioned, low-tech, and inefficient technology. Sellen and Harper (2002) illustrate this general bias with the story of an individual whose office was piled so high with papers that desks and chairs were almost undetectable underneath stacks of reports, articles, and miscellaneous notes (perhaps not so hard to imagine). While the individual who resided in this office was not considered inefficient or unorganized, company managers wanted to avoid the impression that their organization was inefficient or low tech, so the stacks of paper were boxed and put underneath the stairs when visitors were expected.

Sellen and Harper also note that cost and "interactive problems" associated with paper also perpetuate the notion that paper is low tech and inefficient. For example, paper takes up space—more paper requires more storage space. Paper only presents static information (it cannot display moving images or sounds) and requires physical delivery. Without the right technology, paper cannot be easily replicated or copied. Digital documents are mobile and easily revised. Nevertheless, despite the perception that paper is inefficient and old-fashioned, it remains the most prevalent way of collecting and exchanging information (Sellen and Harper, 2002).

Our air traffic control environment provides a good illustration of the kinds of issues that researchers may experience when comparing an existing technology with a proposed high-tech replacement. First, the paper strips are familiar parts of the controller's arsenal. For a new technology to outperform the old technology in the current workforce, the new technology must outdistance this inherent familiarity advantage. Second, over the years the job itself has adapted to the old technology. Controlling air traffic today is done the way it is done, in part, because strips exist. The job has become optimized to the old technology. Third, high technology that requires interactions with the human operator will often be beyond the experiences of at least the older members of the extant workforce. The more senior controllers have had less experience with, for example, virtual reality, Windows-type environments, computer games, wearable computing, and digital interfaces in general than have their younger counterparts. Fourth, the new technology will be modern, cutting edge, complicated digital replacement that may take time to meld with the job of ATC. Finally, some controllers are so inured in a strip-based system that it is impossible to imagine an alternative to the way things are done currently. Just as our grandparents would have suggested "more ice, more often" when asked for alternatives to their iceboxes rather than chemical refrigeration (Cross, 1992), controllers often find it impossible to suggest alternatives to strips (Durso and Manning, 2002). Some controllers have indicated that doing their jobs without paper strips would be impossible.

Mapping Function onto Structure

Another dimension that distinguishes technologies is how the functions of the technology map onto the structure of the technology. The notion of smart appliances, high technology designed for a specific purpose, has been viewed as a solution to the problems encountered when people interact with computers. The technology has a single function and if the device is designed well, the mapping between that function and the structure that initiates it is obvious.

However, the multifunctionality of ATC makes it difficult to develop a collection of single-function devices. Neither paper strips nor the computer system designed to replace them can be thought of as specific-function devices. In general, both paper and computers are general-purpose technologies. The strip and the computer replacement are both intended to accomplish a number of tasks, from issuing clearances to coordinating information with other controllers. Despite this similarity of functions, the two technologies nevertheless differ in how the functions are mapped onto their structures.

De Michelis (2003) compares the Swiss army knife with the Sardinian pattada. The Swiss army knife is the familiar multifunction tool for which each function has a corresponding physical component. Thus, one way for a technology to have multiple purposes is multiplicity (De Michelis, 2003). Italian shepherds also use a knife with multiple functions. Shepherds and farmers use the Sardinian pattada for a number of tasks: digging, carving, slicing, piercing, whittling, forking, clipping nails, shaving, operating on cattle, and so on. The pattada features a single, sharp, "myrtle-leaf-shaped blade with a whetted point." But unlike the Swiss army knife, the Sardinian pattada does not have its multiple functions mirrored in multiple structures. The pattada technology can be characterized by openness: a single component used for various purposes in various instances (De Michelis, 2003).

Multiplicity and openness have their strengths and weaknesses. For the Swiss army knife, finding the particular blade can be problematic, and extracting it can be difficult. Further, the handle shared by so many blades isn't "ergonomically adequate." For the open pattada, it is trivial to switch from function to function, but as De Michelis notes, the generic handle and unspecialized blade provide only an approximate solution. De Michelis then goes on to imagine the impossible "Swiss pattada," where each function would have the optimal physical incarnation and transferring from one function to another would be accomplished at the moment of use through a transmogrification of the tool. While the Swiss pattada is merely a designer's fantasy, De Michelis notes how the computer has made such a blending of multiplicity and openness possible.

Clearly, paper is an open technology. Even when segmented, as it is to make a flight progress strip, the strip remains open. Computer interfaces, although they could be designed to be open, are more often characterized by multiplicity, since programmers, designers, and marketers want to optimize the particular software they are promoting. Although the goal of combining openness and multiplicity is a noble one, it has not yet been possible to create a controller's Swiss pattada. In earlier generations of planning for advanced automation, one plan was to have a customizable worksite so a controller can set up, type in a code, and all parameters of the workstation would change to fit his or her preferences.

Analog Creatures Looking for Inputs

Nicolas Negroponte, Director of the Media lab at MIT, authored a book entitled *Being Digital* in which he painted an optimistic picture of life in a digital world. He noted many of the valuable features we enjoy today on the Internet, the customizability and personalization of education and of commerce; the empowerment of being able to have your ideas consumed by thousands.

Some social scientists and human factors engineers reacted pointing out many of the issues that still direct research on human-technical systems. Norman's clever response, which he entitled *Being Analog*, for example, talks about how designers don't understand people, how technology is "accuracy based" whereas humans are not so precise, and so on. As Norman says "We are analog beings trapped in a digital world, and the worst part is, we did it to ourselves."

Norman also spoke of affordances, "the fundamental properties that determine just how the thing could properly be used." The term *affordance* was coined by Gibson to help describe what the technology offers the operator. Sometimes, the affordances can be misleading. For example, in the psychology building at Texas Tech, the elevator has enumerated lights that protrude from the side panel of the elevator. The lights are merely indicators of the elevator's position; thus, pushing one will do nothing. Yet they afford "pushability." Thus, the indicator lights are pushed routinely by new and old students. For Gibson, because pushability is a part of the environment system, not the perceived properties, the lights are inherently pushable. The perceiver becomes "attuned" to the affordances, but the affordances are not part of the perceiver's cognitive processes. Hence, a Gibsonian or ecological perspective puts much of the action outside of the head.

To cognitive psychologists, the notions that arise from an ecological perspective (e.g., cognition is in the environment) are often quite foreign, and the ecological approach often has been explicitly eschewed as not supplying the theoretical meat cognitive psychologists would like. Certainly, there is little explanation here in terms of underlying mechanisms. However, there is another kind of understanding; understanding the relationship between two or more generalized categories; understanding that F = m*a, for example. Or in our case, explanation in terms of environment-person relationships.

Cognitive psychologists, in an effort to focus on cognition, simplify the laboratory environment. We have often been criticized out of hand for this strategy, but this simplification strategy often proves to be viable. For example, despite concerns raised by Neisser in his *Memory Observed* (1984), principles gleaned from laboratory research have proven useful, even when moved to "realistic" and presumably anomalous phenomena like flashbulb memories. Moving into the real world, where the environment and technology are not simple, does not *guarantee* that cognitive principles born in the lab will fail, but it does guarantee that the environment will be more important than it was when the principle was born.

It would be prudent for the cognitive psychologist to understand the system, the environment, and the technology. Even to a cognitive psychologist, affordances become an interesting construct when we try to plug the analog operator into the digital technology. Take, for example, the affordances of paper compared with those of glass. Luff, Heath, and Greatbach (1992) speak of several advantages of paper. Most advantages for paper (or disadvantages for glass) are related to the input of information or the flexibility of interaction with the technology: (1) Keyboard entries are difficult; (2) range of input is restricted; (3) sequence of input is restricted; (4) moving information through the workplace is restricted; (5) distinguishing among documents is reduced. Thus, because we are analog beings, comparing an analog technology like paper with a digital one like the computer yields a number of possible advantages for the low-tech, analog paper.

These advantages for paper may not apply in each human-technical system using paper (in fact, we have argued elsewhere that all do not apply in ATC; Durso and Manning, 2002). Nevertheless, it does seem generally true that paper is more flexible than current glass interfaces. In general, researchers should recognize that technologies will differ in their flexibility, with analog technologies typically being the more flexible. Paper allows controllers to write the new altitude for an aircraft slanted up, or slanted down. It allows the new altitude to be written first and then the new speed, or vice versa. Paper even allows the controller to write a planned action that she has never before performed and to write it with as little effort as a planned action she performs daily. She could even, theoretically, write a note to call her supervisor, draw a diagram illustrating an unusual routing, or a reminder to get milk after work. The paper allows it.

One solution to the analog-to-digital problem is to create analog interfaces to digital systems, and these efforts are underway. Voice recognition systems hold promise as does research on electronic paper. Researchers who move into the field are likely to see increasing numbers of hybrid analog-digital systems in operational settings.

Digital technologies, on the other hand, function better with increased standardization. As the opposite of flexibility, standardization has some clear disadvantages. However, there may also be cases where standardization is preferred. For example, communicating about some standardized action is considerably easier than communicating about actions that differ from operator to operator. Imagine, for example, Archie and Mary are completely free to write on the paper flight progress strips in any way they choose. Perhaps Archie, well versed in this sector of airspace, makes a few cryptic and idiosyncratic notes about flights performing differently than he expected. Archie's shift is ending, and he is to be replaced by Mary, who is a novice. Typically, she makes notes that are more extensive and does so even for aircraft that are routine travelers through her airspace. The briefing that Archie would give Mary that would accompany such a shift change would likely be inefficient. The FAA and local facilities acknowledge the problem of too much flexibility, and they have standardized many of the marks made on flight progress strips as well as the location of the marks on the strip. The position relief briefing itself also follows standard guidelines.

Of course, while rigid technologies cannot be made more flexible, flexible technologies can be standardized by operators, either intentionally or by default (few people change computer settings). Whether we should prefer flexibility or standardization depends on the system and task in which the technology and operator will coexist. Although flexibility is desirable in a technology (because it can always be made more standardized), it is not always the case that the additional flexibility is desirable in a human-technical system.

So, humans can use digital systems by standardizing what is entered into the system or allowing analog inputs into the system; as Norman (1998) puts it, by making the human more like a computer or by making the computer more like the human. By natural inclination, since he or she is not a designer, the cognitive psychologist will be better at determining how to change the human to be more like the computer than the reverse. We can do this by training, by personnel selection, and by changing procedures. In the real world, the researcher should be on the lookout for the other solution as well, how to change the environment to be friendly to us.

Intelligent Design vs. Evolution

Technology is usually designed for a specific purpose or set of purposes. Intelligent design and engineering produce products that accomplish the intended goal as quickly, accurately, easily, and cheaply as possible. In the beginning, such was likely the case for the paper flight progress strip. Certainly, such is the case for potential digital flight strip replacements.

However, technologies can come to serve functions other than those originally intended by the designers. In other words, technology can evolve. In fact, the history of technology is replete with stories of unintended uses. Our favorite involves the histories of the radio and telephone (Marvin, 1988; Pandora, 1998). Originally, people thought that the telephone would serve as a deliverer of centralized content. People would dial a number to hear the news, advice, weather, and so on. For radio, people originally thought that the radio would be a person-to-person communication tool. I would call you on the radio to see if you wanted to walk to the big social. As we know today, predictions about the evolution of the two technologies was incorrect—telephones came to be used as radio was intended and radio came to be used as the telephone was intended.

However, unintended uses can evolve in addition to the originally intended use. For example, speed bugs of the MD-80s airspeed indicator have evolved functions other than their originally intended use. If redesign of the MD-80 cockpit did not take into account these other, evolved functions, then negative consequences for workload, situation awareness, and performance would be likely in the new and "improved" aircraft (Hutchins, 1995).

This evolution argument has been made explicitly in the case of flight progress strips. Usually the argument assumes that the flight progress strip has evolved to serve a variety of cognitive functions (e.g., Hopkins, 1991; Isaac and Guselli, 1996). For example, writing on the strip, or physically manipulating it, aids controllers' memory of the traffic. Automating flight data without acknowledging the cognitive benefits of strips, the argument goes, would cause problems for the controller and result in a reduction in ATC safety and efficiency.

Although the argument is a viable one, it is also empirically testable. Over a number of tests, we and the Vortac team (e.g., Albright, Truitt, Barile, Vortac, and Manning, 1995; Truitt, Durso, Crutchfield, Moertl, and Manning, 2000; Vortac, Edwards, Fuller, and Manning, 1993; Vortac, Edwards, and Manning, 1994) have repeatedly shown that reducing or removing strips did not have an effect on controller performance. When significant effects are detected, they are usually in the direction favoring elimination of the strips; for example, Vortac et al. (1993) showed an improvement in prospective memory tasks when the task of marking strips was eliminated. Thus, whereas strips could have evolved particular cognitive functions that would aid performance, they apparently did not—or the advantage of these evolved functions is less than the disadvantages of working with strips.

Summary

We discussed broad ways in which technologies can differ. The old paper strips were thought to be open, analog, low-tech devices that over time may have come to evolve particular benefits for the controller. The new computer display was thought to be a multiplicitous, digital high-tech device, potentially capable of reducing workload and predicting problems, but has yet to evolve to fit the job. Each of the broad categorizations had a number of consequences, or potential consequences. If one takes a human-centered stance on human-technical systems, then it strikes us as important to involve cognitive psychologists interested in the rapid technological changes occurring today.

Psychologists at the Center of Human-Technical Systems

In some sense, cognitive psychologists have led the way in promoting humans to the center of the human-technical system. Thus, the argument that humans are central in human-technical systems should be greeted by nodding acknowledgement of the obvious by many readers of this chapter. Perhaps, for cognitive psychologists, the recognition that other components of the system—the environment, the technology—are equally important may be less apparent. The idea that the environment, system, and technology are as important as the person in the understanding of cognition may be quite foreign. However, this recognition is critical if cognitive psychologists hope to leave the lab.

And they should. Cognitive psychologists are critically needed to help fit modern technology with modern users. They can be of direct value in picking between technologies and, with a little change in focus, of value in designing those technologies. This journey into the real world will not be without dangers and inconveniences, nor can it be made successfully without modifying some of the conceptions that we have calcified in the lab. If experimental psychologists do not address these issues of human-technical systems, then others will—to the detriment of both psychology and society.

How Cognitive Psychologists Can Help

Much of what happens in technology-focused research is deciding which of two technologies is "better"? Do controllers perform better with the new glass system or the old paper strips? Does the new technology *cause* an improvement in performance? Psychologists have been trained to answer exactly this type of empirical question. We can bring to bear an arsenal of methodological and quantitative methods that ensure internal validity, that ensure our ability to pronounce causality with good probability.

We have discussed in this chapter many of the nuances of answering this question. Deciding between the two technologies can often be difficult. It may be, for example, that the new technology is better, but the operators are more familiar with the old technology and thus comparisons of the two will be affected by familiarity. Less obviously, the job may have adapted to the old technology so that what it means to control air traffic becomes inextricably connected to, in our case, the paper strips.

Because the question being asked here is one about causality, the controlled experiment is certainly the methodology of choice. So, go ahead, do experiments. We did. In a variety of high- and medium-fidelity simulations, we put field controllers in within-subjects designs measuring a number of dependent variables and showed, typically, no difference between strips and no-strips, and occasionally an advantage for no-strips. (e.g., Vortac et al., 1993)

However, the experimenter must make concessions to the real world. First, expert operators (such as controllers) are usually a rare commodity. The employees' union, rather than a random number table, might pick your participants. These concessions need not sacrifice the value of experimentation for someone who knows how such restrictions affect the logic of experimentation. Most often, especially in usability research, one hears that the real world moves too fast to allow one to do a good experiment. The production division cannot wait to ship while the experimental psychologist does the experiment right, we are told. Such statements usually come from individuals who confuse the long, time-consuming experiment with the good experiment. Some can take a semester to conduct a confounded, externally and ecologically invalid experiment, and others can take a week to do it right. The trick is to focus on what is important: important to the hypothesis, important to control, and important to measure. Therefore, just learning to do the familiar experiment in the real world will be a valuable aid to researchers of human-technical systems.

Experimental psychologists can also do cognitive fieldwork. Knowledge elicitation methods, cognitive task analysis, and a host of procedures will strike cognitive psychologists as familiar (e.g., naturalistic observation, cognitive interview techniques, and protocol analysis), but the methods may have been tweaked by applied researchers to make them more useful in the field.

Even more unfamiliar and difficult for experimental and cognitive psychologists is the design of new technologies. Of course, the psychologist is not the designer, but he or she is certainly capable of serving on a design team. Others with less scientific understanding and similar amounts of aesthetic insight serve on such design committees.

Psychologists bring valuable components to the design: One is an access to a knowledge base of human abilities and limitations; another is a very special training on how to think about human abilities and limitations. This training, perhaps more than our database of facts, will hold the cognitive psychologist in good stead on a design team. By using a naturalistic observation of air traffic controllers' use of strips in the field (Durso, Batsakes, Crutchfield, Braden, and Manning, in press) we took frequency information, perceived benefits, and importance ratings to make suggestions to designers of future ATC systems (Durso and Manning, 2003). None of the procedures used in that endeavor are unfamiliar to cognitive psychologists.

It's Not Just Cognitive Psychology

Moray (1999) notes that the cognitive processes, such as decision making and attention, are just a small fraction of the constraints that are placed on cognitive behavior. Economic, political, and social constraints on cognitive behavior exist as well.

The cognitive psychologist will notice when she leaves the lab that, unlike her lab participants, people have interests, opinions, and fears. They may have even gotten together with other people to protect those interests, advance those opinions, and allay those fears; that is, they may have formed an employee union with which the researcher must negotiate. For air traffic controllers, the union that replaced the controllers fired by Reagan is the National Air Traffic Controllers Associations (NATCA) and they are involved at every level of our research dealings with field controllers, as are representatives of management (i.e., FAA).

In fact, many aspects of the system, constrain cognitive behavior. Moray (1999) explicitly explores four characteristics of industrial systems that place certain constraints on cognitive behavior that may not occur to cognitive psychologists coming from the lab: size, complexity, timing, and modes of control.

Size, both physical and functional, is an important characteristic of industrial systems. Physical size requires information to be transferred efficiently enough so that all subsystems are interconnected and productive. Within the system, several implications arise from just considering size. An analysis of "worker behavior" and modes of "communication" can influence "shift work patterns." "Worker motivations" and "team and group behavior" interact with "organizational and management behavior" that must adhere to "legal and regulatory rules." Other factors outside the system, such as sociopolitical pressures, can also influence the practices of that system.

The complexity of a given system has implications on how the systems function as a whole. Many subsystems must interact. Because of the interconnectedness of an industrial system, potentially hazardous accidents can result from just one change. While the cognitive aspects associated with the complexity of a system may include perception, attention, and thought, "health and safety regulations," a "safety culture," and evaluations of "system design and work practices" are just some of the constraints that influence these cognitive behaviors.

Third, each type of industrial system operates on different time constraints. For example, the rate at which the events of a system progress affects the rate at which workers are able to make decisions. Therefore, it is important to consider the "constraints on system design and work practices" as well as the "economic pressures" related to temporal characteristics of that system.

A final factor related to the cognitive load of individuals in an industrial system refers to the modes of control, how much of the system is automated and how much is controlled by a human operator. Automated systems that are poorly designed to a specific function can result in a higher cognitive load on human operators and potentially lowered productivity. Again, perception, decision making, thought, and memory, are constrained by safety regulations, legal and liability issues, and political and economic pressures. If a system is ill designed, there is a higher potential for human error that could result in disastrous accidents. Take for example the 1986 accident that resulted in the meltdown of a nuclear reactor at Chernobyl (Monroney, 1995). The accident, a result of human error, was met with environmental and political pressures. Certainly sociopolitical pressures are placed on ensuring such incidents do not occur.

The multitude of influences on technology can also be illustrated by considering the development of the "qwerty" keyboard. Often technology development is based on a series of factors unrelated to cognitive issues. Before the qwerty keyboard was engineered, designs ranged from a circular alphabetical layout that required the lifting of a lever to achieve a sequence of letters, to a keyboard similar to that of a piano. The alphabetical configuration of the keyboard introduced the problem of jammed keys; when typists would press successive letters too quickly, the hammers of early typewriters would get jammed (Tenner, 2003). The solution was to rearrange the keys to prevent them from jamming. In the 1870s, Charles Latham Sholes designed the standard keyboard still used today. The qwerty keyboard, as it was called, referred to the arrangement of the top row of letters beginning with "qwerty." The middle row of letters contained an almost alphabetical arrangement, "dfghjkl," and contained a vowel cluster, "uio." This design was constructed loosely based on letter frequencies similar to newspaper type cases (Tenner, 2003). The qwerty keyboard was able to slow down the operator and prevent jammed keys.

In addition to the solution for jammed keys, the qwerty design was adopted due to a series of events. In the 1880s, speed contests were sponsored by typewriter manufacturers to promote newer machines that would facilitate efficiency with higher typing speeds. These contests became a good means of marketing a product. A contestant who won using a specific typewriter could become a spokesperson for that company. In 1888, Frank R. McGurrin, using a Remington typewriter, competed with Louis Traub and his Caligraph typewriter. McGurrin also happened to be the world's first touch typist. So, as any beginning student in research methods would tell you, it may have been the confound of touch typing, not the configuration of the keyboard, that led to McGurrin's winning the contest. Nevertheless, the marketing impact was irreversible. The failure of the Caligraph and success of the Remington were ensured. Thus, the typewriter developed as it did for reasons other than the technology itself. The cognitive psychologist must realize that even when studying cognition, results will depend on more than cognitive processes.

If Not Us, Then...

If cognitive psychologists stay in the comfort of their labs and their theories, research on human-technical systems will nevertheless continue. In fact, researchers trained or influenced by other disciplines have been heavily involved in analysis of human-technical systems. Just as cognitive psychology stepped in to fill the gaps ignored by behaviorists, anthropologists stand ready to fill the gaps ignored by psychologists.

Obviously, anthropology can supply important information about a variety of human endeavors, but applying anthropological techniques, and only anthropological techniques, to the study of human-technical systems has limits. The Mead-Freeman debate exemplifies the problems associated with the methods that anthropologists use to acquire data. Between 1925 and 1926, Margaret Mead conducted fieldwork in Samoa to explore adolescent behavior. The results of her ethnographic observations and interviews were presented in *Coming of Age in Samoa: A Psychological Study of Primitive Youth for Western Civilization* (1928).

Derek Freeman published *Margaret Mead and Samoa* (1983), in which he reevaluated the validity of Margaret Mead's fieldwork in Samoa. Central to Freeman's criticisms of Mead are her inaccurate data derived from two Samoan adolescent women. Later, Freeman followed with *The Fateful*

Hoaxing of Margaret Mead (1989), with an attempt to show evidence of Mead's inaccurate fieldwork. In 1987, Freeman returned to Samoa and interviewed one of Mead's primary sources for her research. Fa'apua'a Fa'amu, the *taupou*, the virgin of the village in which Mead conducted her study, was Mead's primary source of information. Freeman's interview with Fa'amu, in 1987, revealed that Fa'amu, and another village woman, were untruthful about some information concerning Samoan adolescence. Upon hearing of the publication of Mead's *Coming of Age in Samoa*, the two women set out to rectify the inaccuracy.

Freeman's portrayal of Samoa is greatly different from that of Mead. Contrary to Mead's descriptions, Freeman's Samoa is unfavorable, full of male violence, including a high number of rapes. The Samoans place emphasis on hierarchy and status in Freeman's version of Samoa. Also, Freeman asserted that they guarded virginity very fervently. These inconsistent observations from both Mead and Freeman are evidence of subjectivity that may be encountered in qualitative research. When knowledge is socially constructed it has no special epistemological status (Pool, 2003), and debates can continue without progress. Our interest in the Freeman-Mead debate is not which side of the debate is correct, but that a debate like this could take place at all.

The psychologist, on the other hand, has subscribed to the belief that scientific knowledge is epistemologically special. It is the ability to falsify hypotheses (Pool, 2003) that gives the sciences (including psychology) this special status. Although psychologists can debate, disagree, and challenge, we believe that the scientific method undergirding these debates will ultimately move the field in the right direction. A psychologist may make an incorrect conclusion about a particular set of data, but statistical reasoning allows the psychologist to know the probability that he or she is wrong.

Cognitive psychologists can bring to bear science itself and the epistemologically special knowledge it generates, the ability to make causal statements, the precision of quantification, an arsenal of methods constructed to understand human cognition and behavior, a database of facts about cognition and behavior. If they bother to understand the new environment as thoroughly as would a good anthropologist, their first steps out of the lab should be enjoyable ones. If they understand deeply how technologies differ and how those differences can affect people, then their journey outside of the lab can be productive and profitable. If cognitive psychologists do not serve as the scientific voice when choosing between technologies or designing new ones, then other disciplines will bring to bear their methodologies and science and society will be the poorer for it.

References

Albright, C. A., Truitt, T. R., Barile, A. L., Vortac, O. U., and Manning, C. A. (1995). Controlling traffic without flight progress strips: Compensation, workload, performance, and opinion. *Air Traffic Control Quarterly*, 2, 229–248.

Cox, W. M., and Alm, R. (1998, March 12). Technology and economic growth in the information age, *Policy Backgrounder*, 147. Retrieved from www.ncpa.org/bg/bg147/bg147.html

Cross, K. P. (1992). *Adults as learners: Increasing participation and facilitating learning.* San Francisco: Jossey-Bass.

De Michelis, G. (2003). The "Swiss Pattada": Designing the ultimate tool. *Interactions*, 10(3), 44–53.

Durso, F. T., Batstakes, P. J., Crutchfield, J. M., Braden, J. B., and Manning, C. A. (2004). Flight progress strips while working live traffic: Frequencies, importance, and perceived benefits. *Human Factors*, 46, 32–49.

Durso, F. T., and Manning, C. A. (2003). *Following the paper trail: Design clues from paper flight strips.* Paper presented at Air Traffic Management Conference, Budapest.

_____, and _____ (2002). Spinning paper into glass: Transforming flight progress strips. *Human Factors and Aerospace Safety*, 2(1), 1–31.

Durso, F. T., Truitt, T. R., Hackworth, C., Crutchfield, J., and Manning, C. A. (1998). En route operational errors and situation awareness. *International Journal of Aviation Psychology*, 8, 177–193.

Englander, D., and Downing, T. (1998). The mystery of Luddism. *History Today*, 38, 18.

Freeman, D. (1983). *Margaret Mead and Samoa: The making and unmaking of an anthropological myth.* Cambridge, MA: Harvard University Press.

_____ (1999). *The fateful hoaxing of Margaret Mead: A historical analysis of her Samoan research.* Oxford: Westview Press.

Gibson, J. J. (1979). *The ecological approach to visual perception.* Boston: Houghton Mifflin.

Hopkins, V. D. (1991). Automated flight strip usage: Lessons from the functions of paper strips. In *Proceedings of the AIAA/NASA/FAA/HFS Symposium on Challenges in Aviation Human Factors: The National Plan*, pp. 62–64. Tyson's Corner, VA: American Institute of Aeronautics and Astronautics.

Hutchins, E. (1995). The technology of team investigation. In J. Galegher, R. E. Kraut, and C. Egido (eds.), *Intellectual teamwork: Social and technological foundation of cooperative work* (pp. 191–220). Hillsdale, NJ: Erlbaum.

Isaac, A., and Guselli, J. (1996). Technology and the air traffic controller: Performance panacea or human hindrance? In B. J. Hayward and A. R. Lowe (eds.), *Applied aviation psychology: Achievement, change, and challenge.* Proceedings of the Third Australian Aviation Psychology Symposium. Aldershot, U.K.: Ashgate.

Luff, P., Heath, C., and Greatbach, D. (1992). Tasks-in-interaction: Paper and screen based documentation on collaborative activity. In *Proceedings of CSCW '92* (pp. 163–170). New York: ACM Press.

Marvin, C. (1988). *When old technologies were new: Thinking about electric communication in the late nineteenth century.* New York: Oxford University Press.

Marx, L. (1987). Does improved technology mean progress? *Technology Review*, 71, 33–41.

Monroney, W. F. (1995). The evolution of human engineering: A selected review. In J. Weimer (ed.), *Research techniques in human engineering* (pp. 1–19). Englewood Cliffs, NJ: Prentice-Hall.

Moray, N. (1999). The cognitive psychology and cognitive engineering of industrial systems. In F. T. Durso, R. S. Nickerson, R. W. Schvaneveldt, S. T. Dumais, D. S. Lyndsay, and M. T. H Chi (eds.), *Handbook of applied cognition* (pp. 209–245). New York: Wiley.

Negroponte, N. (1995). *Being digital.* New York: Alfred A. Knopf.

Neisser. U. (1983). Snapshots or benchmarks? In U. Neisser (ed.), *Memory observed: Remembering in natural contexts.* (pp. 43–48). New York: Freeman.

Norman, D. A. (1988). *The psychology of everyday things.* New York: Basic Books.

_____ (1998). *The invisible computer.* Cambridge, MA: MIT Press.

Pandora, K. (1998). "Mapping the new mental world created by radio": Media messages, cultural politics, and Cantril and Allport's *The Psychology of Radio. Journal of Social Issues, 54,* 7–27.

Pool, R. (2003). How society shapes technology. In A. H. Teich (ed.), *Technology and the future* (pp. 13–22). Belmont, CA: Wadsworth.

Sellen, A. J., and Harper, R. (2002). *The myth of the paperless office.* Cambridge, MA: MIT Press.

Tenner, E. (2003). *Our own devices: The past and future of body technology.* New York: Knopf.

Torenvlivet, G. (2003). We can't afford it! The devaluation of a usability term. *Interactions,* 10(4), 13–17.

Truitt, T. R., Durso, F. T., Crutchfield, J. M., Moertl, P. M., and Manning, C. A. (2000). Test of an optional strip posting and marking procedure. *Air Traffic Control Quarterly, 8,* 131–154.

U.S. Bureau of the Census (1945). *Historical statistics of the United States, 1789–1945.* Washington, DC: Author.

U.S. Census Bureau (2000). *Statistical abstract of the United States* (12th ed.). Washington, DC: Author.

Vortac, O. U., Edwards, M., Fuller, D., and Manning, C. A. (1993). Automation and cognition in air traffic control: An empirical investigation. *Applied Cognitive Psychology, 7,* 631–651.

Vortac, O. U., Edwards, M., and Manning, C. A. (1994). Sequences of actions for individual and teams of air traffic controllers. *Human-Computer Interaction, 9,* 319–343.

Woods, D. D., and Cook, R. I. (1999) Perspectives on human error: Hindsight biases and local rationality. In F. T. Durso, R. S. Nickerson, R. W. Schvaneveldt, S. T. Dumais, D. S. Lindsay, and M. T. H. Chi (eds.), *Handbook of applied cognition* (pp. 141–171). New York: Wiley.

About the Contributors

Reggie Y. Andrews is a recent graduate of Winston-Salem State University.

Jennifer M. Bonds-Raacke is a graduate student at Kansas State University.

M. Anne Britt is an assistant professor of cognitive psychology at Northern Illinois University.

Elizabeth T. Cady is a graduate student at Kansas State University.

Dennis J. Crouch is a research associate professor of pharmacology and toxicology at the University of Utah.

Frank A. Drews is an assistant professor of cognitive psychology at the University of Utah.

Francis T. Durso is a professor of experimental psychology and human factors at Texas Tech University. He can be reached via e-mail at Frank.Durso@ttu.edu.

Jeffrey A. Gibbons is an associate professor of cognitive psychology at Christopher Newport University. He can be reached via e-mail at jgibbons@cnu.edu.

Catherine F. Hall is currently a psychology major at Texas Tech University.

Richard Jackson Harris is a professor of cognitive psychology and psycholinguistics at Kansas State University. He can be reached via e-mail at rjharris@ksu.edu.

Jeremy D. Heider is a graduate student at Northern Illinois University.

Douglas J. Herrmann is a professor of cognitive psychology at Indiana State University and founder of the journal *Cognitive Technology*. He can be reached via e-mail at Douglas.Herrmann@Verizon.net.

William A. Johnston is a professor of cognitive psychology at the University of Utah.

Joel E. Lynch is a graduate student at Northern Illinois University.

Katelyn Y. A. McKenna is a research professor in social psychology at New York University. She can be reached at kym1@nyu.edu.

Sandra Nicks is a former faculty member at Christian Brothers University. She currently resides in Gastonia, North Carolina.

Janet Phillips is currently a psychology major at Christopher Newport University.

Brad J. Sagarin is an assistant professor of social psychology at Northern Illinois University. He can be reached via e-mail at bsagarin@niu.edu.

Gwendolyn Seidman is a graduate student at New York University.

Chanda Simkin is a recent graduate of Christian Brothers University.

David L. Strayer is a professor of cognitive psychology at the University of Utah. He can be reached via e-mail at strayer@psych.utah.edu.

Cheryl Taylor is a recent graduate of Christopher Newport University.

Stephen Truhon is an associate professor of developmental psychology at Winston-Salem State University. He can be reached via e-mail at stephent@wssu.edu.

Rodney J. Vogl is an associate professor of experimental psychology at Christian Brothers University. He can be reached via e-mail at rvogl@cbu.edu.

W. Richard Walker is an associate professor of experimental psychology at Winston-Salem State University. He can be reached via e-mail at walkerr@wssu.edu.

Sarah E. Wood is a graduate student in social psychology at Northern Illinois University.

Carol Y. Yoder is a professor and chair of the psychology department at Trinity University. She can be reached via e-mail at Carol.Yoder@Trinity.edu.

Subject Index

Name Index